Competency 5: Engage in Policy Practice	1, 8, 9
A. Identify social policy at the local, state, and federal level that impacts well-being, service delivery, and access to social services	1, 9
B. Assess how social welfare and economic policies impact the delivery of and access to social services	1, 9
C. Apply critical thinking to analyze, formulate, and advocate policies that advance human rights and social, economic, and environmental justice	1, 8, 9

Competency 6: Engage with Individuals, Families, Groups, Organizations, and Communities	1, 6, 10
A. Apply knowledge of human behavior and the social environment, person-in-environment, and other multidisciplinary theoretical frameworks to engage with clients and constituencies	1, 10
B. Use empathy, reflection, and interpersonal skills to effectively eng... constituencies	

Competency 7: Assess Individuals, Families, Groups, Organizations	
A. Collect and organize data, and apply critical thinking to interpret i... and constituencies	
B. Apply knowledge of human behavior and the social environment, person-in-environment, and other multidisciplinary theoretical frameworks in the analysis of assessment data from clients and constituencies	1, 10
C. Develop mutually agreed-on intervention goals and objectives based on the critical assessment of strengths, needs, and challenges within clients and constituencies	1, 3, 10
D. Select appropriate intervention strategies based on the assessment, research knowledge, and values and preferences of clients and constituencies	1, 10

Competency 8: Intervene with Individuals, Families, Groups, Organizations, and Communities	1, 9, 10
A. Critically choose and implement interventions to achieve practice goals and enhance capacities of clients and constituencies	1, 9, 10
B. Apply knowledge of human behavior and the social environment, person-in-environment, and other multidisciplinary theoretical frameworks in interventions with clients and constituencies	1, 10
C. Use inter-professional collaboration as appropriate to achieve beneficial practice outcomes	1, 10
D. Negotiate, mediate, and advocate with and on behalf of diverse clients and constituencies	1, 10
E. Facilitate effective transitions and endings that advance mutually agreed-on goals	1, 10

Competency 9: Evaluate Practice with Individuals, Families, Groups, Organizations, and Communities	1, 9, 10
A. Select and use appropriate methods for evaluation of outcomes	1, 10
B. Apply knowledge of human behavior and the social environment, person-in-environment, and other multidisciplinary theoretical frameworks in the evaluation of outcomes	1, 10
C. Critically analyze, monitor, and evaluate intervention and program processes and outcomes	1, 9, 10
D. Apply evaluation findings to improve practice effectiveness at the micro, mezzo, and macro levels	1, 9, 10

A Field Guide for Social Workers

Sara Miller McCune founded SAGE Publishing in 1965 to support the dissemination of usable knowledge and educate a global community. SAGE publishes more than 1000 journals and over 800 new books each year, spanning a wide range of subject areas. Our growing selection of library products includes archives, data, case studies and video. SAGE remains majority owned by our founder and after her lifetime will become owned by a charitable trust that secures the company's continued independence.

Los Angeles | London | New Delhi | Singapore | Washington DC | Melbourne

A Field Guide for Social Workers

Applying Your Generalist Training

Shelagh J. Larkin

Xavier University

Los Angeles | London | New Delhi
Singapore | Washington DC | Melbourne

FOR INFORMATION:

SAGE Publications, Inc.
2455 Teller Road
Thousand Oaks, California 91320
E-mail: order@sagepub.com

SAGE Publications Ltd.
1 Oliver's Yard
55 City Road
London, EC1Y 1SP
United Kingdom

SAGE Publications India Pvt. Ltd.
B 1/I 1 Mohan Cooperative Industrial Area
Mathura Road, New Delhi 110 044
India

SAGE Publications Asia-Pacific Pte. Ltd.
3 Church Street
#10-04 Samsung Hub
Singapore 049483

Acquisitions Editor: Joshua Perigo
Editorial Assistant: Alexandra Randall
Production Editor: Tracy Buyan
Copy Editor: Erin Livingston
Typesetter: Hurix Digital
Proofreader: Jeff Bryant
Indexer: Scott Smiley
Cover Designer: Candice Harman
Marketing Manager: Jenna Retana

Printed in the United States of America

Library of Congress Cataloging-in-Publication Data

Names: Larkin, Shelagh J., author.

Title: A field guide for social workers : applying your generalist training / Shelagh J. Larkin, Xavier University.

Description: First Edition. | Thousand Oaks : SAGE Publications, [2018] | Includes bibliographical references and index.

Identifiers: LCCN 2018009060 | ISBN 9781506379241 (pbk. : alk. paper)

Subjects: LCSH: Social service—Fieldwork. | Social work education—United States.

Classification: LCC HV11 .L265 2018 | DDC 361.3071/55—dc23
LC record available at https://lccn.loc.gov/2018009060

This book is printed on acid-free paper.

SUSTAINABLE FORESTRY INITIATIVE
Certified Chain of Custody
At Least 10% Certified Forest Content
www.sfiprogram.org
SFI-01028

19 20 21 22 10 9 8 7 6 5 4 3 2

CONTENTS

INTRODUCTION

Welcome to field education. Field is the most challenging and rewarding part of your social work education. As a field director for over 20 years, I have walked many students through this process. In fact, one of the things I love most about being a field director is that I get to be a part of an amazing transformation. I cannot adequately describe what it is I witness each year as I watch students go from their first day in field, unsure of what to do or what to expect, to their last day, confidently exiting field, prepared to enter their chosen profession or move on to their advanced education. But what I can say is that it is significant.

As stated earlier, field is both challenging and rewarding. It is challenging in that you will exist in two worlds simultaneously: the world of the classroom and the world of practice in an agency. This is challenging because it is your responsibility not only to navigate successfully between both worlds but also to integrate those worlds, in many cases while moving seamlessly back and forth. Also, the demands of field education can be an overwhelming part of your education. On top of your classroom responsibilities, you will also be expected to work competently with clients in an agency while juggling other responsibilities in your life, such as work and family. I'm sure as you got ready to enter field, you asked yourself, "Okay, how am I supposed to do this?" Field can also be stressful because it is not controlled and doesn't come with a syllabus per se. Thus, you will be exposed to what I like to call the good, the bad, and the ugly. There can be a great many experiences you will need to process. Some you will realize are not necessary for you to attend to, while others will become important learning experiences. So, you will have some rough days. As I tell students, the learning comes in many unexpected ways.

On the other hand, field education is extremely rewarding. I have seen students accomplish amazing things at their field agencies. For instance, students have translated forms into foreign languages to better serve their clients; developed policies for a treatment group that was being run by the agency in a host setting; designed, implemented, and ensured the sustainability of a program they developed; and redone the agency's assessment form to better reflect a strength-based philosophy. I have had students tell me they have been forever and profoundly changed as a result of their work with just one particular client. Furthermore, field is often where students solidify their belief that they have chosen the right profession and are excited to begin their professional life. Finally, field will provide you with invaluable skills that students tell me they would never have gained had they not been in field. At the end of your field experience, you will see that it was more than worth it.

WHY I WROTE THIS BOOK

I wrote this book for two reasons. First, as a result of researching generalist practice, I developed an approach to field education called the generalist field education approach (GFEA) that I feel will add a great deal to your field experience and professional training as a generalist social worker. Second, this book will offer you the resources necessary not only to get you through field but also to make field a wonderful learning and professional development experience. As the director for field education, I fulfill many different roles, which has provided me with a unique perspective. This perspective enables me to have a deeper understanding of what students need as they navigate through their field experience and illuminates the gaps that can exist between the classroom and field.

HOW TO USE THIS BOOK

This book is geared toward Bachelor in Social Work (BSW) students who are in their junior or senior field courses and Master of Social Work (MSW) foundation students. However, many of the principles can also be applied at the MSW advanced level. Each chapter will provide you with information that is important to your understanding of field education. Also, the book offers guided reflection questions and integrative activities (IAs) to assist you in applying your generalist training to your field experience. Many of the chapters will have a frequently experienced situation (FES) feature that will present common experiences that students have year after year. Each situation I share is a composite of several specific experiences that students have had over the years. I have narrowed down the situations to what I consider the most common. Obviously, the FESs presented are not exhaustive and may not specifically apply to you; however, the situations lead to more general information that all students can relate to and have the potential for reflection, discussion, and learning. It is important to note that if you have a situation that you feel needs attention but is not presented, seek out the assistance of your field instructor, field director, or a faculty member. The FES is presented in the form of a question or statement. The question or statement will be followed by some background and recommendations for how to think about and approach the situation. For each situation, I will provide what I call a *best practice* way of approaching the situation, which, based on my knowledge and experience, has been effective for students in handling the situation. Also, I may provide additional information from the literature to ground your thinking about the situation. One last important thing is that the recommendations presented on how to handle a specific situation are just that—recommendations or guidelines. Therefore, when you are deciding how to handle a specific situation you are dealing with in your field agency, even if it is similar to one presented in this chapter, you must always consult with your field instructor, field director, or a faculty member and follow that person's recommendations. The book also offers many examples from my work as a field director that I use to help illustrate the content or IAs and, again, are composite situations.

An important goal of this book is that it strikes a balance between content and process; that is, it does not repeat content you have already studied in other courses. Instead, this book will provide the necessary amount of relevant content regarding a topic to enable you to conceptualize the content in the context of field education and will provide resources to integrate that content area with your practice experiences in field. The content selected reflects two important criteria: (1) It is the most current at the time of writing, and (2) it is literature, regardless of when written and published, that is particularly salient to field education.

The reflection questions in each chapter provide an opportunity to explore various content and process areas as well as experiences of field. I encourage you to start a reflection journal to record your answers to the reflection questions as well as jot down questions for discussion.

The chapters also offer IAs for you to complete while in field. Some you will complete on your own, and others you will work on with your field instructor during supervision or may even bring to class to discuss. The purpose of the IAs is to provide a way for you to directly link your generalist training to your practice experiences in field. This is accomplished by first reviewing key content and then selecting a specific example from your work to provide the basis of the integration. The purpose of this is to enable you to pinpoint those practice experiences that best exemplify your practice in field.

The content and resources in this book will provide you with the tools necessary to develop and demonstrate competence in the nine core competencies and component behaviors necessary for competent generalist practice. This, however, is not always a clear-cut process; so, at the beginning of the text is a chart that identifies which core competencies are address by which chapter. Also, for those IAs that relate specifically to a core competency, those core competencies will be identified. The difference between developing and demonstrating a competence in the field versus in the classroom is that in the field, you will be completing various practice tasks; thus, a list of suggested field tasks that reflect the chapter's content is provided at the end of each chapter.

ACKNOWLEDGMENTS

I would like to thank my husband, Doug, and my daughters, Maddie and Sarah, for all their support during the process of writing this book. I would also like to thank all of the students and field instructors I have worked with, because without them, this book would not have been possible. In addition, I would like to thank the editors with whom I have worked as well as the following reviewers who provided excellent feedback and suggestions:

Gregory Perkins, Fayetteville State University

Jennifer Pax, Kean University

Kiana Webb-Robinson, Alabama State University

Lynda Snowbel, Hood College

Marta Lundy, Loyola University Chicago

Michelle Meer, University of Indianapolis

Ruth Whisler, Northern Arizona University

Sherry Tripepi, University of Toledo

I especially want to thank Lauren Hendrickson, who served as the research assistant while I was researching generalist practice, and Karen Kirst-Ashman, with whom I consulted.

ABOUT THE AUTHOR

Shelagh Larkin is a licensed independent social worker who obtained her MSW at the University of Kentucky in 1988. She has 30 years of experience in practice and social work education. Her practice experience is in the areas of mental health, child welfare, and eating disorders. For the last 20 years, she has been the director for field education at Xavier University. In the role of field director, she is responsible for all aspects of the field program, including recruiting sites, placing students, training field instructors, conducting liaison site visits, and teaching the integrative seminar course. All of these duties have provided her with a comprehensive and unique view of the needs of students and field instructors. She has published and presented at numerous national conferences in the areas of generalist field education, spiritually sensitive professional development, and interprofessional teaming. Lastly, she has also been awarded several grants, most notable being the Council on Social Work Education's Gero-Ed Center Curriculum Development Institute grant.

FIELD EDUCATION

A Generalist Approach

Field education is an exciting and challenging part of your social work curriculum. The purpose of this chapter is to ground you in an understanding of the role that field education plays in your education and training as a social worker and to prepare you to be successful in your field placement. As part of that grounding, the chapter will provide an overview of social work education with an emphasis on field education and introduce you to the generalist field education approach (GFEA).

SOCIAL WORK EDUCATION

Social work education is organized along multiple levels, and each level has its own educational outcomes and scope of practice. At the baccalaureate level, a student can obtain a Bachelor in Social Work (BSW) degree. The purpose of undergraduate social work education as articulated by the Council on Social Work Education ([CSWE], 2015) is to develop generalist practitioners. At the graduate level, a person can obtain a Master of Social Work (MSW) degree, which is considered the terminal degree of the profession. Master's-level students are trained to be advanced practitioners. Both undergraduate (BSW) and graduate (MSW) social work programs use field education as an important part of a student's curriculum. Many graduate programs offer advanced standing for students who have a BSW degree and meet the academic standards for admissions. *Advanced standing* means that the student is exempt from much of the foundation work and often enters the MSW program in the concentration year. The last level of social work education is a doctorate-level PhD or Doctor of Social Work degree and is usually for individuals interested in conducting research or working as a professor in a university.

FIELD IN SOCIAL WORK EDUCATION

Field education has been a part of social work training and education since its inception. In fact, the first training program in 1898 was a six-week program that involved lectures, agency visits, and field work. That training program went on to become the Columbia School of Social Work in New York (Fortune, 1994).

In the history of social work education, there were two early types of programs—agency based and university based—and each had its own focus and expected outcomes. The agency-based training programs were grounded in the idea of learning by doing, with the student modeling a primary practitioner and focusing on common elements that defined social work methods. The university-based programs focused on social work's purpose in social reform and emphasized research and academic-based knowledge. Interestingly enough, field work in the early university-based programs consisted of "field excursions to observe rather than through actual work" (Fortune, 1994, p. 153). Thus, the emphasis was on learning by observing and thinking rather than on doing.

A third type of education that emerged was undergraduate public education, mostly located in midwestern rural areas that prepared people for public service. According to Fortune, "The legacy of the undergraduate state schools includes the public service and rural missions, responsiveness to localized service needs, and a detachment from the developments and strictures of field education in the other streams" (Fortune, 1994, p. 153).

It was not until 1970 that field became a required part of undergraduate social work education. Since then, models and theories emerged to shape today's field experience (Schneck, Grossman, & Glassman, 1991). Some social work programs emphasized the *doing* and saw field as the last part of a sequence of learning that began in the classroom, while others took a different approach, emphasizing the integration of classroom and field.

In fact, the struggle to define the role and place of field in the curriculum and in the development of professionals continues today (Wayne, Bogo, & Raskins, 2006). In 2008, the CSWE deemed field education the signature pedagogy in its educational policies and accreditation standards (EPAS). According to the 2008 EPAS, signature pedagogy signifies field education as "the central form of instruction and learning" (CSWE, 2008, p. 8). This designation was continued in the most recent revision of the EPAS in 2015 (CSWE, 2015).

Signature pedagogies are elements of instruction and socialization that teach future practitioners the fundamental dimensions of professional work in their discipline—to think, to perform, and to act ethically and with integrity. Field education is the signature pedagogy for social work. The intent of field education is to integrate the theoretical and conceptual contribution of the classroom with the practical world of the practice setting. It is a basic precept of social work education that the two interrelated components of curriculum—classroom and field—are of equal importance within the curriculum, and each contributes to the development of the requisite competencies of professional practice. Field education is systematically designed, supervised, coordinated, and evaluated based on criteria by which students demonstrate the social work competencies. Field education may integrate forms of technology as a component of the program (CSWE, 2015, p. 12).

The intent to elevate field within social work education via the designation of field as signature pedagogy is widely recognized; however, as a result, social work educators have questioned, analyzed, and reconceptualized the profession's understanding of signature pedagogy (Earls Larrison & Korr, 2013; Wayne, Bogo, & Raskins, 2010). Earls Larrison and Korr (2013) state that field is a necessary but not singular component of the profession's pedagogy and argue that social work's pedagogy also occurs in other aspects of a program, such as in the classroom and in the interactions between a student and his or her program faculty and professional social workers. The authors go on to provide a reconceptualization of the profession's signature pedagogy as "a framework that focuses on three integrating features: thinking and performing like a social worker, development of the professional self, and characteristic forms of teaching and learning" (p. 194). These three integrating components offer a more nuanced way of thinking about how the classroom and field curriculum come together to develop competent social workers and "move beyond acquiring conceptual knowledge and check-listing performance actions and toward the reasoned thoughtful application—or practical judgement—of how to engage as a practitioner" (p. 201). Last, even given the elevation of field as the signature pedagogy since 2008, field continues to experience great challenges in meeting this expectation and, specifically, in relying on agencies and social workers to voluntarily prepare social workers (Bogo, 2015). For instance, Carey and McCardle (2011) developed an introductory field experience to combat two problems inherent in field education: the ability of an agency to offer a fully generalist practice experience and the opportunity for students to integrate theory into practice. Given this discussion, it becomes increasingly important for social work programs to support students as they navigate the field experience, which is the foundational goal of this book.

Finding oneself at the intersection of classroom learning, field training, and professional socialization can be challenging for students. I have seen students struggle to meet the often-competing academic and practice demands of field, feeling pulled in multiple directions. Furthermore, students often struggle with their own conceptualizations of what they think field should be and, thus, are often left feeling confused and overwhelmed. Yet, the integration of classroom curriculum into real-life practice experiences and bringing field experiences back to the classroom is the reason you are in field. Field is much more than simply working in an organization. You will form and strengthen the connections between your existing knowledge and practical experience at this intersection of classroom learning, field training, and professional socialization as well as develop new knowledge and skills, all of which will result in deeper understanding and an expected level of competence.

In terms of the structure of field, the EPAS (CSWE, 2015) outline specific guidelines regarding the structure and number of hours required in field. Students at the undergraduate level must complete a minimum of 400 hours in an organization, working under the supervision of a social worker. At the graduate level, students must complete a minimum of 900 hours, although many schools require more. The 900 hours for MSW is for both the foundation and concentration years, thus students who qualify for advanced standing may do less than 900 because they will receive some credit for their BSW field hours. However, the exact number of hours varies program to program, so you will want to check with your program to determine the number of required hours. Field is a significant commitment of time, as reflected in the clock hours as well as when you consider the expectations for the outcomes of field. Thus, I always ask my students to reflect on why they think field is such an important part of their social work education.

REFLECTION QUESTION 1.1

Now that you have a beginning understanding of field and its challenges within social work education, why do you think field education is important? And what role do you think field should play in your education and training as a social worker?

ROOM TO REFLECT

THE GENERALIST FIELD EDUCATION APPROACH

This book is grounded in a conceptualization of field that considers the history and evolution of field education and captures the best of all the early approaches as well as current practices and expected outcomes. This is accomplished by emphasizing *doing*, mentorship with a field instructor, professional development of self, critical thinking, and the conscious and deliberate integration of field training and classroom learning. The primary goal of the GFEA is to assist you in the process of developing and demonstrating your competence as a generalist practitioner while in field. The approach was developed after researching generalist practice and is grounded in three key conceptualizations from the literature (Johnson & Yanca, 2007; Kirst-Ashman & Hull, 2006; Schatz, Jenkins, & Sheafor, 1990). The GFEA is defined as field education that is grounded in, integrates, and impacts curriculum; takes place in an organization under the supervision of a social worker; requires that students engage in multilevel field tasks and the foundational roles of social work; and emphasizes ethical practice, diversity and social justice, critical thinking, and the application of the planned change process, with specific emphasis on multilevel assessment, planning, and implementation. From a practical standpoint, this book offers integrative activities (IAs) that will help you put the conceptual aspects of the approach into practice while in field as well as bring that learning back to the classroom and thus enable you to develop and demonstrate your competence as a generalist practitioner (see Figure 1.1). The IAs can be found throughout the book and are grounded in field tasks that enable you to demonstrate the core competencies necessary for effective social work practice. Each IA will start with the expected core competency and requisite knowledge, values, skills, and or cognitive and affective processes that undergird the component behaviors and will direct you to focus on a specific task or case from field. This will allow you to be more targeted as you develop as competent generalist social work practitioners.

Table 1.1 provides an overview of GFEA. The table identifies each element of the GFEA, corresponding supplemental resources, IAs that relate specifically to that element, and the corresponding activities or paperwork of field and suggested time frame for their completion.

FIGURE 1.1 ■ The Relationship of Classroom and Field in the Development of Competent Generalist Practitioners

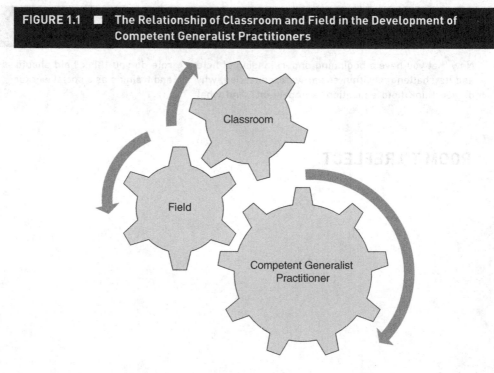

Classroom

Field

Competent Generalist Practitioner

TABLE 1.1 ■ The Generalist Field Education Approach

Element Generalist Field Education	Supplemental Resources	Integrative Activity	Field Activity/ Paperwork Time Frame
1. is grounded in, integrates, and impacts curriculum	• CSWE 2015, EPAS • Department curriculum • Course syllabus	2.3 Curriculum Review 12.1 Curriculum Analysis	• Orientation Weeks 1–3 • End of academic year
2. takes place in an organization	• Organization-based orientation materials	2.1 Orientation and Training 2.2 Agency Analysis 3.2 Identifying Foundational Roles of Social Work in Field 4.1 Field Safety Assessment	• Orientation • training • Weeks 1–3
3. is under the supervision of a social worker		5.1 The Supervision Outline 5.2 The Supervision Agenda 5.3 Documenting Your Supervision Session	• Establish supervision time • Week 1 or 2 • Weeks 3–15
4. requires that students engage in multilevel tasks and the foundational roles of social work	• Agency job description	3.1 Identifying Multilevel Learning Tasks 3.2 Identifying Foundational Roles of Social Work in Field 3.3 Constructing the Field Learning Plan	• Learning plan • Weeks 3–5
5. emphasizes ethical practice, diversity, social justice, and critical thinking	• National Association of Social Workers (NASW) code of ethics • NASW standards and indicators of cultural competence in social work practice • NASW, Association of Social Work Boards (ASWB), CSWE, & Clinical Social Work Association (CSWA) standards for technology in social work practice • Agency code of ethics	1.1 Translating Core Competencies into Field Competencies and Tasks 1.2 The Field Portfolio 1.3 The Field Journal 7.1 The Agency Ethics Audit 7.2 Resolving Ethical Dilemmas 8.1 Understanding Diversity in Field: A Multilevel Approach 8.2 Developing Culturally Competent Practice Skills in Field 8.3 Identifying Social, Economic, and Environmental Injustice in Field 8.4 Policy Analysis and Practice 9.1 Task Analysis 9.2 The Literature Review 11.1 Professional Development of Self Capstone Paper 12.2 Pulling It All Together	• Orientation (Week 1) • Weeks 6–15
6. emphasizes the application of the planned change process with specific emphasis on multilevel assessment, planning, and implementation	• Agency intakes and assessments • Agency service plans • Agency interventions • Agency discharge reports	10.1 The Phases of the Planned Change Process in Field 10.2 The Multidimensional/ Multilevel Assessment 10.3 Identifying Theoretical Perspectives, Practice Models, and Commonly Used Interventions in Field 10.4 Developing and Implementing Multilevel Plans 10.5 The Planned Change Case Analysis	• Week 4 • Weeks 6–15

Note: The following time frame is based on a two-semester academic year with a six-week semester; thus, your particular time frame may vary, depending on your program and agency requirements. Also, not all chapter activities are included in this table, only those that directly relate to the elements reflected in the GFEA.

DEVELOPING AND DEMONSTRATING COMPETENCE IN FIELD

In 2008, the CSWE adopted a competency base approach to social work education that was maintained during its last review in 2015. This approach has been used by other disciplines such as medicine, nursing, and psychology prior to social work's adoption. According to Bogo (2010), "competency-based education shifts focus from input, such as curriculum structure and process, to output or outcomes, expressed as student performance" (p. 56). For social work,

> Competency-based education rests upon a shared view of the nature of competence in professional practice. Social work competence is the ability to integrate and apply social work knowledge, values, and skills to practice situations in a purposeful, intentional, and professional manner to promote human and community well-being. EPAS recognizes a holistic view of competence; that is, the demonstration of competence is informed by knowledge, values, skills, and cognitive and affective processes that include the social worker's critical thinking, affective reactions, and exercise of judgment in regard to unique practice situations. Overall professional competence is multi-dimensional and composed of interrelated competencies. An individual social worker's competence is seen as developmental and dynamic, changing over time in relation to continuous learning.
>
> Competency-based education is an outcomes-oriented approach to curriculum design. The goal of the outcomes approach is to ensure that students are able to demonstrate the integration and application of the competencies in practice. In EPAS, social work practice competence consists of nine interrelated competencies and component behaviors that are comprised of knowledge, values, skills, and cognitive and affective processes. (CSWE, 2015, p. 6)

In the above definition, the ability of the student to demonstrate specific competencies is emphasized. The nine core competencies for social work are articulated in the EPAS and include corresponding component behaviors (CSWE, 2015). The core competencies, corresponding knowledge values, skills, cognitive and affective processes, and component behaviors are presented in Integrative Activity 1.1. For field education, the challenge is to consider how each core competency and component behavior can be demonstrated in practice at your placement. In order to address this challenge, five overarching field competencies that emphasize what is both unique and shared about field and the classroom as they relate to the expected core competencies of generalist social work practice are provided:

1. Student will demonstrate professional and ethical behavior as a social worker in field.

    Learning Objectives:

    a. Student will demonstrate the skills necessary for lifelong learning as a professional social worker.

    b. Student will accurately apply knowledge of organization and history of the profession to practice in field.

    c. Student will use supervision effectively in field.

    d. Student will demonstrate appropriate professional behavior in appearance and oral, written, and electronic communication as a social work student in field.

    e. Student will appropriately utilize foundational social work roles in field and accurately identify the role of other professionals, if applicable.

    f. Student will demonstrate ethical practice in field.

g. Student will utilize an ethical decision-making process to appropriately resolve ethical dilemmas in field using the NASW code of ethics.

h. Student will demonstrate the ability to reflect on practice and professional development in field.

i. Student will demonstrate ethical and appropriate use of technology in field.

2. Student will effectively engage diversity and difference in practice to advance human rights and social, economic, and environmental justice.

Learning Objectives:

a. Student will demonstrate an accurate understanding of the impact of diversity and difference on client systems.

b. Student will demonstrate an accurate understanding of the impact of social, economic, and environmental injustice on client systems in field.

c. Student will develop culturally competent practice skills in field.

d. Student will demonstrate an ability to advance social justice in field.

3. Student will effectively integrate knowledge, values, skills, and cognitive and affective processes acquired in the classroom with the practice experiences of field.

Learning Objectives:

a. Student will use and accurately link knowledge, values, skills, and cognitive and affective processes from courses to practice in field.

b. Student will demonstrate the ability to effectively analyze field tasks using critical-thinking skills.

c. Student will accurately identify policies used by the agency and analyze how they impact practice with client systems.

d. Student will apply an analysis of client systems, using knowledge of human development and the person and environment framework in field.

e. Student will effectively use research in practice in field.

4. Student will demonstrate effective communication skills in field.

Learning Objectives:

a. Student will apply effective oral communication skills in field.

b. Student will apply effective written communication skills in field.

c. Student will apply effective electronic communication skills with client systems in field.

d. Student will evaluate communication skills with client systems in field.

5. Student will effectively use the planned change process with individuals, families, groups, organizations, and communities in field to assist client systems in meeting needs.

Learning Objectives:

a. Student will effectively engage individuals, families, groups, organizations, and communities in field.

b. Student will conduct multidimensional assessment of client systems in field.

c. Student will analyze multidimensional assessment of client systems in field.

d. Student will develop multilevel plans with client systems in field.

e. Student will implement interventions with client systems in field that are grounded in theories and knowledge.

f. Student will terminate effectively with client systems in field.

g. Student will evaluate practice in field with client systems.

In Integrative Activity 1.1, you will have an opportunity to see how the preceding field competencies and student learning objectives (SLOs) link to the core competencies and component behaviors identified in EPAS (CSWE, 2015). For instance, the first field SLO (1.a. Student will demonstrate the skills necessary for lifelong learning as a professional social worker) links specifically to Competency 1 and the specific statement, "Social workers recognize the importance of lifelong learning and are committed to continually updating their skills to ensure they are relevant and effective" (CSWE, 2015, p. 7). This competence expectation will come to life in field as students identify their specialized learning needs and attend trainings to develop their knowledge, values, and skills.

Hand-in-hand with identifying field competencies is identifying the tasks that you can engage in while in field to develop and demonstrate a particular competence. As you can see, Integrative Activity 1.1 also provides a list of possible tasks to engage in while in field. For instance, in order to achieve the competence of developing as a lifelong learner, you can engage in ongoing training and education by attending community- or agency-based trainings, reading the literature, or viewing training videos. For instance, a student in an agency that serves clients who are dealing with addiction will take specific trainings on types of addiction and develop skills necessary to effectively intervene with those client systems. This task will assist the student in meeting this competency in field and lay the foundation in his or her development as a lifelong learner once he or she is practicing as a social worker. As you complete various field tasks, you will develop and demonstrate the field competencies and ultimately demonstrate and achieve the necessary core competencies and component behaviors of social work.

INTEGRATIVE ACTIVITY 1.1
TRANSLATING CORE COMPETENCIES INTO FIELD COMPETENCIES AND TASKS

Purpose: The purpose of this activity is to assist you in the process of developing your understanding of the EPAS (CSWE, 2015), core competencies, and component behaviors and how they relate to the field competencies and SLOs outlined in the book as well as to identify the possible tasks you can engage in to demonstrate that competency in field. The first three columns outline the core competencies; characteristic knowledge, values, skills, and cognitive and affective processes; and component behaviors as identified in EPAS (CSWE, 2015, pp. 7–9). Following those columns are the corresponding field competencies and

SLOs that are linked with that core competency and the tasks you can engage in while in field in order to develop and demonstrate that you have met a particular core competency.

Directions: First, review the first four columns to familiarize yourself with the CSWE EPAS (2015) and the corresponding field competencies and SLOs. Then, review and identify the tasks you can engage in while in field to develop and demonstrate each core competency and component behaviors and discuss with your field instructor in supervision.

Competency: 1–9

Core Competency	Characteristic Knowledge, Values, Skills, and Cognitive and Affective Processes	Component Behaviors	Corresponding Field Competency and SLOs	Field Tasks (Note: The tasks are in no particular order of importance)
Competency 1: Demonstrate Ethical and Professional Behavior	Social workers understand the value base of the profession and its ethical standards as well as relevant laws and regulations that may impact practice at the micro, mezzo, and macro levels. Social workers understand frameworks of ethical decision making and how to apply principles of critical thinking to those frameworks in practice, research, and policy arenas. Social workers recognize personal values and the distinction between personal and professional values. They also understand how their personal experiences and affective reactions influence their professional judgment and behavior. Social workers understand the profession's history, its mission, and the roles and responsibilities of the profession. Social workers also understand the role of other professions when engaged in interprofessional teams. Social workers recognize the importance of lifelong learning and are committed to continually updating their skills to ensure they are relevant and effective. Social workers also understand emerging forms of technology and the ethical use of technology in social work practice.	Social workers a. make ethical decisions by applying the standards of the NASW code of ethics, relevant laws and regulations, models for ethical decision making, ethical conduct of research, and additional codes of ethics as appropriate to context; b. use reflection and self-regulation to manage personal values and maintain professionalism in practice situations; c. demonstrate professional demeanor in behavior; appearance; and oral, written, and electronic communication; d. use technology ethically and appropriately to facilitate practice outcomes; and e. use supervision and consultation to guide professional judgment and behavior.	1. Student will demonstrate professional and ethical behavior as a social worker in field. **Learning Objectives:** a. Student will demonstrate skills necessary for lifelong learning as a professional social worker. b. Student will accurately apply knowledge of organization and history of the profession to practice in field. c. Student will use supervision effectively in field. d. Student will demonstrate appropriate professional behavior in appearance and oral, written, and electronic communication as a social work student in field. e. Student will appropriately utilize foundational social work roles in field and accurately identify the role of other professionals, if applicable. f. Student will demonstrate ethical practice in field. g. Student will utilize an ethical decision-making process to appropriately resolve ethical dilemmas in field.	• Review related course work. • Engage in orientation and training. • Tour agency. • Introduce self to all staff. • Establish supervision time. • Attend and plan for supervision. • Use supervision appropriately. • Demonstrate an understanding of the agency. • Examine and analyze the mission, goals and objectives, programs and services, history, funding, and organizational structure, and relate these to history of profession and organizational theory. • Review and complete field and agency paperwork, time sheets, learning plan, safety assessment, evaluation, mileage reimbursement, incident reports, and such. • Determine your title and role as a student. • Review relevant agency job descriptions. • Discuss the culture of the agency. • Identify a backup for when your field instructor is not available. • Identify your primary role and tasks. • Set up your work space.

(Continued)

[Continued]

Core Competency	Characteristic Knowledge, Values, Skills, and Cognitive and Affective Processes	Component Behaviors	Corresponding Field Competency and SLOs	Field Tasks (Note: The tasks are in no particular order of importance)
			h. Student will demonstrate ability to reflect on practice and professional development in field.	• Obtain an ID and computer/voice mail access.
			i. Student will demonstrate appropriate use of technology in field.	• Set an appropriate voice mail message identifying when you will be in the agency and who should be reached when you are not available.
			3. Student will effectively integrate knowledge, values, skills, and cognitive and affective processes acquired in the classroom with the practice experiences of field.	• Identify your work schedule.
				• Discuss behavioral expectations and appearance standards of the agency, such as dress code.
			Learning Objectives:	• Function independently in the agency.
			a. Student will use and accurately link knowledge, values, skills, and cognitive and affective processes from courses to practice in field.	• Join a social work club, a professional organization such as NASW, or a community group.
			b. Student will demonstrate ability to effectively analyze field tasks using critical thinking skills.	• Identify and engage in philanthropic social action activities.
			4. Student will demonstrate effective communication skills in field.	• Engage a mentor.
				• Attend agency-based, community, or campus trainings and events.
			Learning Objectives:	• Engage in self-care activities and monitor your stress and burnout levels.
			a. Student will apply effective oral communication skills in field.	• Explore professional development of self.
			b. Student will apply effective written communication skills in field.	• Identify key players and the role of each according to the learning triangle (field instructor, field director, faculty field liaison).
			c. Student will apply effective electronic communication skills with client systems in field.	• Identify yourself as a student with client systems.
				• In supervision, identify and discuss personal values and distinguish personal and professional values.

Core Competency	Characteristic Knowledge, Values, Skills, and Cognitive and Affective Processes	Component Behaviors	Corresponding Field Competency and SLOs	Field Tasks (Note: The tasks are in no particular order of importance)
				• Read and review the NASW code of ethics and any agency-based code of ethics or other relevant codes of ethics.
				• Discuss ethical principles and standards and any agency-based ethical standards.
				• Identify and discuss common ethical dilemmas in a practice setting.
				• Conduct an agency audit regarding ethical practices.
				• Identify, analyze, and resolve ethical dilemmas using the NASW code of ethics standards as a guide.
				• Communicate with clients and at the organizational level using oral, written, and electronic communication skills.
				• Evaluate professional communication skills. In supervision, describe and explain practice tasks.
				• Present and analyze client system information.
				• Demonstrate the ability to conceptualize practice.
				• Complete documentation and professional writing.
				• Use reflection to explore your role, tasks, and experiences of field.
				• Articulate your learning from tasks.
				• Explain knowledge, skills, and values developed as a result of field experiences.

(Continued)

[Continued]

Core Competency	Characteristic Knowledge, Values, Skills, and Cognitive and Affective Processes	Component Behaviors	Corresponding Field Competency and SLOs	Field Tasks [Note: The tasks are in no particular order of importance]
Competency 2: Engage Diversity and Difference in Practice	Social workers understand how diversity and difference characterize and shape the human experience and are critical to the formation of identity. The dimensions of diversity are understood as the intersectionality of multiple factors, including but not limited to age, class, color, culture, disability and ability, ethnicity, gender, gender identity and expression, immigration status, marital status, political ideology, race, religion/spirituality, sex, sexual orientation, and tribal sovereign status. Social workers understand that, as a consequence of difference, a person's life experiences may include oppression, poverty, marginalization, and alienation as well as privilege, power, and acclaim. Social workers also understand the forms and mechanisms of oppression and discrimination and recognize the extent to which a culture's structures and values, including social, economic, political, and cultural exclusions, may oppress, marginalize, alienate, or create privilege and power to manage the influence of personal biases and values in working with diverse clients and constituencies.	Social workers a. apply and communicate understanding of the importance of diversity and difference in shaping life experiences in practice at the micro, mezzo, and macro levels; b. present themselves as learners and engage clients and constituencies as experts of their own experiences; and c. apply self-awareness and self-regulation.	2. Student will effectively engage diversity and difference in practice to advance human rights and social, economic, and environmental justice. **Learning Objectives:** a. Student will demonstrate an accurate understanding of the impact of diversity and difference on client systems. b. Student will develop culturally competent practice skills in field. 3. Student will effectively integrate knowledge, values, skills, and cognitive and affective processes acquired in the classroom with the practice experiences of field. **Learning Objectives:** a. Student will use and accurately link knowledge, values, skills, and cognitive and affective processes from courses to practice in field. b. Student will demonstrate the ability to effectively analyze field tasks using critical thinking skills.	• Review related course work. • Identify diversity at the agency- and client-system level. • Increase your knowledge of special populations served by agency. • Identify value-based issues related to engaging diversity. • Review the standards of cultural competence as set forth by NASW. • Develop your cultural competency skills in practice. • Design and implement culturally competent practice interventions.
Competency 3: Advance Human Rights and Social, Economic, and Environmental Justice	Social workers understand that every person, regardless of position in society, has fundamental human rights, such as freedom, safety, privacy, an adequate standard of living, health care, and education. Social workers understand the	Social workers a. apply their understanding of social, economic, and environmental justice to advocate for human rights at the individual and system levels and	2. Student will effectively engage diversity and difference in practice to advance human rights and social, economic, and environmental justice.	• Review related course work. • Identify and discuss issues of oppression and human rights violations that directly impact clients in the agency at all levels. • Identify how the role of advocacy is utilized at the placement site to advance social,

Core Competency	Characteristic Knowledge, Values, Skills, and Cognitive and Affective Processes	Component Behaviors	Corresponding Field Competency and SLOs	Field Tasks (Note: The tasks are in no particular order of importance)
	global interconnections of oppression and human rights violations and are knowledgeable about theories of human need and social justice and strategies to promote social and economic justice and human rights. Social workers understand strategies designed to eliminate oppressive structural barriers to ensure that social goods, rights, and responsibilities are distributed equitably and that civil, political, environmental, economic, social, and cultural human rights are protected.	b. engage in practices that advance social, economic, and environmental justice.	**Learning Objectives:** a. Student will demonstrate an accurate understanding of the impact of social, economic, and environmental injustice on client systems in field. b. Student will demonstrate an ability to advance social justice in field. 3. Student will effectively integrate knowledge, values, skills, and cognitive and affective processes acquired in the classroom with the practice experiences of field. **Learning Objectives:** a. Student will use and accurately link knowledge, values, skills, and cognitive and affective processes from courses to practice in field. b. Student will demonstrate the ability to effectively analyze field tasks using critical thinking skills.	economic, and environmental justice. • Design and implement interventions that target advocacy (case and cause) to address oppression and human rights violations and advance social, economic, and environmental justice.
Competency 4: Engage in Practice-Informed Research and Research-Informed Practice	Social workers understand quantitative and qualitative research methods and their respective roles in advancing a science of social work and in evaluating their practice. Social workers know the principles of logic, scientific inquiry, and culturally informed and ethical approaches to building knowledge.	Social workers a. use practice experience and theory to inform scientific inquiry and research; b. apply critical thinking to engage in analysis of quantitative and qualitative research	3. Student will effectively integrate knowledge, values, skills, and cognitive and affective processes acquired in the classroom with the practice experiences of field. **Learning Objectives:** a. Student will use and accurately link knowledge, values,	• Review related course work. • Identify and discuss how research is used by the agency to support the activities of the organization. • Assist in the agency's annual report and other auditing, program evaluation, client satisfaction.

(Continued)

[Continued]

Core Competency	Characteristic Knowledge, Values, Skills, and Cognitive and Affective Processes	Component Behaviors	Corresponding Field Competency and SLOs	Field Tasks (Note: The tasks are in no particular order of importance)
	Social workers understand that evidence that informs practice derives from multidisciplinary sources and multiple ways of knowing. They also understand the processes for translating research findings into effective practice.	methods and research findings; and c. use and translate research evidence to inform and improve practice, policy, and service delivery.	skills, and cognitive and affective processes from courses to practice in field. b. Student will demonstrate ability to effectively analyze field tasks using critical thinking skills. c. Student will effectively use research in practice in field.	• Identify at least one research question that relates to your placement setting. • Conduct a literature review on a practice area, identifying databases searched and search parameters, and identify both qualitative and quantitative research. • Read varying types of research, discuss and present findings of research in supervision, and explain how it informs practice.
Competency 5: Engage in Policy Practice	Social workers understand that human rights and social justice, as well as social welfare and services, are mediated by policy and its implementation at the federal, state, and local levels. Social workers understand the history and current structures of social policies and services, the role of policy in service delivery, and the role of practice in policy development. Social workers understand their role in policy development and implementation within their practice settings at the micro, mezzo, and macro levels, and they actively engage in policy practice to effect change within those settings. Social workers recognize and understand the historical, social, cultural, economic, organizational, environmental, and global influences that affect social policy. They are also knowledgeable about policy formulation, analysis, implementation, and evaluation.	Social workers a. identify social policy at the local, state, and federal level that impacts well-being, service delivery, and access to social services; b. assess how social welfare and economic policies impact the delivery of and access to social services; c. apply critical thinking to analyze, formulate, and advocate for policies that advance human rights and social, economic, and environmental justice.	3. Student will effectively integrate knowledge, values, skills, and cognitive and affective processes acquired in the classroom with the practice experiences of field. **Learning Objectives:** a. Student will use and accurately link knowledge, values, skills, and cognitive and affective processes from courses to practice in field. b. Student will demonstrate the ability to effectively analyze field tasks using critical thinking skills. c. Student will accurately identify policies used by the agency and analyze how they impact practice with client systems.	• Review related course work. • Obtain and read agency policies and procedures. • Analyze current policies that have an impact on client systems. • Engage in policy development. • Research legislative history of an existing or proposed policy that impacts the client systems served by the agency. • Engage in advocacy of a policy at the legislative or organizational level. • Prepare and present information in support of a policy or program reform.

Core Competency	Characteristic Knowledge, Values, Skills, and Cognitive and Affective Processes	Component Behaviors	Corresponding Field Competency and SLOs	Field Tasks (Note: The tasks are in no particular order of importance)
Competency 6: Engage with Individuals, Families, Groups, Organizations, and Communities	Social workers understand that engagement is an ongoing component of the dynamic and interactive process of social work practice with, and on behalf of, diverse individuals, families, groups, organizations, and communities. Social workers value the importance of human relationships. Social workers understand theories of human behavior and the social environment and critically evaluate and apply this knowledge to facilitate engagement with clients and constituencies, including individuals, families, groups, organizations, and communities. Social workers understand strategies to engage diverse clients and constituencies to advance practice effectiveness. Social workers understand how their personal experiences and affective reactions may impact their ability to effectively engage with diverse clients and constituencies. Social workers value principles of relationship-building and interprofessional collaboration to facilitate engagement with clients, constituencies, and other professionals as appropriate.	Social workers a. apply their knowledge of human behavior and the social environment, person-in-environment, and other multidisciplinary theoretical frameworks to engage with clients and constituencies and b. use empathy, reflection, and interpersonal skills to effectively engage diverse clients and constituencies.	3. Student will effectively integrate knowledge, values, skills, and cognitive and affective processes acquired in the classroom with the practice experiences of field. **Learning Objectives:** a. Student will use and accurately link knowledge, values, skills, and cognitive and affective processes from courses to practice in field. b. Student will demonstrate the ability to effectively analyze field tasks using critical thinking skills. c. Student will apply an analysis of client systems using knowledge of human development and the person and environment framework in field. 4. Student will demonstrate effective communication skills in field. **Learning Objectives:** a. Student will apply effective oral communication skills in field. 5. Student will effectively use the planned change process with individuals, families, groups, organizations, and communities in field to assist client systems in meeting needs.	• Review related course work. • Engage with your field instructor and field setting. • Review phases of the planned change process in field. • Intake and engage with individuals, families, groups, organizations, and communities via phone and in person. • Interview clients, demonstrating the effective use of empathy and interpersonal skills. • Identify how the agency applies knowledge of human behavior and the social environment, person-in-environment, and other theoretical frameworks in the engagement process with diverse clients. • Prepare for client system contacts. • Use empathy and effective interpersonal skills with diverse client systems.

(Continued)

[Continued]

Core Competency	Characteristic Knowledge, Values, Skills, and Cognitive and Affective Processes	Component Behaviors	Corresponding Field Competency and SLOs	Field Tasks [Note: The tasks are in no particular order of importance]
			Learning Objectives: a. Student will effectively engage individuals, families, groups, organizations, and communities in field.	
Competency 7: Assess Individuals, Families, Groups, Organizations, and Communities	Social workers understand that assessment is an ongoing component of the dynamic and interactive process of social work practice with, and on behalf of, diverse individuals, families, groups, organizations, and communities. Social workers understand theories of human behavior and the social environment and critically evaluate and apply this knowledge in the assessment of diverse clients and constituencies, including individuals, families, groups, organizations, and communities. Social workers understand methods of assessment with diverse clients and constituencies to advance practice effectiveness. Social workers recognize the implications of the larger practice context in the assessment process and value the importance of interprofessional collaboration in this process. Social workers understand how their personal experiences and affective reactions may affect their assessment and decision making.	Social workers a. collect and organize data and apply critical thinking to interpret information from clients and constituencies; b. apply knowledge of human behavior and the social environment, person-in-environment, and other multidisciplinary theoretical frameworks in the analysis of assessment data from clients and constituencies; c. develop mutually agreed-on intervention goals and objectives based on the critical assessment of strengths, needs, and challenges within clients and constituencies; and d. select appropriate intervention strategies based on the assessment, research	3. Student will effectively integrate knowledge, values, skills, and cognitive and affective processes acquired in the classroom with the practice experiences of field. **Learning Objectives:** a. Student will use and accurately link knowledge, values, skills, and cognitive and affective processes from courses to practice in field. b. Student will demonstrate the ability to effectively analyze field tasks using critical thinking skills. c. Student will apply an analysis of client systems, using knowledge of human development and the person and environment framework in field. 5. Student will effectively use the planned change process with individuals, families, groups, organizations, and communities in field to assist client systems in meeting needs.	• Review related course work. • Review template tasks and identify specialized learning tasks necessary to achieve field competencies and SLOs on learning plan. • Identify multilevel learning opportunities and tasks. • Complete your field learning plan. • Gather information on client systems. • Identify assessments utilized by the agency. • Conduct assessments (intakes, social histories, ecomaps, genograms, or other agency-based assessments) on client systems. • Review and discuss multidimensional/multilevel assessment and how that looks in the agency. • Identify client systems strengths and limitations. • Identify how agency-based assessment integrates knowledge of human behavior and the social environment and person-in-environment.

Core Competency	Characteristic Knowledge, Values, Skills, and Cognitive and Affective Processes	Component Behaviors	Corresponding Field Competency and SLOs	Field Tasks (Note: The tasks are in no particular order of importance)
		knowledge, and values and preferences of clients and constituencies.	**Learning Objectives:** a. Student will conduct multidimensional assessment of client systems in field. b. Student will analyze multidimensional assessment of client systems in field. c. Student will develop multilevel plans with client systems in field.	• Utilize your knowledge of human behavior and the social environment, person-in-environment, and theory to understand the client. Demonstrate your knowledge of theory by defining and explaining how agency uses theory in assessment. • Identify how the larger practice context and specific issues impacting agency practice direct and impact assessment. • Identify how the agency engages in interprofessional collaboration and how that impacts assessment. • Identify client system goals and objectives and interventions necessary to assist clients in meeting goals and objectives.
Competency 8: Intervene with Individuals, Families, Groups, Organizations, and Communities	Social workers understand that intervention is an ongoing component of the dynamic and interactive process of social work practice with, and on behalf of, diverse individuals, families, groups, organizations, and communities. Social workers are knowledgeable about evidence-informed interventions to achieve the goals of clients and constituencies, including individuals, families, groups, organizations, and communities. Social workers understand theories	Social workers a. critically choose and implement interventions to achieve practice goals and enhance capacities of clients and constituencies; b. apply knowledge of human behavior and the social environment, person-in-environment, and other multidisciplinary theoretical frameworks in interventions	3. Student will effectively integrate knowledge, values, skills, and cognitive and affective processes acquired in the classroom with the practice experiences of field. **Learning Objectives:** a. Student will use and accurately link knowledge, values, skills, and cognitive and affective processes from courses to practice in field. b. Student will demonstrate the ability to effectively analyze	• Review related course work. • Complete field tasks to achieve learning goals and objectives on your learning plan and to develop and demonstrate competence. • Review how this phase of the planned change process looks in field and identify commonly used interventions by the agency. • Identify theories used by the agency or social workers within the agency that direct intervention.

(Continued)

(Continued)

Core Competency	Characteristic Knowledge, Values, Skills, and Cognitive and Affective Processes	Component Behaviors	Corresponding Field Competency and SLOs	Field Tasks (Note: The tasks are in no particular order of importance)
	of human behavior and the social environment and critically evaluate and apply this knowledge to effectively intervene with clients and constituencies. Social workers understand methods of identifying, analyzing, and implementing evidence-informed interventions to achieve client and constituency goals. Social workers value the importance of interprofessional teamwork and communication in interventions, recognizing that beneficial outcomes may require interdisciplinary, interprofessional, and interorganizational collaboration.	with clients and constituencies; c. use interprofessional collaboration asappropriate to achieve beneficial practice outcomes; d. negotiate, mediate, and advocate with and on behalf of diverse clients and constituencies; and e. facilitate effective transitions and endings that advance mutually agreed-on goals.	field tasks using critical-thinking skills. c. Student will apply an analysis of client systems, using knowledge of human development and the person and environment framework in field. 5. Student will effectively use the planned change process with individuals, families, groups, organizations, and communities in field to assist client systems in meeting needs. **Learning Objectives:** a. Student will implement interventions with client systems in field that are grounded in theories and knowledge. b. Student will terminate effectively with client systems in field.	• Identify how the agency integrates knowledge of human behavior and the social environment, person-in-environment, and theory in interventions. • Engage in interventions (implement plans) that integrate knowledge of human behavior and the social environment, person-in-environment, and theory to assist client systems in meeting their goals. • Engage in interprofessional collaboration and practice as indicated to assist clients in achieving their goals. • Demonstrate the roles of negotiation, mediation, and advocacy in serving client systems. • Plan for and implement client and agency termination.
Competency 9: Evaluate Practice with Individuals, Families, Groups, Organizations, and Communities	Social workers understand that evaluation is an ongoing component of the dynamic and interactive process of social work practice with, and on behalf of, diverse individuals, families, groups, organizations, and communities. Social workers recognize the importance of evaluating processes and outcomes to advance	Social workers a. select and use appropriate methods for evaluation of outcomes; b. apply knowledge of human behavior and the social environment, person-in-environment, and	3. Student will effectively integrate knowledge, values, skills, and cognitive and affective processes acquired in the classroom with the practice experiences of field. **Learning Objectives:** a. Student will use and accurately link knowledge,	• Review related course work. • Evaluate progress in meeting goals and objectives of field and core competencies and practice behaviors. • Identify how the agency evaluates practice. • Identify and discuss how the agency integrates knowledge of theory and human behavior

Core Competency	Characteristic Knowledge, Values, Skills, and Cognitive and Affective Processes	Component Behaviors	Corresponding Field Competency and SLOs	Field Tasks (Note: The tasks are in no particular order of importance)
	workers understand qualitative and quantitative methods for evaluating outcomes and practice effectiveness. practice, policy, and service delivery effectiveness. Social workers understand theories of human behavior and the social environment and critically evaluate and apply this knowledge in evaluating outcomes. Social	other multidisciplinary theoretical frameworks in the evaluation of outcomes; c. critically analyze, monitor, and evaluate intervention and program processes and outcomes; and d. apply evaluation findings to improve practice effectiveness at the micro, mezzo, and macro levels.	values, skills, and cognitive and affective processes from courses to practice in field. b. Student will demonstrate the ability to effectively analyze field tasks using critical thinking skills. c. Student will apply an analysis of client systems, using knowledge of human development and the person and environment framework in field. 5. Student will effectively use the planned change process with individuals, families, groups, organizations, and communities in field to assist client systems in meeting needs. **Learning Objectives:** a. Student will evaluate practice in field with client systems. 4. Student will demonstrate effective communication skills in field. **Learning Objectives:** a. Student will evaluate communication skills with client systems in field.	and the social environment in evaluation. • Monitor and evaluate practice strategies. • Evaluate practice in the agency. • Evaluate interviewing skills in field. • Engage in program-level evaluation.

REFLECTION QUESTION 1.2

After reviewing Interactive Activity 1.1, which field competencies are directly linked to EPAS (CSWE, 2015) core competencies and component behaviors and which are indirectly linked? Next, review and identify the tasks that you will need to complete in order to demonstrate the field competencies. Are there any missing, or are there any additional tasks that you think will be necessary to engage in to demonstrate a competency? If so, jot those down to include on your learning plan.

ROOM TO REFLECT

THE WHO'S WHO OF FIELD EDUCATION

Now that you have laid the foundation for the big picture of field education, let's discuss and define the who's who of field education. The *who's who* refers to those individuals who are critical players in your field experience and their corresponding roles and responsibilities.

The Learning Triangle

Sherer and Peleg-Oren (2005) use the term *learning triangle* to conceptualize those involved in field education. They say that "each side of the learning triangle—teachers, field instructors, and students—plays its own part in developing the professional social worker" (p. 316). This concept clearly identifies those involved in field education and reflects the notion that field is unique in that it requires multiple entities—the university, the student, and the agency—to come together and function as a whole. This can be depicted using a Venn diagram such as the one in Figure 1.2.

The Venn diagram provides a visual representation of the distinct yet overlapping roles and responsibilities of each player and demonstrates that field is a unique part of social work education. As a student entering field, it is helpful to understand the following roles and responsibilities of each player.

THE UNIVERSITY

The first member of the learning triangle is the university and, specifically, the social work program within the university. Several roles within your program are important to define. First and foremost is the role of the field director or coordinator. This individual is responsible for overseeing the field program, which includes recruiting sites, placing students, establishing and defining all field paperwork and policies compiled in a field manual, and training students and field instructors. The next important role is the faculty field liaison. The purpose of this role is

FIGURE 1.2 ■ The Learning Triangle

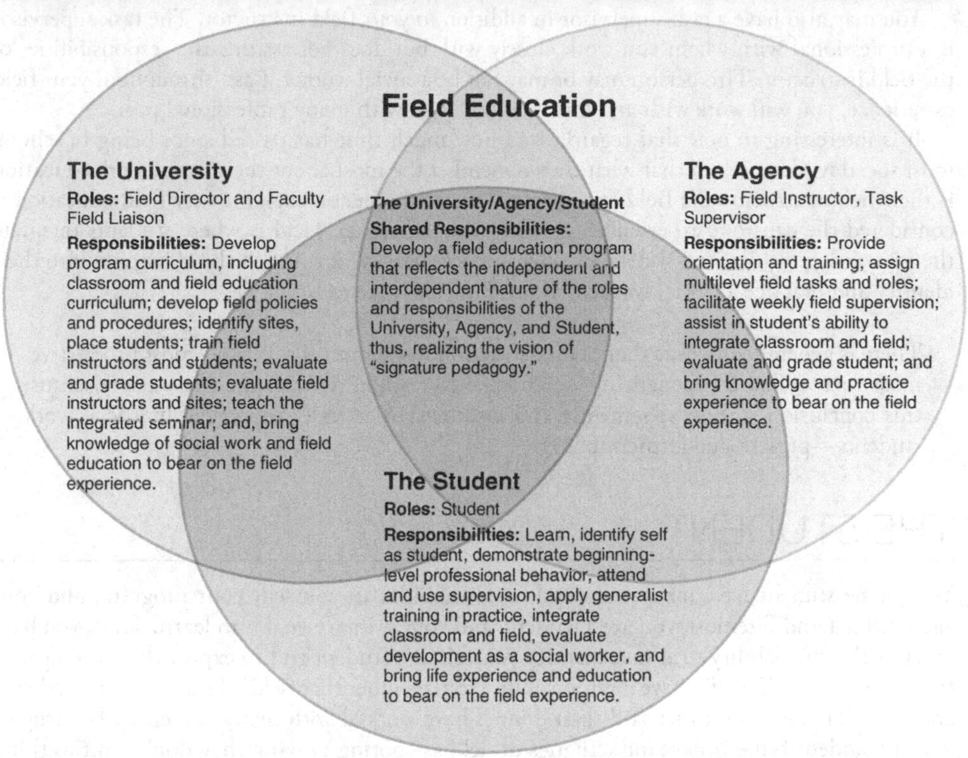

Field Education

The University

Roles: Field Director and Faculty Field Liaison

Responsibilities: Develop program curriculum, including classroom and field education curriculum; develop field policies and procedures; identify sites, place students; train field instructors and students; evaluate and grade students; evaluate field instructors and sites; teach the integrated seminar; and, bring knowledge of social work and field education to bear on the field experience.

The University/Agency/Student

Shared Responsibilities: Develop a field education program that reflects the independent and interdependent nature of the roles and responsibilities of the University, Agency, and Student, thus, realizing the vision of "signature pedagogy."

The Agency

Roles: Field Instructor, Task Supervisor

Responsibilities: Provide orientation and training; assign multilevel field tasks and roles; facilitate weekly field supervision; assist in student's ability to integrate classroom and field; evaluate and grade student; and bring knowledge and practice experience to bear on the field experience.

The Student

Roles: Student

Responsibilities: Learn, identify self as student, demonstrate beginning-level professional behavior, attend and use supervision, apply generalist training in practice, integrate classroom and field, evaluate development as a social worker, and bring life experience and education to bear on the field experience.

to conduct site visits, engage in troubleshooting, and assign a final grade. The preceding roles may be fulfilled by one person or by many; thus, it is important for you to familiarize yourself with your field office and the roles and requisite responsibilities of those in the field office and to print out or obtain a copy of your field manual.

Also, your program may offer an integrative seminar course as part of the curriculum. This course serves an important role. This course usually runs concurrent with field instruction and may be taught by a member of the social work department, the field faculty liaison, or the field director. The purpose of the seminar course is to provide an opportunity for students to meet, usually weekly, and share their field experiences. Furthermore, it provides an additional opportunity to integrate classroom content with practice experiences through the completion of important academic assignments.

THE AGENCY

The agency is the second member of the learning triangle and also provides a critical function. Without the agency, field education could not happen. It is the belief of field educators that some things happen in field that cannot be replicated in the classroom and these experiences are critically important to the development of social workers.

The field instructor is the most important person at the agency. This is the social work practitioner who has agreed to manage the field education experience by planning your orientation and training program, assigning appropriate multilevel tasks, providing weekly supervision, and completing all required program paperwork, all with the goal of developing and demonstrating the competencies necessary to become a social worker. Furthermore, the field instructor brings practice experience and knowledge of the agency to field education. If you are in an agency that does not have a social worker on staff, your field instructor may be a person outside the agency or affiliated with the university.

You may also have a task supervisor in addition to your field instructor. The task supervisor is a professional with whom you work closely with but does not assume the responsibilities of the field instructor. This person may or may not be a social worker. Last, throughout your field experience, you will work with and form relationships with many professional peers.

It is interesting to note that regardless of how much time has passed since being in school, most social workers report that what they remember the most about their social work education is their field instructor and field experience. This phenomenon explains why field education is considered the capstone experience in social work education. Field is where students integrate the knowledge, values, and skills they have learned and are learning in the classroom into their identity and practice as social workers. Kadushin (1991) states,

> There is general consensus that field instruction is the most significant, most productive, most memorable component of social work education. Within the general consensus, this conclusion is most vehemently and most enthusiastically supported by social work students—present and former. (p. 11)

THE STUDENT

You as the student have many roles and responsibilities to yourself, your program, and your agency. First and foremost, you are a student, and your primary goal is to learn. Thus, you have an ethical responsibility to always identify yourself as a student and to expect that your agency treat you as such. You also have a responsibility to remember that field education is an academic endeavor. This is often easier said than done. I have worked with many students who struggle with this, identifying important activities of field as "boring"; saying they don't want to think about "that" (usually some required academic element of field), they just want to serve their clients; or not reading important field documents. I often have to remind students that the only reason they are at the agency is to learn and prepare to be a social worker, which can happen only by integrating the classroom curriculum with all the possible practice experiences at the agency. Therefore, it is absolutely necessary to consider the academic aspect of field while in the field.

Most students enter field with volunteer service or paid work experience; however, regardless of your level of previous experience, it is important to remember that field is the first time you will have entered an agency as a social work student under the direct supervision of a social worker engaging in professional social work tasks.

Also, with all the competing demands you will face, you may be tempted to skim over or not read this guide or your field manual. I encourage you to carve out time to read everything assigned to you, because if you do not, you compromise your learning, training, and professional socialization. Incidentally, it is usually obvious to all involved in your training when you have not done your homework. Thus, I ask you to make a conscious commitment to your learning. I also ask you to trust those in the field office and your field instructor and realize that they have your educational best interest at heart and are not there to make your life miserable. While your field director's complete focus is on field education, your field instructor has multiple responsibilities and sometimes can overlook your academic needs as a student. Although this is understandable, given the demands of practicing as a social worker and being a field instructor, it can place the burden of ensuring the academic focus of field on you, the student. So, if you are not prepared, have not read the manual or the chapter, or have not completed the IA, you may miss an important opportunity to make or strengthen a new connection or increase your level of competence (not to mention your confidence). This book takes this into consideration and is grounded in an approach designed to empower you to assume the role of an active, engaged, and prepared learner.

Finally, it is important to realize that lifelong learning, which is central to being a professional social worker, is not always tested nor graded in the traditional sense you are accustomed to, but it is nonetheless critical to the clients you will work with. Therefore, I encourage you to begin to embrace that now. A great deal of the reading and reflection will not be tested or graded in the way you are used to; however, you will be evaluated, and many of the competencies that you are expected to demonstrate cannot be met without reflection and academic integration.

REFLECTION QUESTION 1.3

Now that you have an introduction to field, reflect on and write about the following. First, reflect on the learning triangle and think about what you will need from each of the members, including from yourself, in order for field to be successful. Second, think about what you are hoping to get out of field. What are you most excited about as you think about field? And finally, what are you concerned about?

ROOM TO REFLECT

PROCESS AND CONTENT IN GENERALIST FIELD EDUCATION

The most exciting thing about field education is that it is both a process- and content-driven experience. In terms of the process, field has a beginning, middle, and an end. As students have reported and I have observed year after year, the first day of field is significantly different from the last. This process reflects a transformation of sorts or the unfolding of an experience that is equally important as the second part, which is the content of field. A competency-based education emphasizes requisite knowledge, values, skills, and cognitive and affective processes that are necessary for effective practice and lay the foundation of the student's ability to demonstrate competence in field. Thus, you will simultaneously integrate educational content while going through an important process of socialization to the profession and professional development.

SOCIALIZATION TO THE PROFESSION

As stated earlier, one of the goals of field education is to assist you in your socialization to the profession and development as a competent social worker. This is accomplished through your ability to develop and demonstrate your professional identity as a social worker. Through a process of

- immersion in a professional organization,
- observation of professional social workers,

- role rehearsal, and

- reflection on current and past conceptualizations of social workers,

you will begin to develop your identity as a social worker. This means that you will begin to conceptualize what it means to you to be a social worker and demonstrate that in your practice behaviors. Earls Larrison and Korr (2013) emphasize the importance of the development of a professional self and, more specifically, "what it means to think and perform like a social worker through the development of the professional self" (p. 200). The authors state that "self-awareness, critical reflexivity, and analytical thinking" are necessary in order for a competent practitioner to recognize the role that the professional self plays in what they do as a social worker (p. 200). These three concepts—self-awareness, reflection, and critical thinking—are integrated throughout the text to assist you as you engage in your own process of professional development.

Field is a unique educational experience because you will have an opportunity to observe real-life professional social work practice in a social work setting. This will be helpful in that you will see behaviors you wish to emulate as well as behaviors you will feel are not a fit for who you are becoming as a professional social worker. In some settings, you will have interprofessional learning experiences in which you will observe other professionals, such as nurses, teachers, administrators, police officers, and psychologists, to name a few. Observing and interacting with professionals from other professions provide an opportunity to compare and contrast those professions with social workers and thus better define who social workers are and the role they play in the lives of clients.

Furthermore, field is an opportunity to determine if social work is the right fit for you as a profession. Many students tell me it is comforting to know that they have made the right choice. Field is also a safe opportunity to try on a particular role as a social worker. As many students tell me they could never work in their field setting again as do students who say their placement experience has confirmed that they have found the right professional practice area. Better yet, I have had students tell me that even though they did not see themselves working with the population they served in their field site, the significant knowledge, values, and skills they gained while working with that population in their field site will stay with them and contribute greatly in their development and practice as a social worker. All of these experiences form the foundation of how students begin to develop their own identities as social workers. These practice experiences are also important because they are real, and students often state that real-life practice experiences are handled very differently than the textbook case examples. Conversely, students have also told me that they have observed practice-based situations in their agencies that they could clearly point to and say, "I learned about that in class."

Your development as a professional social worker is a dynamic and ongoing process. The outcome of this process will be explored in greater detail toward the end of your field experience in Chapter 12. At this time, it is useful to consider the following reflection question as a way to begin to conceptualize professional development.

REFLECTION QUESTION 1.4

What does it mean to you to be a professional? What are the advantages of being a professional versus an employee, and are there any disadvantages?

As you think about yourself as a professional social worker, what excites you and what creates anxiety?

ROOM TO REFLECT

THE USE OF PORTFOLIOS IN FIELD

The GFEA encourages you to be an active learner and to use reflection and various IAs in the learning process. One way to support this type of learning and organize the process is to create a portfolio. A portfolio has been found to be an effective tool in the process of integrating curriculum and field, professional development, and lifelong learning (Alvarez & Moxley, 2004; Cournoyer & Stanley, 2002; Riser, 1999; Schatz & Simon, 1999). Alvarez and Moxley (2004) present the portfolio as a "process, product, and tool" and describe each of these as an important part of the learning process (p. 92). The authors go on to outline the benefits of a portfolio for students that include expanding evaluation beyond traditional tests, providing a way to document accomplishments in learning, requiring that students engage in self-evaluation of their professional development (which can result in defining their professional self), and supporting self-awareness and finding the meaning and totality of their work. Fitch, Peet, Reed, and Tolman (2008) expand the discussion of portfolios to include eportfolios and found them to be effective in helping students become "'self-authors' who integrated competencies across courses, connected course knowledge and skills to field work, and engaged in ongoing self-reflection and peer review processes" (p. 51). Thus, a portfolio can provide a concrete way to link curriculum to practice.

Schatz and Simon (1999) state that "the use of a portfolio assignment supports students' learning through the creation of a tangible product that illustrates practice knowledge and skills" (p. 101). In addition, they go on to say that "a portfolio is a collection of selected materials that demonstrate one's knowledge, skills, and expertise amassed in a notebook or special type of binder" (p. 101). For field, the purpose of a portfolio is to assist you in

1. better understanding and integrating the experiences of field with the curriculum of the classroom by linking various elements to the overarching areas of social work education;

2. improving supervision by providing concrete, tangible products to discuss and review; and

3. displaying your professional development and accomplishments by including your résumé and samples of your work that may distinguish you from another social worker.

A portfolio can be a useful tool when applying for a job, graduate school, or your advanced field placement, or it can become a treasured keepsake of your field experience and education. Regardless of the outcome, developing a portfolio can be fun and educational. Integrative Activity 1.2 outlines a process of creating a portfolio and provides a list of possible elements to choose from to develop your portfolio. This all being said, portfolios can seem overwhelming, confusing, and time-consuming and feel that they are yet another academic assignment that is taking away from your work with clients. In fact, Heron, Lerpiniere, and Church (2010) found that portfolios can "get in the way of practice rather than be informed by it" (p. 13). Thus, care should be taken in considering how best to use the portfolio and what should be included, given that students found that the separate parts of the portfolio were more helpful than the compilation of the portfolio as a whole. But, as Alvarez and Moxley (2004) state, "The portfolio offers a powerful opportunity for students to engage in critical reflection and to make up their minds about the merits of a particular learning experience, as well as to plan their next steps in job, career, and/ or further education" (p. 102). Heron and colleagues (2010) recommend that in order for the portfolio to be helpful, it should complement the student's experience in field, not take attention away from it. In order to meet this expectation, consider how the portfolio can be helpful in both your learning and as a means of demonstrating your competence as a social worker.

INTEGRATIVE ACTIVITY 1.2
THE FIELD PORTFOLIO

Purpose: The purpose of the field portfolio is to (1) have an opportunity to create a tangible record of your work in field, (2) assist you in the process of integrating curriculum with the practice tasks of field, (3) enable you to translate the specific elements of your site to the expected competencies and overarching aspects of generalist practice, and (4) demonstrate competence as a generalist practitioner.

Directions: To create a portfolio, follow these steps:

1. Obtain a binder or accordion folder.

2. Create tabs for the sections; sections can either be the competencies or overarching areas of generalist practice—see the outline for suggestions.

3. Identify and produce an element.

4. Place the element in the appropriate section.

5. Consider or provide a rationale for how that element reflects the competency or aspect of generalist practice.

6. Add elements to your portfolio over the course of your field education experience.

Competency 1: Demonstrate Ethical and Professional Behavior

- use reflection and self-regulation to manage personal values and maintain professionalism in practice situations

Competency 9: Evaluate Practice with Individuals, Families, Groups, Organizations, and Communities

- apply evaluation findings to improve practice effectiveness at the micro, mezzo, and macro levels

Suggested Elements: To assist in the process of selecting possible portfolio elements, a list of possible elements has been provided but is not exhaustive. The items are grouped in sections that reflect the core competencies. For those elements that reflect the overarching aspects of the GFEA, they are bolded. The items that make up the portfolio can come from two primary sources. First, an item may reflect a particular task that you do at your field site. For instance, if you conduct intakes, you could place a sample of an intake in the Competency 6 section. Second, you can choose to do a particular task that is not a normal part of your agency role, such as write a comprehensive social history or complete an ecomap. Either of these items would be placed under Competency 7. Other items can flow directly from the field course, such as IAs from the text and field paperwork (for example, your learning plan and field evaluation). Last, assignments from other courses can also be included.

For agency-based elements, it is critical that you discuss using these with your field instructor and ensure that no identifying client information is included. If you are not able to copy work, you can always create mock-ups of your work using composite clients so as to ensure client confidentiality.

The item selection and the process you go through to create your portfolio are useful in linking curriculum to practice. The portfolio becomes a record of your experiences and can be used to document your competencies and accomplishments with prospective employers, graduate programs, or advanced practice field sites.

Field Portfolio Outline

I. Competency 1: Demonstrate Ethical and Professional Behavior

   a. Course syllabi

   b. Résumé

   c. Integrative Activity 2.3: Curriculum Review

   d. Training certificates related to specialized curriculum

   e. Integrative Activity 12.1: Curriculum Analysis

   f. Orientation materials

   g. Integrative Activity 2.2: Agency Analysis

   h. Agency brochure

   i. Integrative Activity 3.1: Identifying Multilevel Learning Tasks

   j. Integrative Activity 3.2: Identifying Foundational Roles of Social Work in Field

   k. Integrative Activity 5.1: The Supervision Outline

   l. Integrative Activity 5.2: The Supervision Agenda

   m. Integrative Activity 5.3: Documenting Your Supervision Session

   n. Integrative Activity 9.1: Task Analysis

   o. Oral communication skills: Interviewing

      a. Integrative Activity 6.1: Assessing Interviewing Skills

      b. Integrative Activity 6.2: The Process Recording

      c. Audio/video transcript

   p. Written communication skills: Documentation/professional writing

      a. Integrative Activity 6.3: Writing a Case Note

      b. Task or treatment group notes

      c. Program/project report

      d. Meeting minutes

      e. Newsletter article

      f. Agency fliers

      g. Letter to the editor

   q. Electronic communication skills

      a. Copy of professional e-mail

      b. Social media submission

      c. Electronic document submission

      d. Copy of electronic client record submission

   r. Foundational roles

      a. Integrative Activity 3.2: Identifying Foundational Roles of Social Work in Field

      b. Broker

         1. Identify community resources used as referrals

      c. Advocate

      d. Educator

      e. Facilitator

      f. Mediator

      g. Counselor

   s. Integrative Activity 7.1: The Agency Ethics Audit

   t. Integrative Activity 7.2: Resolving an Ethical Dilemma

   u. Integrative Activity 11.1: Professional Development of Self Capstone Paper

   v. Integrative Activity 12.2: Pulling It All Together

II. Competency 2: Engage Diversity and Difference in Practice

   a. Training certificates

   b. Integrative Activity 8.1: Understanding Diversity in Field: A Multilevel Approach

   c. Integrative Activity 8.2: Developing Culturally Competent Practice Skills in Field

   d. Examples of culturally competent practice interventions

   e. Case notes

III. Competency 3: Advance Human Rights and Social, Economic, and Environmental Justice

   a. Integrative Activity 8.3: Identifying Social, Economic, and Environmental Injustice in Field

(Continued)

(Continued)

    b.   Meeting minutes

    c.   Organization membership certificates

    d.   Case notes documenting specific interventions

IV.   Competency 4: Engage in Practice-Informed Research and Research-Informed Practice

    a.   Research papers from other courses

    b.   Research proposal

    c.   Agency-based research

    d.   Client satisfaction survey findings

    e.   Integrative Activity 9.2: The Literature Review

V.   Competency 5: Engage in Policy Practice

    a.   Policy analysis

    b.   Policy paper

    c.   Sample policy from agency practice

    d.   Integrative Activity 8.4: Policy Analysis and Practice

    e.   Letter to representatives

    f.   Testimony to representatives

    g.   Participation in Lobby Day event

VI.   Competency 6: Engage with Individuals, Families, Groups, Organizations, and Communities

    a.   Integrative Activity 10.1: The Phases of the Planned Change Process in Field

    b.   Agency-based intakes

    c.   Case notes documenting engagement

    d.   Integrative Activity 6.1: Assessing Interviewing Skills

    e.   Group icebreakers

    f.   Meeting minutes documenting facilitated introductions

VII.   Competency 7: Assess Individuals, Families, Groups, Organizations, and Communities

    a.   Agency-based assessments

    b.   Integrative Activity 10.2: Multidimensional/Multilevel Assessment

    c.   Ecomap

    d.   Genogram

    e.   Social history

    f.   Mini mental status

    g.   Activities of daily living/Instrumental activities of daily living

    h.   Drug and alcohol

    i.   Risk assessment

    j.   Integrative Activity 10.4: Developing and Implementing Multilevel Plans

    k.   Individualized service plans

    l.   Goal sheets

VIII.   Competency 8: Intervene with Individuals, Families, Groups, Organizations, and Communities

    a.   Sample interventions: Activities completed with client systems

    b.   Case notes documenting interventions

    c.   Materials developed for group session

    d.   Integrative Activity 10.3: Identifying Theoretical Perspectives, Practice Models, and Commonly Utilized Interventions in Field

    e.   Integrative Activity 10.4: Developing and Implementing Multilevel Plans

    f.   Discharge summary

    g.   Closing note

    h.   Transfer note

    i.   Final report

IX.   Competency 9: Evaluate Practice with Individuals, Families, Groups, Organizations, and Communities

    a.   Integrative Activity 10.5: The Planned Change Case Analysis

    b.   Individual client evaluation

    c.   Group evaluation

    d.   Program evaluation

    e.   Client satisfaction survey

X.   Other

Note: All elements in the portfolio must maintain confidentiality either by blacking out confidential information or by creating elements without any identifying information. It is critically important to discuss this with your field instructor.

THE ROLE OF REFLECTION IN FIELD

To achieve the goals identified in the conceptualization of generalist field education—socialization to the profession, professional development of self, and integration of the classroom content with the practice experiences of field—you will need to develop the skill of reflection.

Canda and Furman (2010) emphasize being reflective as a critical part of both personal and professional growth and state that "personal engagement in learning is a transformative experience that requires reflectivity, the practice of introspective self-reflection, and reflection about how one's inner life and the outer world reflect on each other" (p. 17). They relate reflection specifically to what they call *reflective reading* and state that the prerequisite is "silence—that is, quieting in order to know oneself, the inner stirrings of the heart, and the discerning wisdom of the intellect" (p. 17). They go on to explain that reflective silence requires "a willingness to become introspective, to 'get centered,' and to pay gentle consistent attention to oneself and one's situation" (p. 18).

This useful concept can be applied to the reflection process for field education and renamed *reflective experiencing* (Larkin, 2010), which emphasizes the experiential nature of field education. Canda and Furman (2010) discuss the importance of building this skill through being regular, consistent, and disciplined. It is important to set a time for reflection and keep to it by building it into your day or week.

Remember, the overall purpose of reflection and journal writing is to enable you to step back and take a longer, more integrated view of your field experiences. This is particularly important, given that students are often practicing in hectic, chaotic, and high-paced settings in which days can go by before they can come up for air. In these types of situations, it is not uncommon for students to report that they don't even know what they did all week, just that it was crazy. Or, on the other hand, a student may find himself or herself engaged in what can seem to be a boring or mundane task and, without reflection, miss the learning opportunity present in the task. Making a commitment to regular and disciplined reflection becomes critically important to your development as a social worker. As Kiser (2008) states, "You might think of experience without reflection as being somewhat like an unread book sitting on a shelf, or perhaps a book that you have quickly scanned but not carefully read, understood, or thought about" (p. 70). My goal is to help you turn your field experiences into ones that resemble a well-read book, one that shows signs of study, with turned-down corners; fanned pages; items highlighted, underlined, and circled; and extensive notation in the margins. This is the point where field comes to life.

When writing field journals, it is important to go beyond the restating of events. Although setting the stage is helpful, your writing should be more than a blow-by-blow account of the day or a list of activities. The journal entry should express the thinking, feeling, and doing aspects of your field experiences. Reflection and journal writing are skills that do not come easy for all students; you may need to work on developing them. For help in getting started with your reflection and journal writing, see Integrative Activity 1.3. This handout provides several categories you can select to reflect on.

INTEGRATIVE ACTIVITY 1.3
THE FIELD JOURNAL

Purpose: The purpose of this IA is to provide some guidelines and suggested areas of reflection that will assist you in the development of your critical thinking skills through the process of writing reflection journals. It is important to note that writing reflection journals is a skill, and you need to determine how easily journal writing comes to you. The guidelines provided are structural in nature and may be all that you need. If that is not the case, consider the suggested areas of reflection that you can focus on in the context of a field experience. These can provide inspiration or a more structured approach when you write your reflection journals.

(Continued)

(Continued)

Directions: Read and follow these guidelines:

1. Find a quiet place and get comfortable.

2. Write legibly or type your journal entry. Although the length is not as important as the time spent and the content, a general guideline is a minimum of 3–4 pages handwritten or 2–3 typed pages (with standard font and margins).

3. The reflection journal is for you. It is a place to process your experiences, ask questions, and explore your thoughts and feelings about specific content areas, the field process, field experiences, and general questions concerning field.

4. If you hand in your journals and receive feedback, read the comments. One of the purposes of the feedback is to improve *your* journal writing skills so that *you* will get the most from this learning task.

Competency 1: Demonstrate Ethical and Professional Behavior

- use reflection and self-regulation to manage personal values and maintain professionalism in practice situations

Competency 9: Evaluate Practice with Individuals, Families, Groups, Organizations, and Communities

- apply evaluation findings to improve practice effectiveness at the micro, mezzo, and macro levels

Suggested Reflection Areas: Select one significant event or experience of field and explore it, addressing any, all, or one to two of the following specific areas that apply:

1. **Placement Experience:** Describe what happened; identify the significant events, including successes, concerns, and challenges.

2. **Self-Awareness:** What were you feeling, thinking, and doing about the situation? What assumptions do you hold that help you understand what you are feeling, thinking, and doing with regard to the placement experience?

3. **Diversity Issues:** What diversity issues, if any, were present in relation to this event, and how did you deal with them?

4. **Legal and Ethical Concerns:** What significant legal or ethical issues are there in relation to this situation, and what did you do regarding them?

5. **Organizational or Systemic Concerns:** What are the significant organizational or systemic concerns or issues in relation to this event, and what did you do to address them? Include peer and coworker relationships and interactions.

6. **Supervision:** What was discussed with supervisors about this experience? What did you think about how the supervisory meeting went? What did you do with the information?

7. **Learning:** What did you learn from this experience about yourself, the agency, your client, the supervisor, and so on?

8. **Additional Observations:**

FINAL THOUGHTS ON THE IMPORTANCE OF FIELD

Field education is a significant learning experience because it is real life, the living classroom. This means you will have the opportunity to get out of the classroom and work with real client systems in an organization under the supervision of a practicing social worker. Field education is also an opportunity to act while still being a student. Students are usually excited to have an opportunity to practice what they have learned or are still learning in the classroom. Furthermore, the role of a student has interesting qualities of its own.

As a student, you have a unique opportunity to experience a practice setting in a way that you could never experience without being a student. That is, in many ways, you are an insider and outsider at the same time. This provides a unique perspective that will give rise to many important observations. These important observations also often become tough questions about why something is the way that it is or why something is done a certain way. Do not be afraid to ask the tough questions, as they often lead to interesting tasks and accomplishments on the part of the student.

FREQUENTLY EXPERIENCED SITUATIONS

The following is a frequently experienced concern that students have as they enter field and reflects the dynamic nature of field education. Reflect on this situation and discuss it in class or with your field instructor.

What if my clients don't want to work with me because I'm a student?

I'm afraid to tell my clients I'm a student because they might not want to work with me. Do I really have to tell them?

This concern is very common for students going into field. The short answer is yes, you and your field instructor have an ethical responsibility to notify the clients with whom you work that you are a student (NASW, 2017). The long answer is, once you do, you may experience a variety of responses that you might not have fully considered. First, it is possible that a client won't want to work with you because you are a student or that you cannot engage in a learning task because you are a student. This experience and the fear of this happening can cause students to question why they need to tell their clients they are students or, even worse, cause students to not disclose their student status to clients to prevent something such as this from happening.

Indeed, having a client refuse to work with you or being told you can't do something because you are a student can be frustrating and even upsetting. However, if this happens to you, it is important to keep a few things in mind.

First of all, as already stated, you, your field instructor, and the agency are ethically bound to inform the client systems you work with that you are a student. This is not negotiable. Second, in all likelihood, at some point during your field experience, you may have a client refuse to work with you, express concern about working with "the student," or not be able to do something because you are a student, so it is useful to prepare yourself now for how you will respond. The best thing to do is acknowledge that you hear the client and respect his or her wishes. If you feel that you can discuss the situation with the client, it is okay to let the client know that yes, you are a student, but you have been trained and are receiving supervision by a social worker, and you will ensure that the client receives the best possible service. If the client insists that he or she does not want to work

with a student, thank the client for meeting with you and let the client know that you will need to let your field instructor know about the client's request and that someone will be with him or her shortly. Inform your field instructor or agency designee of the situation, and make sure that someone meets with the client. After the client has been taken care of, discuss the situation with a supervisor to see if you or your field instructor can do anything else to keep this from happening in the future.

If the situation involves a learning task such as participating in a meeting, first handle the situation in a similar fashion as suggested in the preceding example. Then meet with your field instructor to determine if the field instructor or agency director can do anything to enable you to participate in that learning task in the future.

A bright spot related to being a student and one that is the opposite of the preceding situation is the fact that a number of students report that a client has opened up to them because they were a student. I have heard many stories of students saying they have met with clients who the social worker said probably wouldn't talk much, but when they met and the client was introduced to the student, the client completely opened up. What often happens is that many clients like the idea of helping a student and thus become engaged. Or the student's status actually becomes an effective engagement tool as they talk about the school, the program, or the student's desire to be a social worker. So, although sometimes your student status may become an issue for your client, there may also be times that it can be an asset. The most important thing you can do when working with clients is to be confident and have clarity about your role as a social work student in your agency and always introduce yourself as a student. This alone will translate into competence for a client.

Finally, try not to take these things personally or overemphasize your student status, because for some clients, anything may be used as a deterrent to the helping process. Or the client may be searching for a way to find some control in a situation that may be making them feel out of control. Or the client may have a legitimate concern that needs to be respected. So, the best course of action is to acknowledge and meet the client's need and move on to the next task at hand.

Suggested Field Tasks

- Review Integrative Activity 1.1.

- Identify key players and the role of each according to the learning triangle (i.e., field instructor, field director, faculty field liaison).

- Determine your title and role as a student.

- Use reflection to explore your role, your tasks, and your experiences of field.

References

Alvarez, A. R., & Moxley, D. P. (2004). The student portfolio in social work education. *Journal of Teaching in Social Work, 24*(1/2), 87–103.

Bogo, M. (2010). *Achieving competence in social work through field education.* Toronto, Ontario, Canada: University of Toronto Press.

Bogo, M. (2015). Field education for clinical social work practice: Best practices and contemporary challenges. *Clinical Social Work Journal, 43,* 317–324. doi. 10.10007/s10615-015-0526-5

Canda, E. R., & Furman, L. D. (2010). *Spiritual diversity in social work practice: The heart of helping* (2nd ed.). New York, NY: Oxford University Press.

Carey, M. E., & McCardle, M. (2011). Can an observational field model enhance critical thinking and generalist practice skills? *Journal of Social Work Education, 47*(2), 357–366.

Council on Social Work Education (CSWE). (2008). *Educational policy and accreditation standards.* Alexandria, VA: Author.

Council on Social Work Education (CSWE). (2015). *Educational policy and accreditation standards.* Alexandria, VA: Author.

Cournoyer, B., & Stanley, M. (2002). *The social work portfolio: Planning, assessing, and documenting lifelong learning in a dynamic profession.* Pacific Grove, CA: Brooks/Cole.

Earls Larrison, T., & Korr, W. (2013). Does social work have a signature pedagogy? *Journal of Social Work Education, 49,* 194–206.

Fitch, D., Peet, M., Reed, B., & Tolman, R. (2008). The use of eportfolios in evaluating the curriculum and student learning. *Journal of Social Work Education, 44*(3), 37–54.

Fortune, A. E. (1994). Field education. In F. J. Reamer (Ed.), *The foundations of social work knowledge* (pp. 151–194). New York, NY: Columbia University Press.

Heron, G., Lerpiniere, J., & Church, S. (2010). Portfolios and practice-based learning: A student perspective. *Journal of Practice Teaching & Learning, 10*(1), 5–26. doi:10.1921/146066910X570267

Johnson, L., & Yanca, S. (2007). *Social work practice: A generalist approach.* Boston, MA: Allyn and Bacon.

Kadushin, A. (1991). Introduction. In D. Schneck, B. Grossman, & U. Glassman (Eds.), *Field education in social work: Contemporary issues and trends.* Dubuque, IA: Kendall Hunt.

Kirst-Ashman, K., & Hull Jr., G. (2006). *Understanding generalist practice* (4th ed.). Pacific Grove, CA: Brooks/Cole.

Kiser, P. (2008). *The human services internship: Getting the most from your experience* (2nd ed.). Belmont, CA: Thomson Brooks/Cole.

Larkin, S. (2010). Spiritually sensitive professional development of self: A curricular module for field education. *Social Work & Christianity, 37*(4), 446–466.

National Association of Social Workers (NASW). (2017). *Code of ethics of the National Association of Social Workers.* Washington DC: Author. Retrieved March 9,

2018, from https://www.socialworkers.org/LinkClick.aspx?fileticket=ms_ArtLqzeI%3d&portalid=0

Riser, E. (1999). Student practice portfolios: Integrating diversity and learning in the field experience. *Arete, 23*(1), 89–96.

Schatz, M. S., & Simon, S. (1999). The portfolio approach for generalist social work practice: A successful tool for students in field education. *The Journal of Baccalaureate Social Work, 5*(1), 99.

Schatz, M. S., Jenkins, L. E., & Sheafor, B. W. (1990). Milford refined: A model of initial and advanced generalist social work. *Journal of Social Work Education, 26*(3), 217.

Schneck, D., Grossman, B., & Glassman, U. (Eds.). (1991). *Field education in social work: Contemporary issues and trends*. Dubuque, IA: Kendall Hunt.

Sherer, M., & Peleg-Oren, N. (2005). Differences of teachers', field instructors', and students' views on job analysis of social work students. *Journal of Social Work Education, 41*(2), 315.

Wayne, J., Bogo, M., & Raskin, M. (2006). The need for radical change in field education. *Journal of Social Work Education, 42*(1), 161.

Wayne, J., Bogo, M., & Raskin, M. (2010). Field education as the signature pedagogy of social work education: Congruence and disparity. *Journal of Social Work Education, 46*(3), 327–339.

THE ORGANIZATION

Orientation and Training

Foundational to the generalist practice field education approach (GFEA) outlined in Chapter 1 is the role of the organization in shaping both your field experience and your professional development. For the purposes of this chapter, *organization* designates the setting where you are completing your field placement, is interchangeable with *agency*, and includes host settings such as a hospital, school, or corrections facility. The first few days at your organization are important because many critical things need to happen for you to maximize your opportunities for learning and have a successful field education experience. But, before you launch into your orientation and training, it is useful to take a step back and think about your entrance into the organization in the context of immersion.

FIELD EDUCATION AS IMMERSION

According to the Merriam-Webster online dictionary (2017), *immersion* is defined as "instruction based on extensive exposure to surroundings or conditions that are native or pertinent to the object of study." In social work education, immersion experiences have been developed to facilitate cross-cultural awareness (Cordero & Rodriguez, 2009; Mapp, McFarland, & Newell, 2007; Roholt & Fisher, 2013), and, of course, international field placements can be considered immersion, given the emphasis placed on preparing a student to manage unfamiliar situations and developing the skills necessary to work in an environment that is very different from what they are used to (Nuttman-Schwartz & Berger, 2011). But immersion has not been applied across field education, even though it offers important pedagogical ways of thinking about the experience.

For instance, Roholt and Fisher (2013) offer three pedagogical approaches used to enhance learning in short-term international courses that are useful when applied to field education, particularly how a student thinks about entering their organization. The three approaches are "experiential learning, transformative learning, and decolonizing pedagogy" (p. 48). Experiential learning is not new to field education; in fact, as presented in Chapter 1 with regard to the history of field education in social work, *doing* has always been an important part of social work education. What is important for you as a student to keep front and center is that your learning will come in many ways and from multiple sources as you engage in the process of "action and reflection" (p. 60), thus the focus on journal writing in field, which supports documenting what you do in field and encourages reflecting on your practice. The next pedagogical approach that is useful to employ as you enter your organization is *transformative learning*, which is grounded in critical reflection and your ability to explore your assumptions that underlie how you interpret your experiences of the organization (p. 61). The latter is what is of most importance in order to make your experiences transformational—specifically, your ability to ask yourself, *What are the assumptions I hold that lead to the conclusions I draw as a result of reflecting on my experiences?* The development of your critical-thinking skills, grounded in both cognitive and affective processes (Council on Social Work Education [CSWE], 2015), is key and will be addressed in more detail later in the text. So, for now, you want to try to be open and allow yourself to take in all that you are experiencing as you enter the organization. The importance of these early experiences will become more apparent later as you reflect on them and synthesize their role in whom you become as a social worker. Finally, the last pedagogical approach and most important offered by Roholt and Fisher (2013) is *decolonizing pedagogy* (p. 62). In the context of international educational experiences, this concept focuses on raising the awareness of global colonization and the "othering" of individuals through practices grounded in colonization. These practices are viewed within the context of understanding power relationships and the students' role in supporting them in their practice. For field education, considering power relationships in the context of how your organization engages in social work practice and what will be asked of you as you practice is important in order to ensure that you are able to uphold the profession's values of dignity and worth of the individual and the importance of human relationships; all while serving within systems in which power differentials between clients and workers exist.

Roholt and Fisher (2013) offer three pedagogical approaches used in their Master of Social Work study abroad programs with the goal of combating what Dewey talked about almost a century ago, which is that educational "experiences can be 'mis-educative' just as they can be educative" (p. 48), and encourage social work educators to develop processes that encourage the latter. The same can be said for field education, as a student immersing yourself in an organization and practice setting that is novel can bring about learning that is both educative and "mis-educative." Therefore, you must be vigilant in your ability to identify what you are doing, reflect on your learning experiences, challenge your assumptions about your conclusions, place this within a context of the power relationships inherent in social work practice, and even challenge the injustices that can occur within the context of helping. In order to begin this process, it is necessary to start by familiarizing yourself with your organization by focusing on two important topics: first, the organization itself and its potential impact on your learning, and second, your orientation and training plan, with specific emphasis on the role of curriculum in orientation and training.

THE ORGANIZATION

The organization you have selected to serve in as your field site is an important aspect of your learning experience in several ways. First, your socialization to the profession depends on affiliation with an organization, your field instructor, agency peers, and other professional organizations with which you interact. Second, your individual development as a social worker will be impacted by the agency, meaning the type of services, culture, and practices of your agency will contribute to who you become as a social worker. Third, you will have an impact on the organization that can be positive and negative. Mallory, Cox, and Panos (2012) identified several benefits and costs to agencies that host bachelor-level social work interns. In terms of benefits, agencies reported both the positive quality and quantity of services provided to clients and that students had a positive impact on the agency in terms of reduced stress of the workers, higher morale, and respect for the creativity and positive attitudes of the interns. With regard to the negative impact, Mallory and colleagues (2012) reported that the vast majority of the sample responded with "none." But for those that did identify a negative, the respondents identified two common issues—unprofessionalism of the student and turnover of students. With regard to turnover, this was identified as a negative due to the impact their departure had on clients who struggled with trust and forming relationships. It is interesting to note that this study did not find time for supervision to be a negative, which was contrary to previous findings and a concern I hear from students year after year. In light of this research, it is helpful to first consider the type and culture of your placement agency and the impact those factors can have on your learning, your experience of social work as a profession, and the type of social work practiced in the agency. Next, focus on how to successfully address the concerns that have been identified in the research to ensure that your presence in the organization doesn't have a negative impact on the organization as a whole. A useful way for you to consider the above is to use the student-in-organization approach, which is presented below.

STUDENT-IN-ORGANIZATION

Person-in-environment is a long-held foundational concept of social work practice that considers the reciprocal nature and interplay of people and their environments; it is "social work's *simultaneous focus* on both the person and the person's environment that makes social work unique among the various helping professions" (Sheafor & Horejsi, 2015, p. 7). This concept is useful when applied to your field education experience and requires you to adopt a student-in-organization perspective.

The student-in-organization perspective considers the reciprocal nature and interplay of you, the student, with your organization. The perspective suggests that your interaction with the organization will shape your field education experience and, in turn, you will impact your organization.

The significance of the student-in-organization perspective can best be understood by considering various aspects of an organization. For instance, the type of agency you selected may matter. If you selected a large bureaucracy, there may be multiple layers of authority and a complex decision-making process. There may also be extensive paperwork, and your role as the social work student may have firm boundaries. The experience of a student in a large, bureaucratic organization will be much different than that of a student whose agency is small and has only one or two levels of authority and decision making and where he or she can be fully integrated not only at the service provision level but also in decision making. One is not necessarily preferable over the other, but it is important to consider the potential impact of the organization on your learning. Furthermore, the culture, role of the social worker, services, and even the leadership style of the director can impact you and your learning.

What I have found fascinating about working with the same agencies and field instructors year after year is how much the organization can impact a student. For instance, one year, a student placed at an agency began to struggle with completing the necessary tasks and started questioning the work of the agency. Field became so difficult for the student that he even questioned whether social work was the right profession for him. After a long and involved process, which included working directly with the student and the field instructor, it was mutually agreed that the student would switch placements.

In the second setting, the student thrived. It became clear that the student needed a more structured setting with clearly defined roles and tasks, which had not been present in the first setting due to the nature of the agency's work. It was interesting to observe the same student in two very different agencies doing very different work and hear his account of how he felt each agency positively and negatively impacted his ability to learn. It is important to note that the first setting was an excellent setting with a highly competent field instructor and where previous students had been successful. I remember discussing this observation with both the student and the field instructor. Each of us realized that the interplay between the agency, the role and services, and the student definitely impacts the learning and, in this case, impacted the student's ability to demonstrate specific social work skills.

The next thing to consider when using the *student-in-organization* perceptive is whether you have any special needs with regard to the setting and the work that may impact your ability to be successful. Hopefully, this was discussed during the placement process but if not, you should discuss any concerns you have with your field instructor and field office during the orientation and training process. With regard to accommodations, for instance, those accommodations may or may not transfer to field. According to Neely-Barnes, McCabe, and Barnes (2014),

> the law requires higher education institutions to make reasonable accommodations, but not substantial modifications to their curriculum or requirements. A program is not required to grant a requested accommodation if the accommodation would fundamentally alter the nature of the curriculum or not require the student to demonstrate proficiency in one or more core areas of competency. (p. 291)

The need to have this conversation is even more important, given that one of the barriers students who have disabilities have had in receiving accommodations was the fear that they would be perceived differently by faculty if they disclosed their needs (Hong, 2015). Some students may have this same concern going into field and think that because field is such a different educational experience, they may not need accommodations. In my experience, it is best to begin to have this conversation while in field for two reasons. One, as a student, you have the support of the university and field office to determine if accommodations are indicated and facilitate the process of implementing them in your field setting. Two, this experience—as a student in field—will enable you to develop the professional skills necessary to address this as an employee and determine exactly what you might need as well as what you won't need to be a competent social worker.

The best way to apply the student-in-environment perspective is to explore your initial observations and reactions to your agency and assess the impact the agency may have on you and your learning as well as the impact you can have on your agency. To prepare for this reflection, spend your first day or two observing your organization. Pay attention to everything: Notice the flow of the day; the interaction between the workers, supervisors and peers, and the workers and clients; hang out in the break room and listen to what the staff are saying and the tone; and pay attention to how you feel in the setting itself. Once you have engaged in this observation, consider Reflection Question 2.1.

REFLECTION QUESTION 2.1

Given your initial impressions of the agency based on your observation day(s) and reflecting on the student-in-organization perspective, what did you notice? How would you describe the agency? What impact do you think the agency will have on you, your learning, and your development as a social worker? Similarly, reflect on what impact you think you may have on your agency.

ROOM TO REFLECT

Once you have had a chance to get acquainted with your agency, the next step in orientation and training is to develop your orientation plan. The purpose of orientation is twofold: one, increase your understanding of the organization in key areas and two, reduce the likelihood of having a negative impact on the organization in the key areas identified by Mallory and colleagues (2012). In the following section, you will be introduced to and shown how to develop a multilevel orientation plan to help you gain your bearings in your new agency.

MULTILEVEL ORIENTATION

The first step is to discuss the plan for your orientation with your field instructor. To develop a successful orientation plan, it is recommended to take a multilevel approach that considers orientation at the individual, agency, and larger system levels. Integrative Activity 2.1 provides an excellent overview of orientation that you can follow as you move through the orientation process. This overview identifies several broad areas to consider, along with useful questions to discuss with your field instructor.

Individual Level

At the individual level, consider what you need to discuss and negotiate with your field instructor. For instance, the first thing is to get to know each other. This discussion is a type of introduction. Although you most likely interviewed with your field instructor during the placement process, it is important to begin to develop a strong working relationship now that you are in the field. The relationship with your field instructor is especially important, given that he or she is the person you will be working closely with and who will be evaluating you throughout your field experience at the agency. In preparation for this discussion, review Integrative Activity 2.1 to assemble a list of useful questions.

First of all, interview your field instructor and ask that individual to share his or her background. This is a wonderful opportunity to learn about your field instructor's journey to the profession. This can include asking the field instructor where he or she went to school; what he or she liked and disliked about their education, specifically focusing on field; and why the individual wanted to be a field instructor. Next, share your background. This can include what brought you to social work, your interest in the agency, and the experiences you bring to the agency.

Next, discuss your learning style and field instructor's teaching style. This is important to determine the fit between the two. If you are a doer, for instance, and your field instructor thinks you need to go through a structured learning process that includes reading and verbal discussion prior to doing, this might be frustrating. On the flip side, perhaps you like to read, discuss, practice, and prepare before you do, but your field instructor believes that it is best for you to get out there, complete a task, and then interweave the training into the discussion of the task. Either of these conflicting styles could become frustrating and even create problems for you and your field instructor. That being said, there may be times when there is not a perfect match between your learning style and your field instructor's teaching style.

For example, I had a student who was very hands-on and described her learning style as that of a doer. This student was in a placement site where the field instructor felt there needed to be a comprehensive orientation and training plan that covered several topic areas and insisted this be completed prior to beginning work as a case manager.

After discussing the situation with both the student and field instructor, it became clear that they had not discussed their learning and teaching styles and that the mismatch was becoming problematic.

I encouraged them to discuss what was going on. The student could explain that the best plan needed to include doing as a part of orientation and training, and the field instructor could explain that the fast-paced nature of the setting and the complex needs of the clients meant that doing should come after a comprehensive orientation and training plan that would improve the student's overall experience. They negotiated a plan that increased the pace and included more direct observation. Once the orientation and training plan was completed, the student could begin working as a case manager, and it became clear to both that the modified plan worked well. The student realized she could provide a more effective service as a case manager due to being well oriented and trained. And the field instructor realized that for this student, having some experience was necessary to give the content a context. What became a situation that needed intervention could have been avoided, had the student and field instructor discussed and negotiated the training plan early in the placement. As you can see, it is important to discuss your learning style and learn about your field instructor's teaching style prior to beginning the work of field.

Agency Level

At the agency level, orientation activities are focused on the organization itself. To begin the process of learning about your organization, if you have not already done so, look over the agency's website and review it in its entirety. Then, google your agency to see if anything comes up about the history, services, or recent events that have impacted the agency.

Next, consider the five *W*s: *who, what, where, when,* and *why*. The *who* involves meeting everyone and getting to know each member of the staff. Ask your field instructor about the easiest way to meet everyone. The introductions can be done at a staff meeting or more informally by walking around the office. Also, ask for the organizational chart. Familiarizing yourself with the organizational chart is part of Integrative Activity 2.2, which will be discussed in more detail later and will help you begin to organize your understanding of who is who. Obviously, you and your field instructor need to consider the size of your agency and determine what is needed. If you are in a very large agency's program, you may not need to know everyone within the entire organization. So, focus your initial introductions on those involved with your program. If you are in a small agency, you may be able to meet everyone on your first day. Last, determine who else you may be working closely with and determine if this person will have an official role in your field experience, such as in the areas of training, coworking, and—even more importantly— evaluation. If this is the case, make sure that your field director or liaison is aware of this to ensure that this person has all of the information necessary to be successful in this role.

The *what* focuses on several different things that are important for you to know. First and foremost, what is the agency's mission? What is the history of the agency? What does the agency do? What are the agency's funding sources? What do each of the staff members you met during the *who* phase do at the agency? It is important to note that the organizational chart will also help you with this. What are the overarching policies and procedures of the agency? What will be your role and primary task(s)? What are your field instructor's expectations of you? What are the professional expectations with regard to behavior and appearance? Last, what are you hoping to accomplish? All of these questions will help you develop competence in two important areas: (1) understanding your role and (2) understanding the context of your agency, such as the agency's history and mission and how they impact practice.

The *where* involves where everything is and goes. This can include the bathroom, client records, office supplies, and kitchen. Also find out where your office will be and where you can keep academic- and agency-based work. Last, make sure to discuss any policies and procedures that go along with the *where*.

The *when* includes the timing of the work tasks. This might involve important training activities, such as completing an agency-based orientation or being trained on a particular client documentation program prior to working with clients. This may also involve the timing of paperwork. For instance, if you will be required to write case notes, the agency may have a policy that all case notes need to be completed within 24 hours of the delivery of the service. Thus, you and your field instructor will need to build in time to discuss the process and provide you with sufficient training to meet this expectation. Also, find out when important regularly scheduled agency-based meetings occur, such as the staff meeting. Finally, and most importantly, ask when you will have your supervision session.

The last thing to consider as you begin your field placement is the *why*. I have found that this is an important but often missed aspect of orientation. It has been my experience that the more a student understands why things at the agency are done the way they are, the easier it is for the student to manage the demands of field, which improves overall learning. So, don't be afraid to ask questions. Also, remember that your field instructor may have been doing a certain procedure for a long time and, most likely, it has become second nature. Therefore, the field instructor may not even think about why he or she does it the way that they do. So, make sure you ask the important and even seemingly mundane questions.

I know many students who have asked important questions and, as a result, challenged the agency to see their services or practices in a new light. For example, I recall a student who had to complete three different forms at intake that all gathered similar information. During a staff meeting, the student asked why there wasn't one central form that could gather all the needed information at one time. The social workers in the agency considered this and asked the student to work on a mock-up of such a form. The student was happy to engage in this organization, macro-level task, particularly since he had brought this up in the first place. As a result, the forms were condensed into one, which met all the various funders' needs and was more client friendly. This positive change came as the result of a simple question.

Larger System Level

The last area of the multilevel orientation is to consider the larger system in which your organization resides. If your field site is a program within a larger organization, familiarize yourself with the overarching organization and your specific program. For instance, one of the sites I have worked with is a program within an agency that has over 20 programs; so, it is important to understand the larger agency as a whole. By understanding your organization as a whole, you can better identify potential learning opportunities to include in your learning plan, which will be discussed in detail in Chapter 3.

Another important area to explore as a part of your orientation is the social service system with which your organization may be intricately connected. For instance, if you are doing your placement at the local public defender's office as a guardian ad litem, it is critically important to understand the relationship between that office and the county children's protective services as well as the larger child welfare system. This may also include understanding any policy or legislation that directly impacts your services, such as the Child Abuse Prevention and Treatment Act, which specifies that courts must appoint a guardian ad litem to represent the best interests of the child.

Last, reflect on the community or neighborhood in which your organization resides and/or serves. You may need to understand important aspects about the community, such as its history and experiences with the larger community, in order to be effective in your placement site. For instance, a neighborhood that is, on the surface, impoverished and may appear not as well maintained as another neighborhood could be misunderstood on first look, especially if you are an outsider. But, when you learn the history, you find out that the neighborhood actually has a high percentage of homeownership and was negatively impacted by the use of eminent domain when a highway was built through the neighborhood, which negatively impacted property values. Furthermore, when considering crime statistics, it could appear that the neighborhood is a high-crime neighborhood but, once you dig deeper, it becomes clear that most of the crime is committed by people who do not live in the neighborhood. Both of these examples drive home the importance of understanding the community's history and connection to the larger community. In order to be effective in an organization that is situated in a community and services members of that community, it is critical that you develop both an understanding of the community and a presence in the community; exemplify the ability to engage the community and its members.

By completing Integrative Activity 2.1, you will have the opportunity to conduct a comprehensive multilevel orientation. The outcome of Integrative Activity 2.1 is that you will feel grounded in your agency and better positioned to reap all the possible benefits from your placement site and to represent the agency to your clients and in the community.

INTEGRATIVE ACTIVITY 2.1
ORIENTATION AND TRAINING

Purpose: The purpose of this integrative activity (IA) is to provide a foundation for developing and completing a multilevel orientation and training plan. The following framework includes general things for you to consider as well as specific questions to discuss with your field instructor.

Directions: In supervision, discuss the plan for your orientation and training using the IA as a guide. First, address the general areas of multilevel orientation indicated by the bullets, and then, discuss the specific questions with your field instructor.

Competency 1: Demonstrate Ethical and Professional Behavior

Social workers understand the profession's history, its mission, and the roles and responsibilities of the profession. Social workers also understand the role of other professions when engaged in interprofessional teams.

- Demonstrate professional demeanor in behavior; appearance; and oral, written, and electronic communication.

Multilevel Orientation

Overarching areas

- Develop a comprehensive orientation plan.
- Engage your field instructor and develop the supervisory relationship.
- Identify how you learn and how your field instructor teaches.
- Identify any other staff with whom you will be working closely.
- Identify expectations for professional behavior and appearance.
- Meet and join with staff.
- Engage clients.
- Develop a comprehensive training plan.
- Identify role and primary tasks.
- Review agency policies and procedures.
- Review safety.
- Discuss the limits of your role as a social work student and any limits to tasks.

Specific questions to discuss in supervision:
Individual Level

1. Get to know your field instructor.
   a. What attracted you to social work?
   b. Where did you go to school?
   c. What did you like and dislike about your education, particularly your field experience?
   d. Why did you want to be a field instructor?
   e. What is your teaching style?
2. Share your background with your field instructor and answer all Questions 1a–1d that apply. For 1e, focus on your learning style, and make sure to address any special needs you may have, including but not limited to accommodations.

Agency Level

1. Does the agency have a structured orientation program?
   a. If so, can I attend?
   b. If not, what do I need to know and how will my orientation be handled?
2. Discuss the five *W*s: *who, what, where, when,* and *why.*
   a. Who: Meet everyone.
   b. What: Review the mission and history, all services and programs offered by the agency, funding, roles, tasks of student, policies and procedures, what everyone does, expectations for professional behavior and appearance, and what you as the student want to accomplish.
   c. Where: Discuss the location of the bathroom, copier, break room, copy paper, client files, student office, student belongings, and so on.
   d. When: Identify time lines for tasks, paperwork, supervision sessions, important agency meetings, and staff meetings.

(*Continued*)

(Continued)

e. Why: Discuss anything you don't understand, rationale for things, why things are done the way they are, and so on. These may need to be revisited over time, particularly as you develop more skills and engage in more complex tasks.

Larger System Level

Learn about the

1. overall organization,
2. interaction of organization with social service system,
3. policies and legislation that are important to organization services, and
4. community or neighborhood issues that impact organization.

Training: To have a successful placement, it is critical that you are trained on the tasks you will be performing in your agency. Develop a training plan using the following guidelines:

1. Review the five-step training plan.
2. Identify the specific training needs.
3. Develop a plan for training; include observation, doing while under observation, and independent work.
4. Engage in and discuss training.
5. Revisit training needs through the placement.

AGENCY ANALYSIS

An effective learning task to engage in at the completion of your multilevel orientation is to conduct an agency analysis. Integrative Activity 2.2 will help you conduct your agency analysis. First, however, it is worth discussing why doing your own agency analysis is essential to your work in field.

Conducting an agency analysis will help you develop and demonstrate the competence of critical thinking, with specific focus on your cognitive and affective process, through your ability to integrate and apply what you have learned about organizations, such as organizational theory, to an analysis of your agency. Second, it relates to the competence of developing the ability to function within your agency, because the better informed you are about your agency, the better you can represent your agency in the community. Third, it enables you to consider the contexts that shape practice by reflecting on the impact your agency has on the larger system and the impact the larger system has on your agency. Last, the more you know and understand about your agency, the better you can serve your clients and advocate for client access to services. Thus, Integrative Activity 2.2 will enable you to synthesize the information you gathered during orientation and develop a comprehensive understanding of your agency.

INTEGRATIVE ACTIVITY 2.2
AGENCY ANALYSIS

Purpose: The purpose of this IA is to assist you in the process of learning about and analyzing your field agency. It is very important to have a complete understanding of your agency, including the programs and services, funding, and history. This knowledge will enable you to function more successfully as a member of the organization and better serve your clients.

In addition, it is helpful to think critically about the purpose, structure, and function of your organization and answer the fundamental question: Is this agency meeting its mission?

Directions: Gather information about each area, and once you have gathered all information, discuss your analysis of your agency in supervision with your field instructor. You may need to contact others in your agency to gather the needed information.

Competency 1: Demonstrate Ethical and Professional Behavior

Social workers understand the profession's history, its mission, and the roles and responsibilities of the profession. Social workers also understand the role of other professions when engaged in interprofessional teams.

1. Gather the following information about your agency:

   - Mission, goals, and objectives

   - History

   - How history reflects the history of the profession

   - Philosophy, values, and culture

   - Type of organization

   - Programs and services offered

   - Funding base, including a budget

   - Organizational structure (obtain or create an organizational chart and locate self on the chart)

   - Supervision function and structure for staff

   - Relationship of agency to larger social service system

   - Current issues impacting the agency

   - Future direction of agency

   - Oversight or accrediting bodies and impact on services

   - Impact of policy(ies) on agency

   - Cultural competence of agency and staff

2. Overall reflection and analysis—once you have gathered all of the above information, ask yourself the following questions:

   - Is the agency meeting its mission?

   - What do you think about the agency? What surprised you?

   - How does the agency's history relate to the history of the profession?

   - Based on your knowledge of organizational theory, how would you conceptualize how your organization functions?

   - What are the agency's strengths?

   - What are the agency's blind spots?

   - If you were in charge, is there anything you would do differently? If no, why? If yes, then what and how?

THE ROLE OF CURRICULUM IN ORIENTATION

A key component of orienting to field is orientating to the academic goals of field education in the context of your particular field agency. As articulated by CSWE (2015), the educational policies and accreditation standards (EPAS), one of the goals of field is the integration of theory and practice. This goal is accomplished by first developing the ability to link the classroom curriculum to the practice tasks of the agency. The second goal of field is to develop and demonstrate the core competencies and component behaviors identified by both the EPAS (2015) and your program at your field agency.

The GFEA states that generalist field education is grounded in, integrates, and impacts curriculum. On the one hand, this is obvious: Students in a social work program take various classes and engage in field education to complete their degree, making the classroom and field curriculum both critical components of social work education. However, there can be a gap between the front-loading of theories taught in the classroom and the practice experiences of field that typically—but not always—come later (Lam, 2004). This means that students can struggle with how to apply their classroom learning to the practice experiences of field. This same gap can also occur in programs where field and classroom courses run concurrently. The linkage of the classroom content to the field and the field to the classroom is often not as clear as you might have first imagined. Miller and Skinner (2013) have developed what they call a "theory-mindedness approach" (p. 280), which can be applied to learning and practices that strive to address or close this gap. This approach will be discussed in more detail in Chapter 10. For now, the focus is on how best to begin the process of linking classroom content to field, which is to discuss and review your curriculum with your field instructor. Integrative Activity 2.3 will ground you and your field instructor in your program's curriculum and the content you are learning. In social work education, a particular program's course work is the curriculum and reflects the values and specific culture of that school.

There are three types of curriculum that are important to discuss in supervision. The first is foundation curriculum, which are the courses, including content and outcomes, taken prior to entering field. The second is concurrent curriculum, which refers to the courses, including content and outcomes, taken while in field. The third type is specialized curriculum, which is knowledge, values, and skills that are specific to your practice setting. The specialized curriculum that you identify may not have been a part of your program's curriculum and will need to be acquired during the field experience. Integrative Activity 2.3 provides an opportunity to plan with your field instructor how that information will be learned. For example, content may be presented in the supervision session or by attending agency- or community-based trainings, reading books, conducting a literature review, and by watching training videos. Identifying and planning for the development of specialized knowledge will be your opportunity to embrace and understand the importance of career-long learning as a professional social worker.

A useful resource in the curriculum review process is to look over your course syllabus. The syllabus will provide useful information, such as course objectives and accreditation standards, and it may even outline specific core competencies and practice behaviors targeted by that course. Also, as a part of the accreditation process, many programs develop curricular maps, which provide a comprehensive understanding of the course and the course objectives as well as the core competencies and practice behaviors targeted by each course. Ask your field director if your program has such a resource for you to review in your discussion with your field instructor.

The review of curriculum will ground you and your field instructor and provide an opportunity to identify the course content and outcomes that will serve as the foundation to your field experience. This activity will also identify any gaps in your learning and provide an opportunity to develop a plan for learning-specialized curriculum. Without you and your field instructor being firmly grounded in your curriculum, it will be more difficult to apply the curriculum to the tasks of field. The curriculum review also organizes what can be overwhelming and often lost prior to entering field: As students enter field, they are often overwhelmed with curricular content and anxious about their ability to enter field and practice. Yet they are equally anxious to get to work and often resistant to more classroom learning. This challenging set of dynamics requires a clear vision for how to approach the field experience to achieve the goals of field education.

The curriculum review task also serves an important role in the engagement process between you and your field instructor. Having the opportunity to inform your field instructor about something you know—your course work, learning, and thoughts about how that course work can be integrated into the setting—provides an opportunity for you to share your expertise. This comes at a time when you may understandably feel in over your head. One question I love to have students ask their field instructor during this process is, "What course(s) did you enjoy the most and why?" Also ask in what, if any, content areas the field instructor felt he or she wasn't prepared enough in and how he or she dealt with that in field practice.

This discussion is also helpful for your field instructor who may have been out of the classroom for some time and may work with several schools that have different course offerings. This will help your field instructor become grounded in an area that is critically important to his or her ability to assist you in linking curriculum and practice.

As you can see, this part of orientation becomes a win–win because this task can help alleviate the initial anxiety you may feel in the beginning of the field experience as well as the anxiety your field instructor may feel about how to help you meet the goal of linking curriculum to practice.

INTEGRATIVE ACTIVITY 2.3
CURRICULUM REVIEW

Purpose: The purpose of this IA is twofold: (1) to ground you and your field instructor in your program's curriculum by identifying courses in the areas of foundation and concurrent curriculum as well as identifying the specialized learning needs and plan for achieving that knowledge and (2) to provide a foundation for later task analysis.

Directions: First, in the areas of the foundation and concurrent curriculum, review your program's social work courses and identify those that stand out. Of those that stand out, identify the learning outcomes. Then, identify how those learning outcomes can be directly applied to your practice at your field agency. Second, in the area of specialized learning, identify the plan for how you will develop the knowledge, values, and skills specific to your practice in field.

Competency 1: Demonstrate Ethical and Professional Behavior

Social workers recognize the importance of lifelong learning and are committed to continually updating their skills to ensure they are relevant and effective.

1. Foundation curriculum—social work courses taken prior to entering field

Courses Taken:	Learning Outcomes:	Application to Field:

2. Concurrent curriculum—social work courses to be taken during field

Courses to Be Taken:	Projected Learning Outcome:	Application to Field:

(Continued)

(Continued)

3. Specialized curriculum—content specific to field site

Content to Be Learned at Field Site:	Projected Learning Outcome:	Plan/Application to Field:

Note: Specialized curriculum tasks are often included on your learning plan.

THE TRAINING PLAN

Once you have begun your orientation process, you need to consider the plan for your training. Refer back to Integrative Activity 2.1, which provides a section on training to guide your discussion with your field instructor. This is an equally important discussion because your training is the best introduction to what social work practice entails at your agency and, more specifically, your role within the agency. The lack of effective training can become a barrier to your learning in one of two ways. First, it can prevent you from being able to perform an important practice task, and second, it can compromise your ability to learn from the task.

For instance, if you are in a placement setting where you provide group treatment but have not been adequately trained to cofacilitate or independently run a group, you may not be able to develop or demonstrate competence as a group facilitator. Furthermore, you may even end up feeling overwhelmed, be unclear about what you are doing, and, even worse, lose your confidence. All of this can prevent you from achieving the necessary competencies related to this task. Thus, it is important to discuss the plan for your training as a group facilitator. Also, discuss with your field instructor the expectations for your level of competence. For instance, if you have never attended or facilitated a treatment or task group, it would be unrealistic to expect that you could independently run an effective group right away. The expectation should be to observe, cofacilitate, develop, and demonstrate a foundational understanding of group work and then facilitate a group session on your own under observation. This entire training process would then culminate in you facilitating group sessions on your own.

In addition to discussing the plan, it is also helpful to consider the pace and process of the plan and negotiate that with your field instructor. A completed training plan will enable you to successfully engage in important tasks necessary to demonstrate various competencies and component behaviors. Far too often, students are thrown into tasks with no discussion about the plan for training, which results in the learning being compromised. To assist you in this process, discuss with your field instructor how you might follow a five-step training plan such as the one outlined in Table 2.1 below. If your agency has its own training plan, be sure to ask questions about that plan and see how it compares. The ultimate goal is to ensure that you develop a plan that meets both your learning needs and follows the expectations of the agency. Structured agency-based orientation and training programs can be very valuable to your learning, so make sure to take full advantage of those opportunities.

Monitoring your training is an ongoing process as you move from task to task and as your skill and ability level develops over time in your agency. I encourage you to discuss your training needs during the first few days each semester in conjunction with putting your learning plan together, which will be discussed in Chapter 3.

TABLE 2.1 ■ Five-Step Training Plan	
Step 1	Identify tasks.
Step 2	Assess baseline competence. Using a 5-point scale with 1 = *not at all competent* and 5 = *completely competent*, assess your level of competence for all tasks identified by the field instructor that require training. This rating will be based on past work, volunteer experience, and degree of specialization of task.
Step 3	Observe task. Shadow field instructor and agency peers engaging in identified tasks.
Step 4	Do task under direct observation.
Step 5	Do task independently. Reassess level of competence, report in supervision, and revisit any necessary steps throughout the placement.

FREQUENTLY EXPERIENCED SITUATION

Below is a frequently experienced situation from field that relates nicely to this chapter. As discussed in the Introduction, these will be included in a few of the chapters to help prepare you by sharing some commonly experienced situations. They are composite experiences that students have shared year after year, and the hope is that they will give you a heads-up for what you might experience. And if you do experience something similar, this will offer some suggestions for how to best approach this type of situation. As always is the case, if you ever experience something that is difficult or out of the ordinary, it is critical that you discuss your particular situation with your field liaison or field director, as this situation is in no way meant to be a directive for how you should handle your particular situation in field.

My agency is so chaotic.

> I think my agency is a mess. I mean total chaos. Everyone seems to do something different when it comes to the clients, and there are times when I disagree with how client situations are handled. I don't even think there are policies for some of the things that I think are really important and for which there really should be a policy. As I think about my training and orientation, I don't see how it is going to work, since there doesn't seem to a uniform way for doing anything. Should I say anything?

I love this situation particularly as you think about orientation and training; to me, it reflects an all-too-common experience of students and an observation that comes from the student who may be a budding macro-practitioner at the organizational level. A student who instinctively sees how the agency is functioning, questions the practices and their impact on clients, and conceptualizes real solutions is confronted with and halted by his or her student status and lack of experience. This situation also illuminates the fact that you will absolutely be impacted by your agency. How you experience your agency and conceptualize yourself as a social worker within the context of your agency is significant and reflects the student-in-organization concept discussed earlier. On the flip side, it is also possible that what you are observing is controlled chaos and that the work is getting done and being done well, just not in a manner that is readily apparent to you as a student. For this type of situation, what became important was to allow the student to first vent about those things that were making her frustrated; second, to encourage her to share her observations with her field instructor in the event that she was misinterpreting the practice; and third, to identify how she might be able to positively impact her agency (organizational practice), an expected part of her generalist training. The student, first and foremost, shared her observations in a professional manner with her field instructor. Her field instructor was very open to her observation, and they began a discussion of possible solutions. Similarly, the field instructor was open to the possibility of the student working on a policy and procedures manual as part of her field experience. The field instructor discussed the task with the agency director, who also thought it would be helpful and sanctioned the student to begin to work on this task. The student was a natural at organizing and prioritizing the needs of the agency as well as at gathering information from other agencies regarding policies and procedures. For that, she developed an outline. Once the outline was approved, the student wrote some specific policies, several of which were ultimately adopted. All of this ended up being a unique way to orient the student to the agency and developed the structure needed for her training. This situation illustrates an important thing for you to remember as a student: Even if your reactions are right on, it is still important to be open and share your observations in a nonjudgmental way. When your observations are confidently and professionally shared, you may have an opportunity to resolve your concerns and not only build skills but actually give back to your agency in a meaningful way. I always tell the students I work with that the agencies that take students tend to be open and encouraging of the observations and feedback students share about their experiences, as this often becomes a way that an agency improves its service delivery.

Suggested Field Tasks

- Discuss your orientation and training plan.
- Complete your orientation and training (Integrative Activity 2.1).
- Attend an agency-based orientation session in person or online.
- Conduct an agency analysis (Integrative Activity 2.2).
- Review related course work with your field instructor (Integrative Activity 2.3).
- Attend agency-based, community, or campus trainings and events.

References

Cordero, A., & Rodriguez, L. N. (2009). Fostering cross-cultural learning and advocacy for social justice through an immersion experience in Puerto Rico. *Journal of Teaching in Social Work*, *29*(2), 134–152.

Council on Social Work Education (CSWE). (2015). *Educational policy and accreditation standards*. Alexandria, VA: Author.

Hong, B. S. (2015). Qualitative analysis of the barriers college students with disabilities experience in higher education. *Journal of College Student Development*, *56*(3), 209–226.

Lam, D. (2004). Problem based-learning: An integration of theory and field. *Journal of Social Work Education, 40*(3), 371.

Mallory, D., Cox, S., & Panos, P. (2012). A participatory outcome evaluation on the impact of BSW interns on agencies. *Journal of Teaching in Social Work, 35*, 502–517.

Mapp, S., McFarland, P., & Newell, E. (2007). The effect of a short-term study abroad class on students' cross-cultural awareness. *The Journal of Baccalaureate Social Work, 13*(1), 39–51.

Merriam-Webster Dictionary. (2017). Immersion. Retrieved May 5, 2017, from https://www.merriam-webster.com/dictionary/immersion

Miller, S., & Skinner, J. (2013). A theory-mindedness approach: Eliminating the need for a gap in baccalaureate education. *Journal of Teaching in Social Work, 33*, 280–296.

Neely-Barnes, S. L., McCabe, H. A., & Barnes, C. P. (2014). Seven rules to live by: Accommodations in social work education and the field. *Journal of Social Work in Disability & Rehabilitation, 13*(4), 279–296. doi:10.1080/1536710X.2014.961113

Nuttman-Shwartz, O., & Berger, R. (2012). Field education in international social work: Where we are and where we should go. *International Social Work, 55*(2), 225–243.

Roholt, R., & Fisher, C. (2013). Expect the unexpected: International short-term study course pedagogies and practices. *Journal of Social Work Education, 49*(1), 48–65.

Sheafor, B., & Horejsi, C. (2015). *Techniques and guidelines for social work practice* (10th ed.). Boston, MA: Pearson Education.

3

THE PLAN AND PACE OF LEARNING IN FIELD

This chapter will explore the plan for and pace of your learning in field. Establishing a plan for your learning is critical and begins with drafting your learning plan. The *pace* of your learning refers to how slowly or quickly you will move from orientation and training to independent practice and requires that you consider several key concepts and steps.

THE LEARNING PLAN

The learning plan is a crucial document in several ways. First, the learning plan provides a sense of direction for your learning that ensures that you have an effective field experience and ultimately accomplish your goals by the conclusion of field. Second, the learning plan helps you pace your learning, meaning it will specifically reference tasks that reflect the process as you move from orientation and training to independent practice. For instance, the learning plan will include tasks that reference shadowing, coworking, and, ultimately, completing tasks independently. Third, the learning plan assists in the fulfillment of the overall purpose of field, which is threefold:

1. to integrate classroom and field,

2. to become socialized to the profession, and

3. to develop as a generalist, ready to apply your generalist training to your practice or to your advanced practice field experience.

It is interesting to note that constructing your learning plan is a useful learning experience in its own right because it mirrors the engagement, planning and contracting, and evaluation phases of the planned change process that you will use with client systems. By developing your learning plan, you are using and integrating what you have learned in the classroom with an important activity of field. Furthermore, writing a learning plan requires competence in professional writing: You need to be able to develop agreed-upon goals and objectives, determine appropriate tasks to meet the goals and objectives, implement strategies identified in the plan, and monitor and evaluate your plan, all of which are important skills for a social worker.

This chapter will provide an overview of the information you need to develop your learning plan and instructions for using your learning plan as an educational tool during field. The chapter covers the elements of a learning plan, including writing learning objectives, selecting the tasks and roles you will engage in to meet your objectives, and developing a plan for evaluation. In addition to this, the chapter will discuss how the learning plan can act as a road map throughout field, with opportunities to consider the pace of learning and monitor progress.

Elements of the Learning Plan

As mentioned earlier, certain elements need to go into a learning plan to make it an effective and useful document. A well-constructed learning plan should include

- the goals and objectives of field,

- the tasks and roles you will engage in at your site to meet the goals and objectives,

- a plan for evaluation,

- demographic information, such as your name and your field instructor's name, the agency's name, dates of the plan, and perhaps your title and role, and

- signatures to document agreement by all involved parties.

To familiarize yourself with your learning plan and identify the preceding elements, review the learning plan required by your program. In all likelihood, this document can be found online or in your program's field manual.

Goals and Objectives

The first step in developing a learning plan is to identify your goals and objectives for field. The ability to identify goals and objectives is grounded in your knowledge of what goals and objectives are and your skill level in writing them. Knowledge about goals and objectives would fall within the curricular area of practice, specifically the planned change process phase of planning and contracting.

In social work practice, a *goal* is defined as a "specific statement of intended outcomes. Goal statements should be clear, meaningful, and attainable. Whenever possible, they should reflect the client's priorities and be stated in the client's own language" (Kagel & Kopels, 2008, p. 69). Obviously, you are not a client, but the ideas reflected in the preceding definition hold true for you in field. That is, the goals you set for field should reflect the intended outcomes of field education. Your goals should be "clear, meaningful, and attainable" (p. 69), in your own words, and reflect your personal goals and interests. Furthermore, goals are the end result: As you are writing your learning plan, ask yourself what you need and hope to accomplish as a result of field.

Although the terms *goals* and *objectives* are often used interchangeably, they are different. Goals tend to be broad, sweeping statements, whereas an objective "is more specific and written in a manner that allows and facilitates measurement and evaluation" (Sheafor & Horejsi, 2015, p. 282). As Sheafor and Horejsi (2015) state,

A properly developed objective meets the following criteria:

- It usually starts with the word *to*, followed by an action verb.

- It specifies a single outcome to be achieved.

- It specifies a target date for its accomplishment.

- It is as quantitative and measurable as possible.

- It is understandable to the client and others participating in the intervention.

- It is attainable, but still represents a significant challenge and a meaningful change. (p. 283)

In the context of field, your goals will reflect large, overarching outcomes of field education and most often include the use of action-oriented verbs such as *to know, to learn, to develop,* and *to demonstrate*. Given that goals tend to be broad and sweeping in their scope, once you have determined the global outcomes of field education, you will then want to break those into smaller, attainable objectives. Objectives, like stepping stones, will help you meet the larger goal, such as getting across a river. An objective tends to be smaller in its scope, specific, well-defined, concrete, and measurable. I particularly like the idea of an objective being challenging and meaningful. To lend each objective concreteness, you need to indicate what you will be doing, how you will do it, and by when. The type of language that is helpful when writing objectives is language that reflects *behavior*, meaning what you will do. Examples of good action words for field objective could include but are not limited to *attend, schedule, participate in, cofacilitate, conduct,* and *write*. Horejsi and Garthwait (1999) state that "a learning objective brings together in a single outcome statement a goal, a description of learning activities, and evaluation criteria" (p. 22). This particular definition is helpful in field. Thus, using this definition as a foundation, look at a possible learning objective for a student:

1. To learn about the cycle of violence . . . (a goal)

2. by reading an article and viewing a video . . . (a description of learning activities)

3. and demonstrating knowledge by presenting content in supervision by end of September and applying knowledge to at least one case by the end of October. (evaluation criteria)

This type of learning objective is useful to you and your field instructor because it is specific and clearly identifies the intended outcome and what you will do to achieve the objective and provides clarity for how you and your field instructor will evaluate whether or not you met the objective. You and your field instructor can easily measure if you read the article and watched the training video by your ability to present the content and apply the knowledge to a specific case in supervision. Thus, having clearly worded objectives takes the mystery out of evaluation and enables you and your field instructor to determine that an objective was met or not met.

Now that we have defined goals and objectives and reviewed the components of an objective of learning, the next step is to consider your learning tasks.

Multilevel Learning Tasks

The tasks that a social worker engages in to assist clients in meeting their goals and objectives are critical to effective social work practice. Sheafor and Horejsi (2008) define a *task* as

some specified and observable problem-solving action or step that can be evaluated in terms of whether it was achieved or completed. Preferably, a task is an action that can be accomplished in a matter of days or at the most a couple of weeks. A task can be viewed as one of the many steps or short-term activities that must be completed to achieve an objective. (p. 333)

This definition is applicable to field in that you, your field instructor, and field director will all be participating in identifying what you will be doing at the agency to achieve the objectives of learning. The learning tasks will come from a variety of sources. The first source for identifying learning tasks will come from the agency. You want to consider the activities that relate to what the social worker does in the agency. You can determine many of the expected activities by reviewing the current job description of the position with which your role is most closely aligned. By reviewing the job description, you will obtain useful information to translate into your learning plan. Additional sources for researching and identifying your learning tasks will come from activities related to the population served and activities that reflect the social problems addressed by the agency. Second, you should consider your own personal interests related to your development as a social worker. Again, reflect on what you would like to get out of the field experience and identify tasks aligned to the work you might do. Third, you should consult with your field instructor for ideas for possible tasks that may not be readily apparent. For instance, perhaps you can get involved with a special project or current issue that the agency is experiencing, such as research or program evaluation. Last, look to your program, field director, faculty field liaison, or department faculty for suggested and possibly required learning tasks as well. For instance, many programs require that students complete process recording. The purpose of gathering options from all these sources is to ensure that you are engaging in a comprehensive array of learning tasks.

In addition to identifying the specific learning tasks that you will engage in at your agency, you also need to consider the scope of the learning tasks that you need to develop as a competent generalist practitioner, ready to practice or to apply your generalist training to advanced field instruction. As you will recall from Chapter 1, the generalist field education approach (GFEA) requires students to engage in multilevel tasks. By including multilevel tasks in your learning plan, you ensure that you develop the skills necessary to practice at multiple levels. This is important in order to prepare you to assume a variety of different types of positions and job responsibilities after you complete your education.

Multilevel tasks fall within four primary levels or areas of practice that are specifically referenced in the educational policies and accreditation standards (EPAS) (Council on Social Work Education [CSWE], 2015). The primary levels are *micro* (individuals and families), *mezzo* (treatment and task groups), and *macro* (organizations, communities, and may include policy/legislature and research). In addition, given field education's emphasis on socialization and professional development, the last level or area of tasks would be those that contribute to your professional socialization.

Sometimes it is hard to identify at what level—micro, mezzo, macro, or professional socialization—a specific field task fits within and or to take advantage of a particular task that may present itself. This most often occurs when students engage in mezzo, macro, or professional socialization tasks, such as attending staff meetings, engaging in administrative tasks, reading training materials, conducting research, and completing documentation. However, when a task is clearly defined and linked to a particular level of practice, students are better able to identify the purpose the task can play in their development as a social worker. As a result, the student develops a better understanding of the depth and breadth of social work practice at all levels of practice.

So far, the necessity of having multilevel practice experiences has been established; however, in all likelihood, your tasks will be clustered in one or two levels that reflect the services and role of the social worker in the agency, meaning you may have more tasks in one area than the other areas. This is understandable because you probably selected the agency in part due to the services and role of the social worker and had a desire to learn to practice in that particular area. Yet, your development and socialization as a generalist practitioner may be hampered if you don't have opportunities to complete tasks at other levels as well. Thus, you may need to look beyond the social worker's role within the agency to identify additional opportunities, as many social workers provide specific tasks within an agency.

For example, I worked with a student at an agency who provided primarily micro-level case management services to individuals. The student loved the agency and services and was receiving an excellent learning experience. However, the experiences were heavily focused on practice with individuals. As a result of the need to engage in multilevel tasks, the student identified two mezzo-level learning tasks: (1) cofacilitate a group and (2) conduct educational presentations in the community. These particular services were done by another group of social workers in the agency, so the field instructor had to connect the student with the other social workers. Fortunately, it ended up being a fairly easy process to set up the learning tasks. As a result, the student added two mezzo practice tasks to the learning plan, and to the field instructor and field liaison's satisfaction, the student reported that the work not only complemented the case management services but also helped develop important group practice skills. By the completion of the field experience, the student felt better prepared as a soon-to-be professional social worker.

To facilitate the process of identifying the multilevel learning tasks, complete Integrative Activity 3.1. Once you have identified your multilevel tasks, include them in your learning plan. The list came from several sources, namely agencies, the literature (Birkenmaier & Berg-Weger, 2007; Hendricks, Finch, & Franks, 2005; Plionis, Bailey-Etta, & Manning, 2002; Riebschleger & Grettenberger, 2006), and input from students, faculty, and field instructors. The list is not exhaustive; you can engage in a task that is not on this list as long as it is a social work task and can be linked to a goal statement.

INTEGRATIVE ACTIVITY 3.1
IDENTIFYING MULTILEVEL LEARNING TASKS

Directions: Identify the tasks that you will engage in at your agency by placing a check mark in the box next to each task. You must select tasks from all four areas.

Educational Policy 2.0—Generalist Practice

To promote human and social well-being, generalist practitioners use a range of prevention and intervention methods in their practice with diverse individuals, families, groups, organizations, and communities, based on scientific inquiry and best practices. The generalist practitioner identifies with the social work profession and applies ethical principles and critical thinking in practice at the micro, mezzo, and macro levels.

Professional Socialization	
	• Set a supervision time. ❑
	• Attend supervision sessions. ❑
	• Develop and use an agenda during your supervision session. ❑
	• Keep supervision session notes. ❑
	• Orient to the agency and field education. ❑
	• Tour the agency. ❑
	• Introduce yourself to all staff. ❑
	• Conduct an agency analysis. ❑
	• Examine your mission, goals, and objectives. ❑
	• Learn about programs and services. ❑
	• Learn about funding and review a budget. ❑
	• Review the organizational structure, identify or place yourself on the organizational chart. ❑
	• Obtain and read agency policies and procedures. ❑
	• Develop and complete a training plan. ❑
	• Review and complete agency documentation. ❑
	• Complete professional paperwork, such as mileage reimbursement or incident reports. ❑
	• Review agency client system records. ❑
	• Write reports. ❑
	• Identify your title. ❑
	• Identify your primary tasks. ❑
	• Set up your work space; obtain computer/voice mail access. ❑
	• Identify your work schedule. ❑
	• Discuss the dress code. ❑
	• Engage in ethical behavior. ❑
	• Read the National Association of Social Workers (NASW) code of ethics and any agency ethical standards. ❑
	• Identify common ethical dilemmas in a practice setting. ❑
	• Identify and analyze ethical dilemmas using the NASW code of ethics. ❑

(Continued)

(Continued)

	• Conduct an ethics analysis of agency practices. ❑ • Develop a professional identity. ❑ • Join a social work club or professional organization (i.e., NASW, community group). ❑ • Identify philanthropic activities. ❑ • Engage a mentor. ❑ • Attend agency/community/campus trainings/events. ❑ • Engage in self-care activities and monitor your stress and burnout levels. ❑ • Complete field paperwork. ❑
Micro—individuals and families	• Shadow services to individuals and families. ❑ • Reach out to individual clients and families by telephone or in writing to set up appointments for interviews. ❑ • Conduct intake interviews. ❑ • Conduct assessments with individuals and families. ❑ • Complete a social history. ❑ • Complete an ecomap. ❑ • Complete a genogram. ❑ • Engage in casework/case management services with individuals and families. ❑ • Establish a caseload. ❑ • Contract with a client to develop a service plan. ❑ • Develop and implement interventions and plans. ❑ • Complete documentation. ❑ • Complete case notes. ❑ • Make referrals—broker on behalf of clients. ❑ • Analyze your communication skills. ❑ • Complete your interview checklist. ❑ • Complete process recording. ❑
Mezzo—group tasks/treatments	• Observe a treatment group. ❑ • Cofacilitate a treatment group. ❑ • Gather information to determine client interest in a group (needs assessments). ❑ • Develop an outline for planning a group. ❑ • Develop curriculum/group session activities. ❑ • Complete group notes and other required documentation. ❑ • Increase your knowledge of types of groups/research group skills. ❑ • Facilitate group sessions. ❑ • Attend team meetings, interdisciplinary treatment team meetings, and individualized education program meetings. ❑ • Attend a task group/join a committee. ❑ • Cofacilitate a task group meeting; develop an agenda, write minutes, learn parliamentary procedure from *Robert's Rules of Order* by Henry Robert. ❑ • Complete meeting minutes. ❑ • Facilitate a task group. ❑
Macro—organizational practice or community policy/legislature, or research	• Engage in organizational practice. ❑ • Participate in fund-raising activities. ❑ • Engage in grant writing. ❑ • Engage in research activities to support activities of the organization; assist in the agency's annual report and auditing. ❑ • Explore/participate in program evaluation. ❑ • Write flyers, brochures, or newsletters regarding agency services or programs. ❑ • Attend board meetings. ❑ • Analyze social/agency policy(ies). ❑ • Write a policy. ❑

- Develop and implement a program. ❑
- Engage in community organizing. ❑
- Conduct a community needs assessment. ❑
- Participate in a community action/coalition group/task force. ❑
- Develop an agreement to work with another agency, including establishing funding. ❑
- Engage in policy development. ❑
- Research legislative history of an existing or proposed program. ❑
- Engage in advocacy at the legislative/bureaucratic level. ❑
- Prepare and present testimony in support of a policy or program reform. ❑
- Engage in political practice. ❑
- Participate in voter registration. ❑
- Organize and disseminate information regarding a levy or important issue. ❑
- Participate in a campaign. ❑
- Engage in canvassing, tabling, or phone banking. ❑

Sources: This task list was developed from *Learning to Teach, Teaching to Learn,* by Hendricks, Finch, and Franks, 2005; *The Practicum Companion for Social Work,* by Julie Birkenmaier and Marla Berg-Weger, 2007; and the Generalist Practice Scale, developed by Riebschleger and Grettenberger, 2006.

If you are asked to complete a task that is not on the list, you will want to determine if it is an appropriate task. To determine if a task is appropriate, explore two things. First, find out if the task is normally completed by the social workers at the agency. If that is the case, then it is fine for you to engage in that task. For example, suppose you were asked to provide child care for the parents in a substance-abuse group meeting. In doing so, you learned that all the social workers in the agency rotate through the role because attendance at the group is better if child care is offered. In this case, taking on the task might fit the criterion of being part of a multilevel learning experience. That being said, the student still needs to consider how the task relates to the larger goals and objectives. Assisting in child care could be linked to diversity and cultural competence if working with the children increases the student's understanding of child development, or it could be linked to professional development in the area of fulfilling the role of the social worker in the agency. However, the student also must consider the appropriateness of the task in the context of the time available and as compared to other task opportunities. In other words, a student may not want to spend time each week engaging in child care when other learning options are available. Therefore, a thorough discussion with the field instructor to evaluate all of the preceding possibilities is necessary.

On the other hand, if the agency doesn't normally provide child care and you are asked to do that or if other non–social work staff provides child care most of the time, this might not be an appropriate task for you. For instance, suppose that a student is asked to watch the child while the social worker meets with the child's mom to discuss the case. If child care is usually provided by a non–social work staff member and providing child care is not normally what the social worker would be doing, then attending to the child probably is not an appropriate learning task. Taking care of the child, while undoubtedly important to the work, may actually be taking away from your learning because you would otherwise be observing the social worker working with the mom. Again, the student and field instructor need to discuss and determine the purpose of a task and how the task is linked to the achievement of the student's goals and objectives.

Second, it is important to determine if a particular task has merit and will contribute significantly to your learning, the latter being the most important. However, making a determination about the value of a particular task is not always cut and dry. For instance, suppose you are asked to cover the phones because there is a crisis in the agency and all the staff are pulled into a meeting. Answering the phones at the front desk is not the job of the social worker, but you can help out, as all professionals do from time to time, and the task actually becomes a great learning experience in that the student can speak to clients firsthand and get a sense of the types of calls the agency gets and what to do with the callers. At the end of the day, this particular task proves to be beneficial, even though it was clearly situation specific; that is, you will not answer the phones on a regular basis, but on that day, doing something that wasn't the social worker's job ended up being productive.

One last example is the opposite of the preceding scenario. In this particular situation, a student was asked by a staff member of the agency to complete a task not normally done by the social worker. It involved performing physical care activities with the client. At the time, the student thought it might not be an appropriate task, but the field instructor was not at the agency and the student did not feel comfortable saying "no." The student completed the task but was very upset about being asked in the first place. Fortunately, the student completed the task without any harm being done to themselves or the client, and the student even reported some benefit in completing the task. However, in a later discussion with the student about the situation, it became clear that the task could have put the student at risk, and the student reported being extremely uncomfortable. The student was told to discuss the situation with the field instructor and establish a plan for determining appropriate tasks and how to handle situations that may come up when the field instructor is not at the agency. This is an example of a situation where a student is asked to do something that is not appropriate or productive and even created some concern on the part of the student.

As shown from all the examples offered, it is extremely important that you determine your primary tasks, ensure that everyone in the agency knows your role and primary tasks, and feel empowered to evaluate the requests that will come up from time to time in your agency. The best way to provide clarity with regard to your tasks is to

- create a well-constructed and comprehensive learning plan,

- identify the tasks and roles you will regularly engage in on the learning plan,

- ask your field instructor to let others in the agency know your role and primary tasks, and

- when and if you are asked to do something outside of your learning plan, pause and reflect on the appropriateness of the task and, if necessary, ask the purpose and goal of the task. If you are still unsure, consult with your field director or faculty field liaison.

The goal is for you to join the agency fully as a team member, which may require flexibility on your part from time to time, while at the same time ensuring that you are not asked to do things that are clearly not related to your development as a social worker.

Now that you are familiar with multilevel learning tasks, the next thing to think about as you are putting your learning plan together is the foundational roles of social work that you may use in conjunction with a task.

Foundational Roles of Social Work Practice in Field

The GFEA outlined in Chapter 1 requires that students engage in the foundational roles of social work. This is due to the fact that, from a generalist perspective, the foundational roles that the professional social worker uses are critically important to effective practice, as can be seen in its inclusion, implicitly or explicitly, in various definitions of *generalist practice*. I often hear students use the terms *case manager*, *advocate*, *facilitator*, and *educator*, but the students do not usually identify these as foundational roles of social work practice. Instead, students use them in more general ways or understand that a particular role happens to be the name of a particular job, as is the case with the term *case manager*. Conversely, students rarely state, "I brokered today," but regularly talk about referring a client to a service, which is the function of the role of the broker. Thus, it is important to increase your understanding of the foundational social work roles and how those roles are referred to in your agency and to ensure that you have opportunities to use the roles in your practice in field. This will, in part, be accomplished by including various foundational roles in your learning tasks as well as increasing your knowledge and understanding of the roles you are providing in the context of your position at the agency. For instance, if your agency identifies the primary role of the social worker as a case manager and you will be fulfilling that role as a student, ask yourself, *what does that mean to be a case manager? What is the role of a case manager? How do I manage a case?* As a result of this focused examination and answering these questions, you will become more grounded in that particular role. Last, the more familiar you are with the foundational roles used by the social worker(s) in your agency, the better you will be able to develop competence in attending to your professional roles and boundaries, a practice behavior associated with identifying and conducting yourself as a professional social worker.

Kirst-Ashman and Hull (2009) identify eight foundational roles of social work: counselor, educator, broker, case manager, mobilizer, mediator, facilitator, and advocate (pp. 25–26). With regard to the use of the foundational roles of social work practice, DuBois and Miley (2005) state that

> rather than the social worker's starting with the roles or strategies and then determining the plans of action, the nature of the situation should drive the selection of roles and strategies. Client systems' challenges, rather than the preferred methods of practitioners, generate strategies. (p. 229)

The notion of fitting the role to the need versus providing the role because that is what the social worker or agency does at the agency is a critical concept for you to grasp in your practice in field and one that can be complicated by your overarching role within the agency.

In addition to identifying the role of the social worker at the agency and the foundational roles used by the social workers to assist their clients, it is also key to identify the role of other professionals with whom you will work, when applicable. The CSWE (2015) added interprofessional practice to the EPAS, given the increased awareness about the benefits of interprofessional practice for client system outcomes (World Health Organization, 2010). Schaefer and Larkin (2015) provide an overview of how interprofessional education learning opportunities were infused throughout the curriculum in one undergraduate program to ensure the goal of developing this important competency in students. They go on to state that "social work's strength as a profession, rooted in collective practice, can be used to move social work into a leadership position in IPE [interprofessional education]" (Schaefer & Larkin, 2015, p. 179). Thus, it is important to extend this training to field by providing students with the necessary opportunities to develop and demonstrate this competency in their practice. The Interprofessional Education Collaborative identifies the ability to "use the knowledge of one's own role and those of other professions to appropriately assess and address the health care needs of patients and to promote and advance the health of populations" (2016, p. 10) as one of the four core competencies necessary for interprofessional collaborative practice. The best way for you to develop this competence is to increase your understanding of both your role and the role of other professionals in your field setting.

To assist you in the process of meeting all of the expectations above, review and discuss Integrative Activity 3.2 in class or with your field instructor. The first thing this activity asks you to do is to discuss and clarify your role, the role of other professions with whom you will work closely (if applicable), and the foundational roles used by the social worker in his or her practice with client systems. To guide you in this exploration and discussion,

- review the agency job description to determine your role,

- identify the other professions with which you will work closely and determine their role,

- review the professional roles of social work practice and consider the opportunities for using the various roles within the agency, and

- link the various roles to your multilevel learning tasks.

INTEGRATIVE ACTIVITY 3.2
IDENTIFYING FOUNDATIONAL ROLES OF SOCIAL WORK IN FIELD

Purpose: The purpose of this activity is threefold. First, it will assist you in identifying your role in the agency and the role of other professionals, if applicable. This is accomplished by you and your field instructor (1) reviewing the agency job description of the social worker and (2) deciding together, based on the opportunities, learning objectives, and your interests, what your primary role will look like. Second, the activity will provide you with the opportunity to identify the other professionals with whom you work and their roles. Last, you will review the foundational roles of social work practice and identify tasks in which you will be able to integrate those roles and thus, develop competence.

Competency 1: Demonstrate Ethical and Professional Behavior

Social workers understand the profession's history, its mission, and the roles and responsibilities of the profession. Social workers also understand the role of other professions when engaged in interprofessional teams.

Educational Policy 2.0—Generalist Practice

To promote human and social well-being, generalist practitioners use a range of prevention and intervention methods in their practice with diverse individuals, families, groups, organizations, and communities based on scientific inquiry and best practices.

Role of Social Worker in Agency	Primary Role as Student
(Review the job description of a social worker in the agency and describe it.)	(Identify and describe the student's primary role.)

Role of Other Professionals
(Identify other professionals with whom you will work closely and describe their role within the agency.)

Foundational Social Work Role	Role Defined	Field Task: Identify the field task(s) and targeted client systems that will enable you to fulfill the identified role.	Processing and Evaluation: Identify how your ability to perform the role will be processed and evaluated.
Counselor	This role is fulfilled by the student when the student provides support, encouragement, and suggestions and assists the client in the planned change process. For example, a student might listen to, support, and explore options for how a mother might handle her child's problems in school.		
Educator	This role is fulfilled by the student when he or she provides information and teaches within the client system. For example, a student will provide information to the client system about anger management in the context of a group for urban youtwh.		

Broker	This role is fulfilled when the student links a client system with a needed resource. For instance, the student might refer the client to an Alcoholics Anonymous or a Narcotics Anonymous group.
Case Manager	This role is fulfilled by the student when he or she coordinates needed services provided by different community agencies. For instance, the student might coordinate the services for a client who is being discharged from the hospital.
Mobilizer	This role is fulfilled by the student when he or she convenes community people and resources to identify needs. For example, a student might encourage community residents to address crime that is not being addressed through a community policing program.
Mediator	This role is fulfilled by the student when he or she resolves disputes and conflicts between system members. For instance, the student might work as a go-between for members of a neighborhood and local developers.
Facilitator	This role is fulfilled by the student when he or she leads groups. For instance, a student might run a group for girls in a community youth program.
Advocate	This is fulfilled by the student who stands up for and represents the needs or interests of a client so that the client receives resources. For instance, the student may contact the landlord on behalf of the client requesting an extension on an eviction notice.
Other:	

One role that you as a student in field can target is that of *brokering* or linking clients with needed resources. This is a vital role and can be accomplished by first researching and updating community resources and then linking your clients to a needed resource. Other common roles that students will practice while in field are case manager, advocate, counselor, facilitator, and educator.

In terms of your professional socialization and development, it is necessary to have opportunities to explain your role to clients, staff in the agency, other professionals, students in courses, and faculty. Thus, it may be useful for you to develop a student job description.

Once you have reviewed the eight foundational roles, when you are developing your learning plan and identify tasks, integrate a role into the task whenever possible. For example, going back to the student who was able to add the two mezzo practice tasks, both tasks included a foundational role of social work practice in the task: (1) facilitate a support group and (2) educate clients by conducting community-based presentations. As you can see, both *facilitate* and *educate* were included in the learning task and specifically reference a foundational social work role. By writing your learning task in a way that includes a role, whenever possible, you will become grounded in the roles themselves and ensure that you are having opportunities to use the role in your practice. One last thing to consider is that some learning tasks will not include a foundational role. This may be due to the fact that the task is very straightforward, as in the example of reading an article and viewing a video to develop knowledge. In fact, many of the orientation and training-related learning tasks may not involve a role. It is when the student moves from orientation and training to practice that the roles become clearer.

Now that you have reviewed multilevel learning tasks and how to integrate the foundational roles of social work into a learning task, the last part of the learning objective is the plan for evaluation.

The Plan for Evaluation

If you refer back to the guiding definition of a *learning objective*, you will recall a well-constructed learning objective also includes a plan for evaluation. It enables you and your field instructor to determine if the learning task was completed and the corresponding goal and objective met. A well-constructed learning objective includes information that identifies how the objective will be evaluated (the evaluation plan), which ultimately sets the stage for the final field evaluation process.

The evaluation plan includes information such as due dates, the number of times something is done, and the activities or resources used to measure an objective for learning and goals. Referring back to the sample learning objective, notice that several things are identified to assist in evaluating that learning objective. For instance, you and your field instructor can readily determine if a specific due date when something is to be completed was met and if an activity, such as discussing in supervision and applying content learned to a case, has been completed. Obviously, meeting a due date or completing an activity will not be the only standard by which an objective is evaluated, particularly in the context of the final field evaluation, but starting with a well-constructed objective will set the stage. The final field evaluation will most likely take place at the end of each semester or quarter and weighs heavily in the grade you receive for field. A well-constructed final evaluation will reflect the learning plan and relate directly to the goals and objectives you and your field instructor have set forth. The evaluation process should involve both you and your field instructor, along with any other critical players in the agency, in reviewing your progress and determining an overall evaluation of your performance. Make sure to conduct a self-assessment and be ready to discuss your assessment as well as hear your field instructor's assessment of your performance. If you have any concerns or questions about the outcome of your evaluation, discuss those with your field instructor first, as he or she may be able to resolve them. If that discussion does not sufficiently address your concerns, take them to your faculty field liaison or field director.

Table 3.1 offers a way to think about and practice developing learning objectives for field that integrate all of the areas discussed previously; namely, a goal statement, learning tasks with an integrated role, and a plan for evaluation.

TABLE 3.1 ■ Developing Objectives for Learning		
Objective for Learning		
1. Goal Statement	2. Learning Task(s) (with an Integrated Role)	3. Plan for Evaluation
Sample Goal Statement:		

As you can see, an objective for learning consists of a goal statement, learning task(s), and a possible integrated role and plan for evaluation. This format is in keeping with Horejsi and Garthwait's (1999) definition of *learning objectives*, but instead of the objective being one multi-faceted sentence, the objective for learning is broken down into three parts: (1) a goal statement, (2) learning task(s) with integrated role, and (3) plan for evaluation, which makes it easier to write and evaluate. Using Table 3.1, construct one sample objective for learning.

REFLECTION QUESTION 3.1

Now that you have had a chance to review the elements of the learning plan, specifically focusing on goals and objectives, tasks and roles, and a plan for evaluation, the first thing to think about is what you are hoping to accomplish. In your answer, jot down goal statements. Next, consider expectations for field as identified by your program, field instructor, and the agency. Then, start thinking about the kinds of multilevel tasks and roles you can engage in as well as those that you want to engage in. Last, identify ways in which your tasks, objectives, and goals can be evaluated.

ROOM TO REFLECT

Developing Your Learning Plan

In order to develop a well-constructed learning plan that includes all the information discussed thus far, complete Integrative Activity 3.3. This activity will give you all the necessary information to draft your program's learning plan as well as develop your skill in writing learning objectives.

INTEGRATIVE ACTIVITY 3.3
CONSTRUCTING THE FIELD LEARNING PLAN

Purpose: The purpose of this activity is to assist you in gathering the information you will need to complete your program's learning plan as well as to develop your skill in writing objectives for learning.

Directions: Referring back to Integrative Activities 3.1 and 3.2 and using the guideline set forth in Table 3.1, complete all areas.

Competency 7: Assess Individuals, Families, Groups, Organizations, and Communities

- develop mutually agreed-on intervention goals and objectives based on the critical assessment of strengths, needs, and challenges within clients and constituencies

1. **Primary role within agency: (Refer to Integrative Activity 3.2)**

2. **Primary tasks: (Refer to Integrative Activities 3.1 and 3.2)**

Micro
Individuals:
Families:
Mezzo
Groups: (Indicate Type/Treatment and/or Task)
Macro
Organization:
Community: (Indicate Type of Community, Policy/Legislature, or Research)

3. Identifying learning objectives:

List all of the goals and objectives you are hoping to accomplish as a result of your field experience. To gather this list, consider the goals of the social worker(s) at the agency; your personal interests, goals, and objectives as a professional social worker; goals and objectives that relate to the population served or services offered; special projects or issues impacting the agency; and goals and objectives for field as outlined by your university field director, faculty field liaison, and course work.

In each of the five overarching areas of field competence (see Chapter 1), practice writing learning objectives, including multilevel learning tasks integrating the foundational roles of social work and the evaluation plan. Refer back to the list you developed above and link it to the five overarching goal areas.

Goal Area 1: Socialization and professional development as a social worker in field.

Learning Objective:	Learning Tasks with Roles:	Evaluation Plan:

(Continued)

(Continued)

Goal Area 2: Ethical practice and consideration of diversity and social justice.

Learning Objective:	Learning Tasks with Roles:	Evaluation Plan:

Goal Area 3: Integration of knowledge, values, and skills acquired in the classroom with the practice experiences of field

Learning Objective:	Learning Tasks with Roles:	Evaluation Plan:

Goal Area 4: Effective communication skills in field

Learning Objective:	Learning Tasks with Roles:	Evaluation Plan:

Goal Area 5: Application of the planned change process with individuals, families, groups, organizations, and communities in field

Learning Objective:	Learning Tasks with Roles:	Evaluation Plan:

(Continued)

(Continued)

Other: Competence specific to field site and program

Learning Objective:	Learning Tasks with Roles:	Evaluation Plan:

Effective Use of the Learning Plan

As discussed at the beginning of this chapter, the learning plan provides direction and assists you in achieving what you hope to accomplish in field. You need to consider how to best use the document as a tool in your learning and development as a competent social worker. The first and most obvious use is to keep a copy of the learning plan and periodically review it on your own and in supervision with your field instructor. Students have asked me countless times for a copy of their learning plan so they and their field instructor could complete the final field evaluation. I am usually surprised and concerned that neither the student nor the field instructor had a copy to begin with, and I question their ability to have effectively monitored their progress in field without having referenced their learning plan. Second, if issues come up with regard to your tasks, such as being asked to engage in a task that is not on your learning plan or not having an opportunity to complete a task that is on the learning plan, use the learning plan as a way to resolve the issue. For instance, a student had a task on the learning plan that the student was not getting to complete because the student was spending too much time each day completing another task. By reviewing the learning plan and discussing the agreed-upon tasks with the field instructor and identifying the issue (the fact that the student wasn't getting to a particular task because the other task was taking up so much time), the student renegotiated the days at field. This renegotiation of the time spent on tasks allowed the student to have the time necessary to complete all the agreed-upon tasks. When you have your learning plan and refer to it, you often can avoid issues in the first place and more swiftly resolve an issue if one does come up. Last, use the learning plan to monitor your progress. This helps develop your confidence as you cross off tasks that you have accomplished and helps you refocus your time to complete those tasks that may have fallen through the cracks and have yet to be accomplished. Remember, the number of hours spent per week in field will seem like a lot at first, but once you are working, the time goes very quickly. So, it is important to stay on top of your time and use it in the most productive ways possible.

The Pace of Learning

Once you have completed your official learning plan, it is helpful to consider how the learning plan can facilitate the pace of your learning. This refers to how quickly or slowly you move from orientation and training to independently practicing as a social work student. The learning plan should include tasks that reflect the pace, with some involving shadowing and cofacilitating to others reflecting independence. The first thing to discuss related to the pace of your learning is your transition from shadowing to independent practice.

From Shadowing to Independent Practice

The transition you will make from shadowing to practicing independently as a social work student is similar to the steps involved in training (see Chapter 2), with an important step in your training plan being shadowing. However, how you move from that first day when you shadowed the social worker doing a home visit as part of your training to conducting home visits with your own cases as an independently practicing social work student is an important process to consider. There is no hard-and-fast rule; a lot of this process will be individualized to the style of your field instructor, the training process at your agency, the needs of your role, and your skill level as the student. However, you can do a few things to facilitate this transition.

First, make sure you have opportunities to shadow and observe many different social workers doing a variety of tasks and roles. Observing other social workers is an excellent learning experience for three reasons:

1. You are exposed to a lot of different styles of social workers.

2. You meet a variety of clients experiencing a variety of issues.

3. You begin to reflect on how you will handle a similar situation when you are practicing.

All of this becomes important as you move from shadowing to independent practice. As a part of your shadowing experience, make sure you can observe your field instructor providing various tasks and roles whenever possible. Observing your field instructor will give you a sense of who that person is as a social worker and an opportunity to see a more experienced worker. This contributes to your development and often helps you identify more targeted goals or markers of competent practice. For instance, a student observed the field instructor conducting intakes and, as a result, identified the skill level of the field instructor, specifically the instructor's ability to seamlessly engage the client and gather the needed information. The student noted that the style was very conversational. As a result, the student wanted to be able to do that. The ability of the student to target a skill as something they hoped to accomplish became very useful with regard to establishing the pace and steps involved in meeting that goal.

Next, begin to perform a task while under direct observation. As nerve-racking as this can be, it is an important part of the process. Year after year, at the end of field, students tell me they wish they had had more opportunities to be observed and to be given specific targeted feedback. To bridge this gap, I encourage you to do a few tasks under direct observation. The reason this is such a helpful task is because it is the best way to get feedback. Also, in terms of the learning process, you can engage in a task without having to know everything or be expected to handle every eventuality because your field instructor or agency designee is there with you. Once you get over the nervousness of working under direct observation, you will notice that it is actually comforting to have someone there completing the task with you.

The last step is to complete learning tasks independently. You have defined your role within the agency, been orientated and trained, and have clearly identified your learning tasks in the learning plan; now it is time to engage in those tasks independently. Let's discuss what this might look like. In most agencies, it will be very straightforward: You will be assigned a caseload, project, or task that you will complete independently. However, in some agencies, independent work will need to be defined and perhaps even negotiated. For instance, in some agencies, a student cannot have official case assignment, meaning the student cannot be identified as the primary social worker on the case. However, it is necessary for a student to have some version of a caseload and independent role on the cases; so, even if the student cannot be the *official* caseworker, he or she can still learn the cases and work as independently as possible. Another way to think about independent practice as a social work student is to describe what something should not look like; for instance, a student who comes to field every day and is randomly assigned to workers, cases, and tasks, or a student comes to field each day and has to find work to do. Both situations can happen, and they tend to create a hectic learning environment that is not effective. How casework should actually look is as follows: The student is assigned certain cases to work and coworks those cases with the agency social worker. *Coworking* refers to the student and social worker working in tandem, with the student leading sessions or visits, asking questions to gather needed information, and completing any documentation, which is then reviewed and signed off on by the agency social worker. Another example is in the case of a student who is in an agency where official and legal reports are completed and presented. In this case, the student can work on the report and write a rough draft; based on that, the social worker completes the final version and presents it to the recipient (such as in a court hearing) with the student present. The primary goal of all field tasks, regardless of how the task has to be structured for a student, is to give the student a sense of continuity through case assignment and the ability to practice as independently as possible. Other students will be in a setting that easily translates to independent practice, thus the preceding situations will not be an issue. Either way, it is important that the learning plan reflect the plan for your eventual independent practice and that you discuss this process with your field instructor during the first few weeks of field.

As a final thought, it is interesting to note that macro-level tasks that target the organization—such as updating the resource manual, researching evidence-based practices, or developing a new program—lend themselves nicely to independent practice. Take, for example, a student who will be developing a new policy for the agency. Once the student and field instructor determine the plan for how best to approach this task (such as researching the policy need, identifying other agencies that have the policy, and finding resources that can assist in developing the policy), the student will have a great deal of control over completing this task independently.

REFLECTION QUESTION 3.2

As you think about practicing independently, what does that look like in your agency? What are you excited about, and what are your concerns? What do you need from yourself, your field instructor, and the field director or faculty field liaison to become independent at your field site?

ROOM TO REFLECT

Troubleshooting—Discussing the Pace of Learning

From time to time throughout your field experience, the pace of your learning may ebb and flow. This can be due to a number of variables and may require troubleshooting. During various points in the process of going from shadowing to independent practice, issues can arise, such as a student feeling that he or she is endlessly shadowing and not having opportunities to begin coworking; has no real opportunity for independent practice; or, conversely, is thrown into running a group the second week of field and has no idea what he or she is doing. Last, a student might be avoiding independent practice because the student is unsure about whether he or she can be effective.

All of the preceding situations can happen and, in fact, they are more common than not. So, it is important to discuss the pace of your learning in supervision. For some, this conversation will flow easily and naturally, but for others, it may be more difficult. This is one of the reasons why attending and using supervision is a professional socialization task, but sometimes it is not easy to develop this relationship and use it to discuss your learning process. Once again, this is where your learning plan can be an effective tool, but only if it clearly identifies the tasks that will assist you as you move from shadowing to independent practice.

If you are having issues with the pace of your learning, bring the learning plan to your field instructor and discuss your progress on various tasks. Also, your field director, faculty field liaison, and site visit can be effective resources to use to address any concerns you are having with regard to the pace of your learning. The bottom line is to ensure that you, the university, and the agency are all doing their part to create the best learning environment and experience possible.

FREQUENTLY EXPERIENCED SITUATIONS

The following is a frequently experienced situation that relates well to this chapter. Review the situation and consider how you might go about handling this situation should it happen to you.

I'm not doing what I thought I would be doing; can I get a new placement?

I'm so frustrated; I'm not doing any of the things I thought I would be doing. To make matters worse, my field instructor keeps asking me to do things that I don't think I should be doing. Can I get a different placement?

Although this was touched on in this chapter, this is a common experience that often requires specific attention. First and foremost, any time you have a question about the tasks you are or are not engaging in, you must discuss this openly and honestly with your field instructor.

In fact, whenever students or field instructors bring up issues about field, I ask each person if they have discussed the issue with the other party. I can't tell you how often I am told, "No." I always send each party back to discuss the situation with the other. I realize that this may be easier said than done, so let's talk about discussing your concern about tasks with your field instructor.

First of all, you can refer to your learning plan. If the task you are not getting an opportunity to engage in is on the learning plan, you can refer to the learning plan and discuss how to incorporate that task into your days at field. If the task is not on your learning plan, you can say that you have several tasks already included on the plan, some of which you are having a hard time getting to, and that you won't be able to complete the requested task at this time. Tell your field instructor that you are open to discussing including the task, but you will have to drop another task due to the time constraints of the field placement.

Finally, the student's leap to wanting to switch placements is not so uncommon. My position with the students I work with has always been that the problems that come up while in field are often important learning opportunities. If a student switched placements every time there was an issue, (1) they would be constantly switching and (2) they would miss out on an

(Continued)

(Continued)

important learning opportunity to develop professional skills that will be necessary when practicing. Those skills include assertiveness, being one's own advocate, and professional communication. If a student is particularly nervous about discussing an issue with their field instructor, I encourage the student to write down

what he or she wants to say, practice with me or the other students, and fully prepare for the meeting.

If the problems do not get better, then you may need to discuss with your field director if the placement is appropriate. But this should be the last conversation to have, not the first.

Suggested Field Tasks

- Identify your primary role and tasks.
- Review the social worker's job description.
- Identify other professionals with whom you work and learn about their roles.
- Identify learning opportunities and objectives.
- Develop a learning plan.

- Identify multilevel tasks to achieve the goals and objectives identified on your learning plan.
- Evaluate your progress in meeting the goals and objectives of field and core competencies and practice behaviors.
- Discuss the pace of learning.

References

Birkenmaier, J., & Berg-Weger, M. (2007). *The practicum companion for social work: Integrating class and field work*. Boston, MA: Pearson Education.

Council on Social Work Education (CSWE). (2015). *Educational policy and accreditation standards*. Alexandria, VA: Author.

DuBois, B., & Miley, K. (2005). *Social work: An empowering profession*. Boston, MA: Allyn and Bacon.

Hendricks, C., Finch, J., & Franks, C. (2005). *Learning to teach, teaching to learn: A guide for social work field education*. Alexandria, VA: CSWE Press.

Horejsi, C., & Garthwait, C. (1999). *The social work practicum: A guide and workbook for students*. Boston, MA: Allyn and Bacon.

Interprofessional Education Collaborative. (2016). *Core competencies for interprofessional collaborative practice: 2016 update*. Washington, DC: Author.

Kagel, J., & Kopels, S. (2008). *Social work records*. Long Grove, IL: Waveland Press.

Kirst-Ashman, K., & Hull Jr., G. (2009). *Understanding generalist practice* (5th ed.). Belmont, CA: Brooks/Cole.

Plionis, E., Bailey-Etta, B., & Manning, M. (2002). Implementing the generalist model in practice: Implications for curriculum and best practices. *Journal of Teaching in Social Work, 22*(3/4), 103–119.

Riebschleger, J., & Grettenberger, S. (2006). Assessing graduating BSW field students' preparation for generalist practice. *The Journal of Baccalaureate Social Work, 12*(1), 184.

Schaefer, J., & Larkin, S. (2015). Interprofessional education in undergraduate social work education. *The Journal of Baccalaureate Social Work, 20*(1), 179–188.

Sheafor, B., & Horejsi, C. (2008). *Techniques and guidelines for social work practice*. Boston, MA: Pearson Education.

Sheafor, B., & Horejsi, C. (2015). *Techniques and guidelines for social work practice*. Boston, MA: Pearson Education.

World Health Organization. (2010). *Framework for action on interprofessional education and collaborative practice*. Retrieved March 8, 2018, from http://www.who.int/hrh/resources/framework_action/en

4

SAFETY IN FIELD

As students leave the classroom and enter the agency, safety in field education becomes a relevant issue that many students often don't fully consider. Several studies—in particular, Criss (2010); Dunkel, Ageson, and Ralph (2000); Ellison (1996); and Tully, Kropf, and Price (1993)—point to this fact. A national study in 2001 found that field directors felt there was a need to pay greater attention to the safety of students in field and that risk to students was increasing (Reeser & Wertkin, 2001). Thus, as a field director, I consider your safety and well-being a top priority. With regard to violence encountered by students, either verbal or physical, according to a national study of Master of Social Work (MSW) and Bachelor in Social Work (BSW) students, 41.7% reported direct exposure to violence, with the most common type being verbal abuse at 37.5% (Criss, 2010). Ellison's (1996) national study of BSW and MSW field programs found that "out of a total of 17,650 students in field (N = 11,557 MSW; 6,093 BSW), a relatively small number of students experienced any type of violence while in field" (p. 86). Ellison goes on to report, "The bad news is that 77 students experienced some type of violence while in their field program" (p. 86). Although Ellison's study indicates that the vast majority of students will not experience an issue related to violence, the author encourages caution because the study looked specifically at reported or known instances and may not have captured all instances of violence that students may have experienced.

Tully and colleagues (1993) surveyed both social work students and field instructors to identify safety issues and found that undergraduate and graduate students as well as field instructors experienced instances of violence, both physical and verbal. Interestingly enough, the incidence of violence (verbal and physical) was higher for field instructors than students. The authors concluded that this may be due to the fact that student status protects students more from potential harm. Students in this study also reported safety concerns related to their agency, such as having to work with potentially dangerous clients, working in neighborhoods that have high rates of violence, and being exposed to various communicable diseases. This is important because it expands the discussion beyond violence to the need to consider safety more broadly. Moylan and Wood (2016) found that 55% of the 515 BSW and MSW students surveyed experienced at least one incident of sexual harassment in their field placement, most often perpetrated by other staff or clients. All of these findings indicate the importance of preparing students to manage potential instances of sexual harassment in field.

Thus, it is important to increase your understanding of potential safety issues, as all these studies emphasize the importance of placing the threat of violence and harassment and even the fear that a student may have about the possibility of experiencing violence or harassment front and center. Dunkel and colleagues (2000) suggest that not addressing the threat of violence and fear of violence "will compromise the social worker/client relationship, the professional delivery of services, and in the case of graduate and undergraduate students, negatively impact learning, as well" (p. 6).

Before you consider how best to address safety in your field placement, it is helpful to review what the literature says about safety in both social work programs and in agencies. Wood and Moylan (2017) found that only half of the participants reported having received training on sexual harassment as a part of their formal preparation for field and less than half had an informal discussion of sexual harassment in their classes or with coworkers and classmates. With regard to social work programs, Faria and Kendra (2007) found that 11 of 19 programs or 67% include safety in their curriculum. The six schools that stated they did not include safety in the curriculum reported relying on field agencies to address this content.

This particular study had a very low response rate—only 19 of the 200 surveys sent were returned; thus, these findings may not accurately represent social work education. That being said, given the potential expectation of social work programs that agencies will address safety for students, it is helpful to consider what agencies are doing. Tully and colleagues (1993) looked at agencies' policies and training concerning violence and found two important things. First, most of the students in the study reported that their agencies did not have policies regarding violence or they were not made aware of them if the agencies did. Second, few students received any training on safety at their agency. Interestingly, there was a gap between the field instructors' reports that their agencies had safety policies and the students' reports that they knew the policies. This is even more concerning in light of Wood and Moylan's (2017) findings that of the 55% of students surveyed who reported having experienced an incidence of sexual harassment, only 5.6% pursued formal reporting mechanisms within the agency or campus, even with knowing to whom to report. Furthermore, it was found that about 49.1% of the students who experienced an incident did not report it at all. With regard to reasons why they didn't report, 55.5% of the participants said they did not think the incident was serious, and 28.2% thought that others would not think it was serious. This begs the question: What do you need to know to reduce your risk in field and be prepared to address instances of safety in field? DiGiulio (2001) indicated that universities have a responsibility to consider safety and to "acknowledge potential risks associated with field education and to minimize those risks by providing knowledge and preparation in safety procedures" (p. 69). The need to equip students with the resources to ensure their safety and reduce their risk becomes extremely important, especially in light of the concern that students are impacted by the culture of their agency and how they are responded to by field instructors. Lyter (2015) suggests that some social workers may cause a student to feel shame for expressing their concerns, end the conversation, and thus engage in denial or share horror stories that glorify their bravery and risk taking; others will provide an honest discussion of concerns and actually increase students' skills. The latter is what is preferable. Even more important is the fact that your university and social work program have a responsibility to ensure your safety and well-being, especially given that field is a required part of your program. In order to prepare you to navigate through all of the above potentialities, the SAFE field education approach and an overview of three important areas of personal and professional well-being are offered and explained in detail below. Although *safety* is the common term used in the literature, Dunkel and colleagues (2000) prefer the term *risk reduction*, as they feel that *safety* implies an idealized goal—the ability to control one's environment—and can perpetuate denial, whereas *risk reduction* "describes a set of achievable interventions aimed at recognizing, managing or avoiding dangerous situations" (p. 7). Thus, risk reduction undergirds the discussion of safety and well-being in field throughout this chapter.

SAFETY IN FIELD EDUCATION

SAFE Field Education

As you think about safety in field education, it is useful to take a holistic approach that incorporates risk reduction and personal and professional well-being. The SAFE field education acronym (see Table 4.1) begins this process by offering a quick way to consider four foundational aspects

TABLE 4.1 ■ SAFE Field Education	
Self	Carry liability insurance.
	Identify yourself as a student.
	Communicate your whereabouts.
	Employ physical safety measures.
Agency	Know the safety policies and procedures of the agency and how they are related to the university and the program.
	Assess the culture of the agency with regard to issues of safety.
	Consider the client population served.
	Ensure your professional well-being.
	Attend supervisory sessions.
	Practice within your role as a student.
	Know legal liability.
	Review mandated reporting and your duty to warn/prevent harm.
Feelings	Trust your gut.
	Ensure psychological well-being.
	Engage in self-care; think of the oxygen mask metaphor.
	Manage stress and potential burnout.
	Educate yourself and be aware of vicarious trauma.
Environment	Assess internal and external agency environment—lighting, parking, and so on.
	Assess the type, location, and time of day of service (i.e., in office, in home, or community based).

of safety in field, along with specific areas for each. The *S* stands for *self* and encourages you to reflect on those areas that you can address to increase your personal safety and reduce your risk. For instance, one area of importance is ensuring that you have liability insurance and perhaps exploring carrying your own policy in addition to what your program offers. The *A* stands for the agency and includes those areas of safety that are agency specific, such as knowing your university's, program's, and agency's policies and procedures concerning safety and—even more importantly—following them. The *F* stands for *feelings* and places your feelings front and center in your field experience. Educate yourself about vicarious trauma and have a plan in place should you notice that you are experiencing symptoms. Last, the *E* stands for *environment* and reinforces the importance of environment, which includes the physical space of the agency and any risks inherent to the setting.

THREE AREAS OF PERSONAL AND PROFESSIONAL WELL-BEING

Next, we will explore three overarching areas of safety that are grounded in well-being. The emphasis on well-being aims to shift the conversation away from only considering safety to actually enhancing your personal and professional self within field. The three areas are physical, psychological, and professional well-being.

Physical Well-Being

The first area to consider is physical well-being. This specifically addresses your bodily well-being when coming to and leaving your field site and while in your day-to-day activities at your agency and targets reducing your risk of experiencing physical violence.

The first thing you want to consider is your primary mode of transportation to and from your field site. For example, if you are driving, identify where you will be parking. If you are taking the bus or train, how far do you need to walk to the stop from your home or the university and to your agency? During the winter months and if you are working in the evening, consider your safety needs at night. Are the stops well-lit and public, or are they dark and remote? In addition, consider the lighting of the building itself and the parking lot. If you do not consider your travel in the evenings to be safe, discuss this concern with your field instructor. If you are traveling to and from home visits or working in neighborhoods and in the community, you will want to make sure you know where you are going and whether there are any safety issues related to the neighborhood where you will be working. If you are driving, make sure you have a full tank of gas and that your car is in good working order. Also, always make sure you know where you are going, have a charged cell phone, and are aware of your environment.

While working one-on-one with clients or in a group setting, always consider the population you are working with to determine whether there are any client population–based physical safety issues. Make sure to discuss this with your supervisor, as some agencies have safety measures that they use in their day-to-day practice. For instance, an agency may have a panic button that a social worker can take along to an individual or group session or a code word to be used over the phone system should the social worker need assistance. So, review and know your agency's safety policies and procedures.

You also can consider other things to ensure your physical safety when in the office, at a client's home, or in the community, such as how to position yourself in a room with a client. To increase your physical safety, make sure the client does not block the doorway and you have a clear exit. You always want to be aware of your client's behavior and of any change in behavior, as well as any change in your surroundings. By all means, trust your gut. If something seems wrong or different, make sure to ask for assistance. I always tell my students that it is okay to abandon a task if they do not feel safe for whatever reason.

When coming and going throughout your workday, it is very important that someone knows where you are at all times. This is best handled in agencies that have in/out boards so staff can get a clear visual of who is out and who has not returned. If your agency does not have a structured in/out system, establish an informal system with your field instructor or agency secretary. The goal of this system is that if you do not return, someone will look for you. Additional safety measures can entail using the locator device on your cell phone, if your phone has one. This will send out a GPS signal if someone tries to locate the phone. Make sure your field instructor has emergency contacts should something happen and you need assistance. Finally, when going out into the community, have some form of identification on your person at all times. The best form of ID is an ID badge from the agency with your picture, name, title as social work student, and agency name. Most ID badges also include a number on the back to contact in the event of an emergency. If your agency does not have photo ID badges for students, use your university photo ID and carry a card in your wallet with your agency name, number, and field instructor contact information.

Last, be aware of the potential for health risks through exposure to serious communicable diseases such as tuberculosis and other bothersome issues such as lice, scabies, bedbugs, and standard viruses that can cause a cold or the flu. The best prevention is, first of all, to be educated with regard to the potential risks specific to your work, and second, to employ the number-one precautionary practice: regular hand washing. In specified settings with specific populations, you may need to employ more targeted and elaborate health safety measures. If this is the case, discuss health safety measures, policies, and best practices with your field instructor.

Psychological Well-Being

The next area for you to consider is your psychological well-being. This relates specifically to the thoughts and feelings you will experience as a result of your work and how you manage them. The concepts of *vicarious trauma*, *stress management*, *burnout*, and *self-care* are important to discuss with both field faculty in your program and your field instructor. Vicarious trauma can occur after a worker or student is exposed to trauma experienced by a client; "social workers and other helpers may themselves show symptoms of trauma, such as intrusive thoughts and images, sleeplessness, bystander guilt, and feelings of vulnerability, helplessness, self-doubt, and rage" (Sheafor & Horejsi, 2015, p. 515). This can happen as the result of being exposed to traumatic client situations, unusual case experiences, photos, and client records. In a study of BSW students and their field instructors on *indirect trauma*, a term developed by the study author to include secondary traumatic stress, vicarious trauma, and compassion fatigue, Knight (2010) found that students were at greater risk for vicarious trauma than their field instructor and participants in previous studies.

I remember early on in my practice at a mental health crisis agency, I had a client come in for short-term crisis counseling. During the first session, the client, a young woman, recounted in graphic detail her rape by a family member and the current symptoms, including flashbacks that were triggered when she was in a room that reminded her of where the rape took place. Needless to say, I was stunned and could not get the details out of my head. The client never returned. That was more than 20 years ago, and I can still recall the entire session in vivid detail: what the client looked like, what the room looked like, and the story. I continued to notice difficulties I was having working at the crisis center with clients who were experiencing domestic violence, incest, and suicide and realized, after disclosing my difficulties sleeping and various intrusive thoughts to my supervisor, that I was experiencing vicarious trauma. After processing this issue and engaging in deliberate self-care, I was able to combat the effects of working in a crisis center. Fortunately, with increased practice experience, I was able to develop the skills necessary to process difficult client situations in a variety of settings that included a child welfare setting that again challenged me with experiences of vicarious trauma. I think my practice experiences have made me increasingly sensitive to the experiences of my students and the need to prepare them for managing what they will experience in field.

I have worked with students who have developed symptoms of vicarious trauma and the most important thing I was able to do for them was to reassure them that what they were experiencing was normal. Next, I worked with them and their field instructor to address their needs. One critically important tool in managing vicarious trauma is discussing in supervision the issue and the feelings you are experiencing. Knight (2010) found that compassion fatigue was higher for students who didn't talk to their field instructors or who felt they could not talk to their field instructors. Thus, it is important for students to build a strong relationship with their field instructor and peers at the agency so that when they experience difficult cases, they can freely discuss their concerns. One agency I worked with handled issues of vicarious trauma extremely well by first normalizing the experience and then engaging in a debriefing session to assist the student and field instructor in processing the difficult details of the case.

Some of the warning signs of vicarious trauma can be loss of energy, lack of self-care, disconnecting from others, increased sensitivity to fear or threat, change in worldview, and a feeling of hopelessness or despair. It is important to regularly check in with your field instructor during your supervision session about how you are feeling and what you are noticing about yourself as you are experiencing field. Dane (2002) states that "personal life events can influence the work and induce vulnerability for the student who is a survivor of trauma. It is important for new social workers to monitor their reactions and responses" (p. 9). Also, your area of practice may increase your risk of experiencing vicarious trauma. Knight (2010) found that students in child welfare settings demonstrated more signs of vicarious trauma.

If you are not getting what you need at your agency or, for whatever reason, you cannot discuss your concerns with your field instructor and especially if you are in a higher-risk setting, it is critically important to contact your field director or faculty field liaison. That person will be able to assist you in the process of identifying the vicarious trauma, notifying your placement site, and working with you and your field instructor to develop a plan to address the issue. If your program has an integrated field seminar course, you (as a student) can also go there to share your reactions to the work you are doing and to gain support from students who may be experiencing similar issues.

Intricately woven with vicarious trauma are stress management and burnout. These refer to the difficulties you may experience associated with field education in general and your particular work at your agency. For instance, I tell my students that field is stressful. As you recall, the introduction to this book discussed the challenges associated with field in general. Similarly, your unique situation (course load, outside work and family demands, field schedule) and field site setting (challenging population, chaotic work environment, tough cases) may create sources of stress for you as well. As a part of your personal well-being, it is important to continuously monitor your level of stress and be aware of the potential for burnout while in field. "The concept of burnout has been used to understand workers' reactions to the demands of the work environment" (Dane, 2002, p. 5). Dane goes on to say, "Burnout is perceived as a negative experience, and can appear as physical and emotional exhaustion, negativity about accomplishments, and depersonalization" (p. 5).

It is very important that you employ good stress management and self-care techniques so that the cumulative stress of the field placement does not lead to burnout. I like to use the metaphor of the oxygen mask to explain why it is so important to engage in self-care. When you fly on an airplane, the flight attendant will instruct you that in the event of a drop in cabin pressure, you should put on your oxygen mask. They go on to say that if you are traveling with young children or people who may need assistance, it is critical to put your own oxygen mask on first and then assist the other person.

REFLECTION QUESTION 4.1

Why do you think the airline personnel instruct people to put their oxygen mask on first before assisting others, and how do you think this relates to field education?

ROOM TO REFLECT

The most obvious reason is that as a social worker, you will be assisting individuals who are in need and they need to know that you are there, at your best, ready and able to assist them. The better off you are, the better you will be able to serve your clients. Interestingly enough, good self-care will also protect you better from overall stress and burnout. Self-care will be discussed in more detail in Chapter 11, when we discuss the professional development of self.

Professional Well-Being

The last area of consideration is professional well-being. I consider professional well-being to be analogous to issues of ethical practice and professional liability or malpractice. With regard to ethical practice, as a student, you are bound by the ethical conduct standards of the agency and the profession as outlined in the National Association of Social Workers (NASW) code of ethics. Ethical practice and dealing with ethical dilemmas will be discussed in more detail in Chapter 7. With regard to issues of professional liability and malpractice, Lynch and Versen (2003) state that "professional liability or professional malpractice is defined as a form of negligence on the part of practitioners" (p. 58). Consideration of liability in field will develop your understanding of your current and future liability concerns as a student and practicing social worker.

It is critical to realize that all members of the field education endeavor, the university (field director/faculty liaison), the student, and the agency (field instructor) share in liability (Zakutansky, 1993). Lynch and Versen (2003) state that the "prudent practice of social work today requires that social workers at all levels and settings have an awareness of malpractice liability issues and risk management strategies" (p. 58). The need to be aware of liability issues extends to you, the student. In fact, your field instructor experiences what is referred to as *vicarious liability*. This means that your field instructor is ultimately responsible for what you do. In fact, Lynch and Versen reported that students and their field instructors have been named in lawsuits. So, it is important that as you enter your agency in the capacity of a social work student under supervision of a social worker, you first know the professional responsibilities that relate to issues of legal liability and then meet these responsibilities through best practice. Your ability to reduce your and your field instructor's level of risk will directly impact your placement and possibly your future as a professional social worker. A few best practices will reduce your level of risk and increase your overall professional well-being.

First and foremost, as you enter your field agency as a social work student under the supervision of a professional social worker, it is critically important that you carry malpractice or liability insurance. Most programs offer this through the university, and the student or university pays the cost. If your agency wants a copy, either request one from your field director, or your university bill may have an actual line item that says *liability insurance*. The purpose of liability insurance is to protect you, the university, the agency, and the client should something happen that results in you being sued. If your university does not offer malpractice insurance, you can obtain it through the NASW or other private insurance companies. Some students even carry their own personal liability insurance in addition to the coverage offered through the school.

The next thing to do to ensure your professional well-being is to inform all the clients you come in contact with that you are a student. Your field instructor is responsible, according to the NASW code of ethics, to ensure that this happens. Interestingly enough, year after year, I have seen students enter agencies and be given tasks, but never be introduced properly to their clients. In fact, one of my students was observing a treatment group but was never introduced by the social worker nor did the student introduce herself. As a result, the student was mistaken for being a member of the group. It became very awkward for the student to run the group later. Therefore, it is very important to discuss this ahead of time with your field instructor and determine who will be introducing you. Furthermore, if you ever find yourself in a professional situation where you have not been properly introduced, go ahead and introduce yourself. This is an excellent way for you to show assertiveness and the ability to be proactive as well as to ensure that you are meeting this important ethical standard.

Another way to ensure your professional well-being is to attend supervisory meetings regularly. It is critically important that you and your field instructor be very clear about your tasks and the plan for your work. I encourage you to keep notes on your supervision sessions so that if something happens with a client, you will be able to reference your notes on the supervision session in which you discussed the case. Notes are also a wonderful way to document your progress on a case as well as write down questions you have for future supervision sessions. If you are taking notes, make sure not to write down any identifying information so as not to breach confidentiality and to keep your notes at the agency.

If supervision is not happening, for whatever reason, it is important to notify your field director or faculty field liaison so that the issue can be discussed and a plan of action implemented to address the situation. I am always surprised by these occurrences, given the vicarious liability that field instructors incur when they agree to supervise a student. That being said, as a field instructor who was also providing direct service and functioning as a supervisor, there were times when a crisis occurred and I had to cancel a student's supervision session. If this happens to you, it is very important that you reschedule immediately, and sometimes *you* will be the one approaching your field instructor and requesting that you reschedule. The previous scenario is different from a chronic pattern of not having supervision; that is a much more serious issue, particularly in light of professional well-being, and it must be addressed. The inability of the field instructor and agency to resolve this could necessitate you having to secure a different placement.

The next best-practice area is to know your role as the social work student and practice only within the boundaries of that role. As social workers, we have an ethical responsibility to practice only within our area of expertise. If you encounter a client situation that is beyond your training or role, it is critical that you obtain supervision and assistance for the client.

Unfortunately, practicing beyond your level of expertise or role can happen in an agency more easily than you would think. Remember the example from Chapter 3 in which the student was asked to complete a task that was not on her learning plan; this is also an excellent example of when a student is asked to practice outside the scope of his or her role. As you will recall, the student was asked to make a home visit and check on the client's well-being. The visit entailed tasks in the area of daily living activities, such as using the toilet and bathing. The student was not trained to fulfill these tasks and, by agreeing to make the home visit, put herself at risk should something have happened to the client during the visit. After discussing the situation, the student determined that she should have declined the request and stated that she can only perform tasks that are within her role and area of expertise.

The last and perhaps most important areas of risk reduction involve mandated reporting, duty to warn, and preventing harm. These are extremely serious issues, so much so that I recommend you have a specific discussion addressing these potential practice situations with your field instructor, field director, and field faculty liaison. If you are ever in a situation in which you suspect abuse or neglect or a client is expressing homicidal or suicidal ideation, notify your field instructor immediately. Of course, if you are experiencing an emergency, contact the police and emergency personnel first and then your field instructor and field director.

I always tell students to watch out when your field instructor or agency task supervisor asks you to do a task that is routine or involves a case that is "easy," because you never know what will come up. Make sure you have the names and numbers of your field instructor's supervisor and other agency personnel, should your attempts to contact your field instructor fail.

In short, it is always important to be prepared. The following example from a student I was supervising when I practiced illustrates how important it is to be prepared for anything, even during a routine task. I asked the student to go on a home visit and obtain the client's signature on a needed release-of-information form. I told the student that this case was going well, that the client was pleasant, and that it would be fine to touch base with the client and see how things were going. I was sitting at my desk about half an hour after the student had left when I received a frantic call. The student was on the phone and told me that the client had disclosed suicide ideation, and the student didn't know what to do next. I told the student to stay with the client and that I would be there shortly to provide the student with supervision to deal with the crisis. Needless to say, the student did the right thing to contact me, the field instructor, given the risk associated with the situation. The student and I were able to get the client to agree to a psychiatric assessment at a local hospital's psychiatric emergency services. The client was ultimately admitted and referred for a psychiatric consultation.

REFLECTION QUESTION 4.2

Now that you have had a chance to review the three areas of physical, psychological, and professional well-being, how do you think these areas relate to your field site? What, if anything, are you now aware of related to your safety and well-being in your field agency?

ROOM TO REFLECT

Assessing Safety in Field

Now that you have had a chance to review and consider SAFE field education and the three areas of physical, psychological, and professional well-being, complete and discuss Integrative Activity 4.1 with your field instructor. The educational policies and accreditation standards (EPAS) added the need for programs to indicate how they support student's safety in field as a part of accreditation (Council on Social Work Education, 2015).

INTEGRATIVE ACTIVITY 4.1
FIELD SAFETY ASSESSMENT

Purpose: The purpose of this integrative activity is to help you and your field instructor assess your safety at your field site in three primary areas: physical, psychological, and professional. It will also help you increase your understanding of your level of safety and identify issues that can impact safety.

Directions: Review and discuss this assessment with your field instructor and identify any areas that need specific attention to reduce the level of risk. Circle the appropriate answer; simply put the acronym *NA* (*not applicable*) if any items do not apply to your field agency and write in any written answers. Once you have answered all the questions, assess the agency's level of safety and your ability to address your safety needs. Last, identify any plan(s) to address safety overall and in the three specific

areas of physical, psychological, and professional well-being.

Accreditation Standard: 2.2 Field Education

2.2.7 The program describes how its field education program specifies policies, criteria, and procedures for selecting field settings; placing and monitoring students; supporting student safety; and evaluating student learning and field setting effectiveness congruent with the social work competencies.

Competency 1: Demonstrate Ethical and Professional Behavior

- demonstrate professional demeanor in behavior; appearance; and oral, written, and electronic communication

I. Orientation			
a. Does the agency have safety policies?		Yes	No
b. Does the agency offer safety training as part of the orientation?		Yes	No
c. Are you familiar with the safety policies?		Yes	No
d. Have you participated in safety orientation or training?		Yes	No
e. Have you and your field instructor reviewed your university's and program's safety guidelines?		Yes	No
f. Will you be receiving any special training related to safety? If so, please specify.		Yes	No
II. Physical Well-Being			
A. Getting to and from the Agency			
1. What is your mode of transportation to and from your placement site? Circle your answer. 　　Car　　　　　Bus　　　　　Train　　　　　Walking　　　　　Bicycle			
2. How easily accessible is your primary mode of transportation to the agency?		Easy	Difficult
a. Will you be walking far to get to the agency?		Yes	No
3. Does your agency offer an escort service to your mode of transportation?		Yes	No
4. Does the area neighborhood present increased risks?		Yes	No
5. How do you assess the physical surroundings of your agency?		Safe	Unsafe
6. Is the agency well-lit both inside and out?		Yes	No
7. Are there fire procedures in place?		Yes	No
8. Is the parking lot well-lit?		Yes	No
B. Working Outside the Office			
1. What is the procedure for traveling to home visits and outreach activities?			
2. If you drive your own vehicle to your placement site, are you expected to use your own vehicle for these visits?		Yes	No
3. What is the insurance plan for using your vehicle while in field?			
4. Have you discussed your program's policy regarding use of your personal vehicle while conducting field work and transporting clients?		Yes	No
5. Does your agency have any specific safety procedures regarding home visits and outreach activities, such as • sign-in/sign-out procedure? • call-in procedure? • buddy system? • escorts?		 Yes Yes Yes Yes	 No No No No

If other procedures are used, please explain:

6. If none, what is the plan you have developed to address your safety while conducting home visits or outreach work?

(Continued)

(Continued)

7. Do you have an identification badge?		Yes	No
8. Does someone know where you are at all times?		Yes	No
9. What is the plan if you find yourself in a situation with a potentially violent or threatening person?			
10. How are high-risk neighborhoods or areas identified?			
a. What is the plan for maintaining your safety when working in high-risk neighborhoods or areas?			
11. Will you be doing any after-hours or evening work?		Yes	No
12. If yes, what safety practices are recommended?		Yes	No
13. Does your field instructor have your emergency contact information?		Yes	No

C. Health

1. Are there health risks in this agency setting, such as risks for communicable diseases?		Yes	No
2. If yes, what are those risks, and what precautions are you taking?			
3. Have you been trained on precautionary procedures and prevention, particularly from communicable disease or infections, as well as parasites such as lice, scabies, and bedbugs?		Yes	No
4. If not, what is the plan for training in this area?			

III. Psychological Well-Being

A. Vicarious Trauma

1. Does the population or issues of practice present a risk for vicarious trauma?		Yes	No
2. If yes, what have you discussed with your field instructor about how you will prevent and manage risks related to vicarious trauma? Please describe.			

B. Stress Management and Burnout		
1. Have you discussed your level or risk for burnout and reviewed stress-management techniques?	Yes	No
2. What are ways you manage your stress at your placement?		

C. Self-Care		
1. What are your primary self-care techniques? (List below.)		

IV. Professional Well-Being		
A. Liability Insurance		
1. Do you currently have liability insurance?	Yes	No
2. Have you discussed and reviewed issues of ethical practice in supervision with your field instructor?	Yes	No
B. Supervision		
1. Do you have a set time for supervision?	Yes	No
2. Are you attending regular supervisory sessions?	Yes	No
C. Role and Training		
1. Do you know your role?	Yes	No
2. Have you been trained to fulfill your primary role?	Yes	No
3. Are you practicing within your role?	Yes	No
D. Crisis Management		
1. Have you (in supervision) discussed mandated reporting, duty to warn, and preventing harm?	Yes	No
2. Do you know whom to contact if there is a crisis?	Yes	No
3. Do you know whom to contact if you can't reach your field instructor?	Yes	No

V. Overview of Safety Assessment		
1. Overall, how safe would you rate the agency? (Safe, Somewhat Safe, Unsafe)		
2. How would you rate your own preparedness at this time to participate safely in your field experience? (Well Prepared, Somewhat Prepared, Not at All Prepared)		
3. Have you discussed the results of this safety assessment with your field instructor?	Yes	No

(Continued)

(Continued)

4. What, if any, specific plan(s) of action will you implement as a result of this assessment in order to address your overall safety in field? And what plan(s) of action will you implement in the following specific areas?		
a. Overall		
b. Physical		
c. Psychological		
d. Professional		
5. Have you discussed the results of this assessment with your field director or faculty field liaison?	Yes	No

Now that you have considered all the information addressed in the assessment and determined the overall level of safety at your agency, discuss anything that needs to be done to increase safety with both your field instructor and field director or faculty field liaison.

Suggested Field Tasks

- Complete the safety assessment.

- Discuss any risks specific to your field setting related to safety and develop a plan to reduce risk.

- Attend supervision regularly.

- Engage in self-care activities and monitor stress and burnout.

References

Council on Social Work Education. (2015). *Educational policy and accreditation standards*. Alexandria, VA: Author.

Criss, P. (2010). Effects of client violence on social work students: A national study. *Journal of Social Work Education*, *46*(3), 371–390.

Dane, B. (2002). Duty to inform: Preparing social work students to understand vicarious traumatization. *Journal of Teaching in Social Work*, *22*(3/4), 3–19.

DiGiulio, J. F. (2001). The power of collaboration: Developing a safety training program for student interns. *The Journal of Baccalaureate Social Work*, *7*(1), 69–77.

Dunkel, J., Ageson, A., & Ralph, C. (2000). Encountering violence in field work: A risk reduction model. *Journal of Teaching in Social Work, 20*(3/4), 5–18.

Ellison, M. (1996). Field can be hazardous to your well-being: Fact or fiction? *The Journal of Baccalaureate Social Work, 2*(1), 79–89.

Faria, G., & Kendra, M. A. (2007). Safety education: A study of undergraduate social work programs. *The Journal of Baccalaureate Social Work, 12*(2), 141–153.

Knight, C. (2010). Indirect trauma in the field practicum: Secondary traumatic stress, vicarious trauma, and compassion fatigue among social work students and their field instructors. *The Journal of Baccalaureate Social Work, 15*(1), 31–52.

Lynch, J. G., & Versen, G. R. (2003). Social work supervisor liability: Risk factors and strategies for risk reduction. *Administration in Social Work, 27*(2), 57–72.

Lyter, S. (2015). Safety and risk management in social work field directors. In C. Hunter, J. Moen, & M. Raskins (Eds.), *Social work field directors: Foundations for excellence* (218–238). Chicago, IL: Lyceum Books.

Moylan, C. A., & Wood, L. (2016). Sexual harassment in social work field placements: Prevalence and characteristics. *Affilia: Journal of Women in Social Work, 31*(4), 405–417.

Reeser, L., & Wertkin, R. (2001). Safety training in social work education. *Journal of Teaching in Social Work, 21*(1–2), 95–113.

Sheafor, B., & Horejsi, C. (2015). *Techniques and guidelines for social work practice.* Boston, MA: Pearson Education.

Tully, C. T., Kropf, N. P., & Price, J. L. (1993). Is field a hard hat area? A study of violence in field placements. *Journal of Social Work Education, 29,* 191–199.

Wood, L., & Moylan, C. (2017). "No one talked about it": Social work field placements and sexual harassment. *Journal of Social Work Education, 53*(4), 714–726. doi:10.1080/10437797.2017.1283270

Zakutansky, T. J. (1993). Ethical and legal issues in field education: Shared responsibility and risk. *Journal of Social Work Education, 29*(3), 338–347.

5

FIELD SUPERVISION

This chapter will review both the functions and structure or logistics of field supervision as well as provide the resources needed to develop a successful supervisory relationship. In addition, the chapter will include information necessary for you to use the supervision session effectively, thus empowering you to cocreate a supervision environment that enables you to meet the goals of field education.

FIELD SUPERVISION

Critical to effective field education is the supervision you receive from your field instructor at your field agency. Field supervision is multifaceted; that is, it has several different functions and structural or logistical aspects. There is much in the literature that documents the important and complex nature of field supervision (Abramson & Fortune, 1990; Barretti, 2004; Bennett & Deal, 2009; Davys & Beddoe, 2009; Ellison, 1994; Fortune & Abramson, 1993; Knight, 1996, 2001; Okundaye, Gray, & Gray, 1999; Webb, 1988). According to Fortune and Abramson (1993), "students were more satisfied if they discussed learning needs in depth, had supervision scheduled regularly, and discussed evaluations prior to getting a formal document" (p. 103). The authors also found "that the critical aspect of a satisfying placement is a balanced approach in which the student may engage in self-directed learning while also having sufficient structure and conceptual challenge" (p. 108). So, as you enter field, it is critical that you focus on

1. defining the functions of supervision and

2. establishing the structure or logistics of the supervision.

FUNCTIONS OF FIELD SUPERVISION

Kadushin (1991) states that "while both field instructors and agency supervisors engage in the three principal cluster functions of supervision—administrative, educational, and supportive—their effective implementation is even more difficult for field instructors than it is for agency supervisors" (pp. 11–12). In a study on the anxiety that students felt when entering field, Gelman (2004) found that 28% of the students surveyed were concerned about the quality of the supervision they would receive. Of the concerns related to supervision, Gelman found that students were most concerned about the content and time of supervision as well as the ability of the field supervisor to evaluate the student fairly. Developing effective field supervision is a challenge for both students and field instructors. To combat this challenge and alleviate the anxiety that you may feel as you enter field, we will discuss each function specifically.

Administrative Function of Field Supervision

Field supervision has several administrative functions. First and foremost, the field instructor is responsible for the overall management of your field placement. This means your field instructor is responsible for your orientation, training, and task assignment as well as for setting and monitoring your schedule. Second, your field instructor is responsible to assist you in the completion of all necessary agency and university-based paperwork. In terms of the agency, this may include fingerprinting, background checks, and mandatory orientation meetings. With regard to the university-based paperwork, the field instructor is responsible for completing the initial paperwork, affiliation and cooperative agreements, time sheets, learning plans, and final field evaluations.

The field instructor is also responsible for evaluating your performance while in field. The evaluation the field instructor provides will take many different forms, both formal and informal. In terms of the informal evaluation provided, it will be in the form of ongoing feedback throughout the placement experience about your performance in any given task. In terms of the formal evaluation, it will be in the form of the final field evaluation, which will also include a recommended grade. It is important to note that you will be intricately involved in this process through self-evaluation and providing feedback on the final evaluation. In terms of a midterm evaluation, that will either be formal or informal, depending on your program's requirements. Even if your program does not require a midterm evaluation, I recommend that you touch base with your field instructor and ask for feedback on how you are doing. During this meeting, I also encourage you to share your thoughts about how you think the placement and your learning process is going. The field instructor will also be involved in reviewing and evaluating your agency-based work, such as reviewing case notes, observing you, providing various professional tasks, and processing your casework. Last, the field instructor may review and evaluate important academic work (such as process recordings) and assist in various academic assignments.

Educational Function of Field Supervision

In terms of the educational function, the main purpose of field supervision is to assist you in the learning process. The difference between field supervision and employee-based supervision is that the focus of field supervision is on education and learning. By placing the emphasis of the supervision session on learning and not only on training, this will address the challenges you may face as you sit down for a supervision session. Students report that often when they meet with their field instructor, they briefly check in, run through the work tasks, identify any training needs, and are done fifteen minutes later. Based on this description, the student is missing important opportunities for learning in a variety of areas. Furthermore, students often report that they don't know what is supposed to happen in the field supervision session, so when the session is missed, they don't necessarily think it is a problem. Or, because they work closely with their field instructor and discuss things all day, they see no need for formal supervision. Thus, by focusing the session on education, this can open the door for a variety of effective learning tasks. One educational activity of supervision that can be added to the weekly supervision session is to deliberately target the integration of curriculum into practice at field. An example of this is to review, each week in the supervision session, one of the ethical standards from the National Association of Social Workers code of ethics and apply that standard directly to practice situations at the agency. This learning activity is different in many ways from your previous classroom-based learning on ethics in that the exploration of the code of ethics and the various standards are now specifically applied to client-based situations in the agency, thus providing you the opportunity to apply the code to real case situations as opposed to cases in your book. Your supervision session truly becomes field-based learning through this process of targeted integration of curriculum with practice.

Supportive Function of Field Supervision

The last function of supervision is supportive. For you, support can look and feel like many different things. One, it is being made to feel that you matter and are welcomed into the agency. Two, you will see your field instructor making time for you and engaging in activities in which you can get to know one another. Third, your field instructor will advocate for your learning needs and explain your role and presence in the agency to the other staff. Last, when you have concerns or problems, your field instructor will listen and assist you in a problem-solving process. As you can imagine, the relationship you build with your field instructor is critical to meeting this function, not only for your learning but also to contribute to the quality of your field experience and socialization as a professional. Barretti (2004) conducted a study on the professional socialization of undergraduate social work students and found that "positive relationships and identifications with their role models were reported as helping students become better people, better listeners, and more whole, functional, happy, confident, and self-aware" (p. 20). Ensuring that this function can occur becomes critical to your success in field and is often challenging, due to multiple factors. Your field instructor will have multiple demands that can take precedence over your supervision; your agency may be chaotic and crisis oriented at times, which can result in you not being able to plan for the day; and you may be anxious about what the relationship between you and your field instructor will entail. All of the preceding can present barriers to the development of the supervisory relationship, and without developing a supportive relationship, it may be more difficult for the other functions to be achieved.

We have discussed the three primary functions of field supervision, all of which are important. That being said, getting the weekly supervision session to happen on a consistent and set basis is the first hurdle to overcome in order for the functions discussed previously to be realized. Knight (1996) found that of 12 schools surveyed, "more than 20%" (p. 411) were not meeting the one hour a week of required supervision. Unless supervision occurs on a regular basis, none of the functions can be met. It is important to focus on the structure and logistics of supervision; this has to do with the when, where, and what and ensuring the supervision's consistent presence in your field experience.

THE STRUCTURE AND LOGISTICS OF SUPERVISION

It is important that you and your field instructor discuss the structure and logistics of field supervision. With regard to the overall structure, first consider the supervision model you will be experiencing, as different models have unique features. In terms of the models, the most traditional model of an on-site social worker who is supervising you may not be how your placement is structured. Additional models include the use of group supervision and an on-site task supervisor with an off-site social worker. Zuchowski (2016) studied the latter and found unique challenges, such as the importance of the off-site supervisor knowing the agency context and the barrier of not being able to observe the student. This chapter most closely aligns with the traditional model, but the content can easily be adapted to other models. For assistance in this process, make sure to discuss any concerns with your task instructor, field instructor, and field director. Regardless of the overall structure or model of supervision your field experience is using, it is important to focus on the actual supervision session and those elements that are necessary to maximize its effectiveness in your learning:

1. timing
2. content
3. tools

Timing

The first thing to consider is timing; this refers to the day of the week, time of day, and length of the session. The best way to address the timing of supervision is to establish a regular and consistent time, write it in your calendar, and stick to it. This should be the first thing you do during your first week of field. For instance, some students like to start the week off in supervision, so they meet at 9:00 a.m. on their first day of the week. Other students like to end the week with supervision, so they meet at 4:00 p.m. on the last day of their week. It really doesn't matter when you meet, as long as you have a set time and stick to it. In terms of the length of the session, most programs require a specific amount of time; check with your program to ensure that you are meeting the requirement. An hour a week is a fairly standard guideline.

Having a set time is particularly important in the beginning of field because this will get you used to attending supervisory sessions and will assist in your ability to develop competence in the use of supervision. It is also helpful to have a set time because you will develop the ability to determine what can wait until supervision and what needs to be answered immediately. Finally, day-to-day life in an agency can become hectic, and days and even weeks can slip by; so, it is important to know you have your supervision time well established.

In some settings, the student may work side-by-side with the field instructor. This can be a wonderful experience and often results in immediate ongoing supervision. Regardless, it is important to realize that there is critical learning that may not occur in those types of contact and that will, in fact, only occur during uninterrupted structured supervision sessions. In other settings, students may not see their field instructor on a daily basis, so it is critical to have that supervision time set aside in both the student's and field instructor's schedules. It is also important to note that attending the supervision session is a task that falls in the professional socialization category of the multilevel field tasks discussed in Chapter 3. As presented earlier, an important outcome of using supervision appropriately is the ability to demonstrate what can wait and what cannot. That is, what do you need to ask or tell your field instructor or task supervisor immediately and what can wait until your scheduled supervision session? This skill will not be readily developed or demonstrated if you do not have a set time. A set time allows you to plan for the session and determine what needs to be addressed when, thus enabling you to demonstrate competence in one of the important ways social workers effectively use supervision.

Content

The content of a supervision session refers to what will be discussed. The two primary areas of discussion will be agency-based content and education-based content. Agency-based content will focus on the agency, such as your orientation, training, task assignment, role, clients served, services, policies and procedures, and important events impacting the agency. Education-based content will focus primarily on two overarching goals of field education: your socialization and development as a social worker and the integration of the classroom and field.

A way to help you identify potential content for the supervision session is to complete Integrative Activity 5.1. The supervision outline will assist you and your field instructor in designing the layout of the supervision sessions over the course of a semester or quarter and is similar to designing a curriculum for a course or a group.

There are four columns. The first column is the week; it includes 16 rows. This is based on a standard semester time line; if this is not the time line of your program, please adjust accordingly. You may want to add in your actual supervision date and time or any other dates that are important. The second column is for agency-based content. This is where you will identify the agency-based content you want to talk about during the supervision session. For instance, during the first few weeks, you may want to include orientation and training, policies and procedures, an overview of all the services offered by the agency, and safety. The third column includes any supervision tools you may need for that session, such as your learning plan, a case note, or a process recording. This might also include course syllabi and assignments, expectations of field,

INTEGRATIVE ACTIVITY 5.1
THE SUPERVISION OUTLINE

Purpose: The purpose of this outline is for you and your field instructor to develop a curriculum for field supervision. This will include the content you and your field instructor want to discuss in each supervision session as well as any materials you need to bring to the supervision session.

Directions: In the first column, **Week**, include the specific date and time of your supervision session and any other dates that are important. In the second column, **Agency-Based Content**, write in the content you and your field instructor need to discuss that relates to the agency; this could be important training and orientation material. In the **Supervision Tools** column,

identify any materials, including any paperwork, handouts, and worksheets, that you will need to go over or interactive activities you want to engage in with your field instructor during the session. In the next column, include **Field Education–Based Content** that needs to be discussed; for information, look at your course syllabus and field manual.

Competency 1: Demonstrate Ethical and Professional Behavior

- use supervision and consultation to guide professional judgment and behavior

Week	Agency-Based Content	Supervision Tools	Field Education–Based Content
1 Date: Time:			
2 Date: Time:			
3 Date: Time:			

4 Date: Time:			
5 Date: Time:			
6 Date: Time:			
7 Date: Time:			
8 Date: Time:			

(Continued)

(Continued)

9 Date: Time:			
10 Date: Time:			
11 Date: Time:			
12 Date: Time:			
13 Date: Time:			

14 Date: Time:			
15 Date: Time:			
16 Date: Time:			

Note: This is based on a 16-week semester, so you can modify as needed. Also, you may need to use this for more than one semester, so make a copy or pencil in entries that can be erased later.

field assignments, and evaluations. The last column is for field education–based content, such as reviewing course work, assignments, midterm and final evaluations, and any other content specific to field that is not covered within the agency-based content.

The purpose of this activity is to help you plan ahead for the entire semester or quarter in terms of identifying important due dates and content that needs to be discussed that is time sensitive and to ensure that you and your field instructor have considered the big picture of supervision. For instance, on the outline, you may include the need to discuss the learning plan and final field evaluations as well as their due dates to ensure that you can meet them. You may also include a discussion of important trainings that are time sensitive, such as a documentation training that you must attend before you can input case notes into the computer system. You may also want to identify midterm and a plan to discuss your progress to date. Furthermore, refer back to Integrative Activity 2.3 for the specialized content identified, determine when and how that will be obtained, and place that on your outline. Last, for other ideas, look to your course work or ask your field instructor for ideas of content-related items that can be included in the outline. Both you and your field instructor should keep a copy of the outline with the designated time, location, and content of the session.

Having an outline of the supervision sessions will allow you and your field instructor to plan ahead and thus better use your supervision time. When the weekly sessions are designed like a syllabus or curriculum for a course or group, the individual supervision sessions will have more focus and be better integrated with the goals of field education.

Now that you have considered the big picture of your supervision needs over an entire semester or quarter, the next step is to begin to think about how you want to structure the flow of content of a specific session. Integrative Activity 5.2 will assist you in this process by encouraging you to jot down agenda items for discussion in a session in several categories:

1. agency-based content

2. education-based content

3. other

By completing this activity and identifying the content to be discussed prior to the start of each session, you will ensure that you are focusing equally on all areas as well as demonstrating leadership for the development of the content of a particular session.

At the onset of your field experience, you will look to your field instructor to lead the supervision session because much of the focus will be on orientation and training and establishing the critical tasks of field. However, as you move toward independent practice, it is critical that you

INTEGRATIVE ACTIVITY 5.2
THE SUPERVISION AGENDA

Purpose: The purpose of this activity is to help you develop an agenda for your supervision session.

Directions: In each of the following areas, list items that you want to discuss in your next supervision session that correspond with each area. For subsequent supervision sessions, refer back to this activity to organize your thinking and identify content for discussion.

Competency 1: Demonstrate Ethical and Professional Behavior

- use supervision and consultation to guide professional judgment and behavior

1. Agency-based content:

2. Education-based content:

3. Other:

4. Questions:

begin to demonstrate leadership in the use of the supervision session. Many of the integrative activities already discussed in this book assisted you in the process of structuring the supervision session. For instance, in discussing your curriculum (as a result of completing Integrative Activity 2.3), you were sharing in the development of the content for that session. Your shared leadership, in the use of the supervision session, will increase throughout the field experience as you focus more on your client system tasks, and you will ultimately demonstrate your competence in your effective use of supervision. As you take on more leadership in determining the agenda, you are also developing and demonstrating your professional communication skills.

Interestingly enough, communication in the supervision session is an area in which students express some anxiety; they often state they don't know what to say. By planning out and even practicing what you want to discuss or share in the supervision session, you will be better prepared to demonstrate competence in this important area.

The last thing to consider with regard to the content of the supervision session is to keep supervision notes. Writing supervision notes supports the development of your competence in professional writing and also provides a record of the specific plans developed for client system work and your learning process.

Integrative Activity 5.3 below suggests that you keep a record of your supervision session by documenting the date, the content discussed, and the plan of action or next steps.

INTEGRATIVE ACTIVITY 5.3
DOCUMENTING YOUR SUPERVISION SESSION

Purpose: The purpose of this activity is to assist you in the development of your note-taking skills as well as provide a record of your supervision session.

Directions: Select a supervision session, and in each of the following areas, document the content discussed; be specific so that you can refer to your notes for direction.

Competency 1: Demonstrate Ethical and Professional Behavior

- use supervision and consultation to guide professional judgment and behavior

1. Agency-based content:

2. Education-based content:

3. Other:

4. Questions:

The Tools of Supervision

It is helpful to consider the tools of supervision that you might use while in field. The tools of supervision refer to specific, concrete, tangible items that may be brought to the supervision session to augment a discussion, or they may be specific interactive activities that you engage in with your field instructor. For instance, a concrete, tangible item that can be used as a tool in supervision is a written document such as a case note, an assessment, an outline of a program you are working on developing, an integrative activity, or an academic assignment such as a process recording. The concrete item, brought to and used in the supervision session, provides an opportunity for learning that is specific. By reviewing a case note that you wrote on a specific client contact, you will end up having a more directed learning experience than if you were to discuss case noting in general. Examples of an interactive supervision tool could be to watch a video or listen to an audio recording of a client session, coworking a session with a client, or receiving training information in the supervision session. It is important to note that an interactive supervision tool may happen in the supervision session or outside the session. For those tools that happen outside the session, it is important to process them right after the activity or in the next session. Similar to the outcome of the use of a concrete, tangible tool, the use of an interactive tool in supervision maximizes your learning and increases the likelihood that supervision will be more than a quick review of your tasks or setting the plan for the week.

REFLECTION QUESTION 5.1

Now that you have had an opportunity to consider the functions and logistics of field supervision, what are you hoping to get out of supervision? What do you need from your field instructor for supervision to be a productive and helpful activity? What are your concerns, if any, about field supervision? What do you need to do to benefit from supervision? What specific tools are you hoping to use in and outside your supervision session?

ROOM TO REFLECT

Identifying the learning tools that will be used in the supervision session is important in that it will ensure that all possible activities that can assist in the learning process are being used. These tools may be incorporated in the learning plan and thus contribute to the evaluation process. Year after year, the students with whom I work give me feedback that they want more concrete learning opportunities in and outside of the supervision session, such as going over their case notes, observing their field instructor and discussing their observations, and being directly observed. This discussion will hopefully identify all the possible tools for learning and negotiating their use.

FREQUENTLY EXPERIENCED SITUATION

This particular situation is again one that students with whom I have worked have experienced and relates well to this chapter. Thus, it is helpful for you to consider this situation and how you might go about addressing this if it is something you experience.

I don't think my field instructor likes me.

> My field instructor makes me uncomfortable. I don't think she likes me. I really like the agency, though. Sometimes I just don't know what we are supposed to be doing in our supervision session, so does it really matter if we meet? Also, she keeps canceling on me and I get all my questions answered by the other social workers anyway; it just seems like a waste of my time.

This situation is tough because, on the one hand, a student's relationship with the field instructor is important and formative; it is often what students remember the most from their education. On the other hand, sometimes a student won't have an amazing relationship with their field instructor, yet that student can learn and have a positive field experience. The latter is the most important thing to reflect on when you are struggling in your relationship with your field instructor. First and foremost, what a student needs to do when faced with this type of situation is to assess if he or she is learning and having a positive experience. If the answer is yes, then the student can work on improving the relationship. If not, then it may be important to discuss the situation with their field director or faculty field liaison.

In the given situation, the student was having a positive experience and was learning, so he didn't want to leave his agency. But he was also struggling with how to manage what he saw as a challenging relationship. He also brought up two other issues in conjunction with his concerns about the supervisory relationship, which involve both the logistics and the content of the supervision session. First, his supervisor kept canceling. This is really important to troubleshoot because supervision is key to your learning; supervision also maintains your professional well-being and the well-being of the client systems with whom you are working. Second, he appeared to be questioning the role of supervision and how best to use the supervision

session. In all likelihood, the challenges in the relationship may be impacting the supervision session, so it becomes necessary to separate these two issues and discuss each individually.

First, it was helpful for the student to express his concerns and articulate that he felt his field instructor didn't like him. By doing so, he could feel some initial relief and seek out assistance. When assessing the quality and experience of a relationship, particularly an important one like your supervisory relationship, you want to look at many different things and be cautious about making rash judgments. It was important for the student to consider that his perception of not being liked may not have been true and what he was interpreting as not being liked could have been related to several variables. For instance, he and his field instructor could have very different personalities and expectations for the relationship, and what he was interpreting as dislike simply may have been related to his field instructor's style.

With regard to supervision being cancelled and his questioning of the role of supervision, it may be helpful for him to reflect on the possibility that the cancelling is interfering with his ability to form a working relationship, and he may want to address this head-on and/or reach out to the field liaison or director to develop a plan to ensure regular meetings. It is essential to remember that the field instructor agreed to the supervision requirement at the time of the placement, so make sure to address this in a straightforward manner. Next, his discomfort in the relationship could be affecting the supervision session, or the other way around—how he was approaching the supervision session could have been impacting the relationship. So, I reviewed the importance of the supervision session and discussed ways that the student could improve the session, such as preparing ahead of time for the session, sending a reminder e-mail with an agenda, discussing expectations, and focusing on how he wanted to present himself, even in light of his concerns about the relationship.

Last, I reiterated that developing the professional skills necessary to manage a challenging working relationship, particularly when it involves supervision, can be an excellent learning experience and one that will benefit him in his professional life. This reframing enabled him to take on the learning

(Continued)

(Continued)

challenge and discuss his concerns directly with his supervisor. The result was that the supervisor took responsibility for the cancelled session, set a regular time, and reassured the student that she was very pleased with his work and look forward to continuing to work together.

Suggested Field Tasks

- Establish a supervision time.

- Complete and review the supervision outline with your field instructor.

- Attend supervisory sessions and plan for supervision.

- In supervisory sessions, describe and explain practice tasks.

- Complete documentation and professional writing.

References

Abramson, J. S., & Fortune, A. E. (1990). Improving field instruction: An evaluation of a seminar for new field instructors. *Journal of Social Work Education, 26*(3), 273–286.

Barretti, M. (2004). The professional socialization of undergraduate social work students. *The Journal of Baccalaureate Social Work, 9,* 10–30.

Bennett, S., & Deal, K. H. (2009). Beginnings and endings in social work supervision: The interaction between attachment and developmental processes. *Journal of Teaching in Social Work, 29,* 101–117.

Davys, A. M., & Beddoe, L. (2009). The reflective learning model: Supervision of social work students. *Social Work Education, 28*(8), 919–933. doi:10.1080/02615470902748662

Ellison, M. (1994). Critical field instruction behaviors: Student and field instructor views. *Arete, 18*(2), 12–21.

Fortune, A. E., & Abramson, J. S. (1993). Predictors of satisfaction with field practicum among social work students. *The Clinical Supervisor, 11*(1), 95–110.

Gelman, C. (2004). Special section: Field education in social work anxiety experienced by foundation-year MSW students entering field placement: Implications for admission, curriculum, and field education. *Journal of Social Work Education, 40*(1), 39–54.

Kadushin, A. (1991). Introduction. In D. Schneck, B. Grossman, & U. Glassman (Eds.), *Field education in social work: Contemporary issues and trends.* Dubuque, IA: Kendall Hunt.

Knight, C. (1996). A study of MSW and BSW student's perceptions of their field instructors. *Journal of Social Work Education, 32*(3), 399–414.

Knight, C. (2001). The process of field instruction: BSW and MSW students' views of effective field supervision. *Journal of Social Work Education, 37*(2), 357–379.

Okundaye, J. N., Gray, C., & Gray, L. B. (1999). Reimaging field instruction from a spiritually sensitive perspective: An alternative approach. *Social Work, 44*(4), 371–383.

Webb, N. (1988). The role of the field instructor in the socialization of students. *Social Casework, 69*(1), 35–40.

Zuchowski, I. (2016). Getting to know the context: The complexities of providing off-site supervision in social work practice learning. *British Journal of Social Work, 46*(2), 409. doi:10.1093/bjsw/bcu133

EFFECTIVE COMMUNICATION SKILLS FOR FIELD

Central to competent practice in field is developing and demonstrating effective communication skills. *Communication* can be defined as "a process in which one individual conveys information, intentionally or unintentionally to another" (Sheafor & Horejsi, 2015, p. 112). This chapter will lay the foundation for you to develop and demonstrate competence in your oral, written, and electronic communication with individuals, families, groups, organizations, communities, and colleagues and provide resources for you to assess and analyze your communication skills.

COMMUNICATION SKILLS FOR GENERALIST PRACTICE

As you think about using your communication skills in field, the first thing to consider is how you will adapt the skills you have learned in your course work to the multilevel tasks you will be engaging in at field. As you begin to think about this, you may realize that some of the skills will be used in the same way, regardless of the task, while others will need to be adapted. To help you develop an understanding of the multifaceted nature of communication in field, let's review multilevel communication.

First and foremost, most social work students consider their micro-level communication with individuals and families as foundational to being a social worker. When working with individuals and families, you focus on developing and demonstrating active listening, reflecting back, question asking, and summarizing. The next level is communicating at the mezzo level, which focuses on how you use your communication skills when working in treatment or task groups. When working in groups, you continue to practice the skill of active listening but may use reflecting back in a different way than you might with an individual client. For instance, with one-on-one contacts, the communication is directed specifically to the individual client. However, when running a group, you may be reflecting back what an individual member has said but directing the reflection to the entire group and adapting what you say to apply more generally to the group as a whole as opposed to just the individual who first made the comment. This is done intentionally and reflects the goals and structure of group work versus individual work. As a result of your reflecting-back statement, another member of the group may respond, which shows that reflecting back may look different, depending on the task. Similarly, when facilitating and/or participating in a task group, how you use your foundational communication skills will vary, depending on the composition of the group and the goals. For instance, if you are cochairing the fund-raising committee of your agency, your communication may be informal. But if you are presenting material you have researched to the program and services subcommittee of the board, your communication may need to be more formal and professional.

Last, consider your communication at the macro-level within your organization and in the community. This involves communication within the agency and on behalf of the organization in the community and encompasses a variety of skills. For instance, how you communicate in the break room with the other social workers, at the annual agency retreat, or in the community at a meeting where you are representing your agency will all differ and require varying skills. Communication at the macro-level will reflect both formal and informal styles of communication as well as your ability to discern the appropriate type of communication, depending on the practice situation. You will pick up on the formal and informal communication patterns as you become more comfortable at the agency. One example is the joking around that may take place during lunch versus the serious and more professional communication style of a staff meeting that is looking at a funding crisis. The ability to recognize these variations when communicating at different levels is important for communicating effectively in field.

REFLECTION QUESTION 6.1

Now that you have had a chance to review multi-level communication, identify the primary multi-level communication you will be engaging in at your site. What types of communication—oral, written, and electronic—will you engage in with individuals, families, groups, organizations, and communities at your agency? What, if any, concerns do you have about multilevel communication at your agency? Where do you see your current strengths related to communication, and what will you need to work on while in field?

ROOM TO REFLECT

ORAL COMMUNICATION SKILLS

At the heart of effective oral communication are the following core interpersonal qualities (Chang, Scott, & Decker, 2009; Sheafor & Horejsi, 2015):

1. warmth

2. empathy

3. respect

4. genuineness

Your ability to demonstrate these qualities when communicating orally in field will lay the foundation for your interactions with individuals, families, groups, organizations, communities, and colleagues. In addition to the core qualities that ground your contacts with clients, you will also need to develop and demonstrate several basic communication skills, such as

- active listening,
- expressing understanding through the use of reflecting back,
- using questions to gather information,
- information giving,
- reframing,
- summarizing,
- seeking clarification,
- using positive confrontation,
- establishing goals,
- planning, and
- evaluating (Chang et al., 2009; Sidell & Smiley, 2008).

These communication skills lay the foundation for effective communication in field. The most useful task to engage in at field in order to develop and demonstrate competency of these foundational oral communication skills is interviewing.

Interviewing

Interviewing is an excellent task because an interview provides you with the structure necessary to practice many important skills. The first thing you need to do is identify the opportunities you will have in field to engage in interviewing. *Interviewing* is defined as the opportunity to engage a client system in a purposeful conversation that allows for exploration of an issue. It is very important to have an opportunity to sit down with a client system and engage in a conversation.

When interviewing, you will be able to practice the following tasks:

1. introducing yourself as a student

2. explaining your role

3. reviewing and discussing the purpose and plan for the interview

4. discussing informed consent

5. explaining confidentiality and the limits of confidentiality

6. engaging your client in a conversation that is directed to a goal

7. ending the interview, which usually includes summarizing, identifying who will do what, and planning for the next contact, if applicable

These structural and functional aspects of an interview create a rich learning experience for you to practice your oral communication skills. Furthermore, more often than not, you will be able to plan for the contact ahead of time as well as discuss and process the interview in supervision.

Interviewing can look very different, depending on your agency and role. For instance, the interviewing you do may consist of onetime contacts, as in the example of the student who is working at a local social services agency that offers a food pantry, or may involve ongoing contacts, as in the case of an agency that provides medical case management services for individuals who are HIV (human immunodeficiency virus) positive. Regardless of the type of service, you need to develop and demonstrate your ability to open an interview, use active listening, ask questions (open ended and closed ended), reflect back, summarize, and close an interview.

An important part of developing your communication skills is the ability to reflect on and analyze an interview. A helpful way to think about an interview is to visualize a tree. Just as a tree is made up of roots, a trunk, and many branches, the conversation between you and your client (the interview) can also be broken down into the three main parts that reflect the parts of the tree. The roots represent the issues that are bringing the client to your attention. Some of the issues maybe evident to the client (such as the need for housing) while other issues (such as an underlying mental health, a substance abuse condition, or the impact of childhood abuse or neglect) maybe not be as evident. The trunk can embody the overall foundation or purpose of the interview. This takes into consideration the referral, agency and services, your role, and purpose of the meeting. Once the conversation starts, the interview moves up to the branches, with each branch representing a possible direction the conversation can take, based on what the client says to you and what you say or don't say back to your client. You want to be able to think about the direction the conversation takes and develop your skill in directing that conversation as well as have an idea of where the conversation is headed.

Integrative Activity 6.1 offers a way to develop your skill in assessing and analyzing your oral communication skills as well as demonstrating competence in this important component

INTEGRATIVE ACTIVITY 6.1

ASSESSING INTERVIEWING SKILLS

Purpose: The purpose of this activity is to assist you in developing and assessing your interviewing skills and overall competence.

Directions: After an interview, review each skill and blind spot and indicate whether you demonstrated that or not. Once you have completed the check list, reflect on your strengths and weaknesses and use this assessment to build your skills. This may also be used by your field instructor or agency designee to obtain outside feedback while you are under direct observation.

Competency 1: Demonstrate Ethical and Professional Behavior

- demonstrate professional demeanor in behavior; appearance; and oral, written, and electronic communication

Competency 6: Engage with Individuals, Families, Groups, Organizations, and Communities

- use empathy, reflection, and interpersonal skills to effectively engage diverse clients and constituencies

Communication Skill	Demonstrated	Not Demonstrated	Comments
Opening			
1. Greeted the client	☐	☐	

2. Introduced self as a student	❑	❑	
3. Explained the purpose and duration of the interview	❑	❑	
4. Explained your role	❑	❑	
5. Explained informed consent, confidentiality, and limits	❑	❑	
6. Invited the client to talk	❑	❑	
7. Reviewed any necessary paperwork	❑	❑	
Questioning			
1. Asked closed-ended questions	❑	❑	
2. Asked open-ended questions	❑	❑	
3. Listened to answers	❑	❑	
4. Balanced talking with listening	❑	❑	
5. Answered the client's questions	❑	❑	
6. Allowed for silence	❑	❑	

(Continued)

(Continued)

Communication Skill	Demonstrated	Not Demonstrated	Comments
Expressing Understanding			
1. Displayed warmth and empathy to effectively engage the client	☐	☐	
2. Reflected back content	☐	☐	
3. Reflected back feelings	☐	☐	
4. Summarized content and feelings	☐	☐	
5. Expressed understanding of meaning	☐	☐	
6. Managed the client's affect	☐	☐	
Seeking Clarification			
1. Used positive confrontation to increase understanding	☐	☐	
2. Provided information, instructions, directions, or feedback	☐	☐	
3. Used reframing to change the perspective of the situation	☐	☐	
Nonverbal Communication			
1. Maintained eye contact	☐	☐	

2. Used a warm tone of voice	❏	❏	
3. Displayed a relaxed facial expression	❏	❏	
4. Demonstrated interest in what the client was saying	❏	❏	
5. Displayed a relaxed posture	❏	❏	
6. Demonstrated congruence between verbal and nonverbal communication	❏	❏	
7. Demonstrated distracting body movements	❏	❏	
Structure of Interview			
1. Appropriate pace	❏	❏	
2. Effective transitions between questions	❏	❏	
3. A clear beginning, middle, and end to the interview	❏	❏	
Common Interview Blind Spots			
1. Gave advice	❏	❏	
2. Talked too much	❏	❏	

(*Continued*)

(Continued)

Communication Skill	Demonstrated	Not Demonstrated	Comments
3. Demonstrated disconnect, moved from topic to topic	❏	❏	
4. Missed opportunities for expressing understanding	❏	❏	
5. Interrupted client	❏	❏	
6. Jumped to reassure the client	❏	❏	
7. Abruptly ended the interview	❏	❏	
8. Jumped to problem solving	❏	❏	
9. Asked leading questions	❏	❏	
Closing			
1. Indicated that the interview was ending	❏	❏	
2. Summarized the interview	❏	❏	
3. Reviewed the agreed-upon plan	❏	❏	
4. Asked if the client had any questions	❏	❏	

5. Indicated the plan for future meetings, if applicable	☐	☐	
Overall			
1. Demonstrated competence in oral communication.	☐	☐	
2. Demonstrated competence in engaging the client using empathy, reflection, and interpersonal skills.	☐	☐	

behavior identified as part of Competencies 1 and 6 in the educational policies and accreditation standards (EPAS; Council on Social Work Education [CSWE], 2015). The interview assessment is a quick way to determine whether you are meeting the structural aspects of an interview and to focus on effective use of empathy when engaging clients. After an interview with an individual, complete the check list to determine whether you hit the main structural aspects of an interview.

This activity can be used in two different ways: (1) You can use it to self-assess your skill development, or (2) you can conduct an interview under the direct observation of your field instructor or an agency designee you feel comfortable with and have that person provide you with feedback. The latter can provide valuable information to assess your competence in communication skills.

Integrative Activity 6.2 provides a deeper way of analyzing and evaluating the flow and direction an interview takes and determining what you (the social work student) and the client did or did not do to advance the conversation. The process recording is a useful tool that provides a more intensive exploration of an interview as opposed to the interview assessment, which offers a quick structural analysis of the interview (Graybeal, 1995; Mullin & Canning, 2007; Neuman & Friedman, 1997). The process recording can also provide an opportunity to demonstrate your competence in using empathy, reflection, and interpersonal skills to effectively engage a client. In order to create your process recording, identify a client system and contact in which you will have an opportunity to discuss an issue in depth; during the interview, take notes to aid in the process of recalling exactly what was said; and immediately following the interview, write out the process recording. Once you have completed the process recording, ask your field instructor for feedback. Once your field instructor has reviewed it, discuss the interview in supervision. The feedback can focus on your strengths and growth areas as well as on what the field instructor might have done differently. The feedback you get from both your self-assessment and your field instructor's assessment is invaluable to your learning.

Although both Integrative Activities 6.1 and 6.2 are best done with individual clients, they can also be completed with a treatment or task group session as a way to evaluate your communication skills at the mezzo level. It is key to remember that even if your field agency is primarily a macro-level setting in which you work most often within the organization or community, developing micro-level communication skills will aid your macro-level work. I typically share

INTEGRATIVE ACTIVITY 6.2
THE PROCESS RECORDING

Purpose: The purpose of completing a process recording is to assist you in the development and assessment of your communication skills as well as to provide a structured opportunity for demonstrating competence.

Directions: Select a client and, using the following form, provide a detailed account of an interview. The process recording should include the following:

1. who was present and when and where the interview took place

2. the purpose of the interview

3. what phase of the helping process you are in and what you are hoping to accomplish

4. your role and overall goal for the interview

5. a full transcript of the interview, including what you said and what the client said back to you, verbatim; the specific dialogue, back-and-forth (like a script)

6. a detailed description of your thoughts, feelings, and reactions during the interview, addressing what was going on for you

7. your analysis of how you did during the interview. This should include the specific interviewing skills you used (for a detailed list, see Integrative Activity 6.1), what you were trying to accomplish, what was effective, what you think the client was thinking or feeling, and what you would do the same or differently in the future

8. your overall analysis of the client's situation, needs, issues, affect, strengths, and so on, based on the interview

9. your analysis of the outcome of the skills used and/or specific interventions in the interview, incorporating feedback from your field instructor

10. the plan for the next interaction or contact (if any)

11. your level of competence in demonstrating professional demeanor in oral communication and your ability to engage the client using empathy, reflection, and interpersonal skills

Process Recording Format: It is critical that you follow the format laid out below to ensure that you are addressing all aspects of the process recording. In doing so, first provide a description of the background of the interview addressing the first three areas from the preceding list. Then document the specific dialogue of the interaction; that is, write out in a script form what you said and what the client said back to you. In the next column, write down your thoughts, your feelings, and the reactions you were having during the interview; next, document the specific interview skills you used, your analysis, what you were trying to accomplish, and how it went. Once you have completed writing the process recording, review and discuss it in supervision with your field instructor. Ask your field instructor to provide comments in the last column and if necessary, have them sign it to indicate that it was reviewed and discussed. Finally, discuss your level of competence in your oral communication skills and your ability to use empathy, reflection, and interpersonal skills to effectively engage your client.

Competency 1: Demonstrate Ethical and Professional Behavior

- demonstrate professional demeanor in behavior; appearance; and oral, written, and electronic communication

Competency 6: Engage with Individuals, Families, Groups, Organizations, and Communities

- use empathy, reflection, and interpersonal skills to effectively engage diverse clients and constituencies

Interview Background
(See Directions 1–4 above.)

Interview Dialogue (See Direction 5 above.)	Student Thoughts, Feelings, and Reactions (Include the thoughts, feelings, and reactions you had while you were interviewing; see Direction 6 above.)	Student Analysis (Identify the specific interviewing skills you used [see Integrative Activity 6.1 for a list of specific interviewing skills], your reason for selecting that particular skill, and your analysis of the effectiveness of that skill. Did these skills accomplish what you hoped they would? Include what you think the client is feeling or thinking [see Direction 7 above].)	Field Instructor Feedback

Overall Analysis of Interview
(See Directions 8–11 above.)

Field Instructor/Agency Designee Signature
Thank you for taking the time to review, discuss, and offer feedback in the Field Instructor Feedback column on this process recording. Signing below indicates that you have done the above in person with the student.

Name:
Signature:
Date:

Note: The process recording is not limited to one page. This is a template; use additional pages as needed to document the client system contact. Format adapted from Alle-Corliss & Alle-Corliss (1998), p. 240.

that in my practice experience, I often had to use my interviewing skills in interprofessional team meetings, interprofessional education meetings, and committee meetings. So, the development of these skills is necessary for effective social work practice.

Last, the most real-life and ultimately most effective tool for evaluating your communication skills is an audio or video recording of an interview. If you have this opportunity at your agency, take it. There is nothing like seeing yourself working with clients in person.

Telephone Communication

The last and often most challenging oral communication for students is the communication conducted over the phone. Interestingly enough, many students tell me they are most anxious about this form of communication. However, social workers spend much time on the phone with and on behalf of clients. Interestingly, phone work is verbal communication without the corresponding nonverbal communication cues; that is, you do not have the advantage of seeing the client or person you are talking with, so you do not have that important information to aid you in your work. Phone work can involve working on a hotline, calling clients to schedule appointments and gather information, calling clients to complete follow-up wellness checks, and contacting other professionals to discuss client needs and progress. The latter is often referred to as *collateral contacts* and can make up much of your work; it is important to become comfortable with this type of communication.

NONVERBAL COMMUNICATION

So far, we have focused primarily on oral communication. However, the nonverbal communication that accompanies all oral communication is important and worth considering. In fact, research indicates that two thirds of all communication is nonverbal (Beall, 2004).

Some of the nonverbal communications that a client may display and that you will want to pay attention to are

- eye contact,
- facial expressions,
- gestures of greeting,
- body positioning and posture,
- tone of voice,
- dress and appearance,
- movement, and
- whether what a client is communicating nonverbally matches what they are saying orally (Sheafor & Horejsi, 2015; Sidell & Smiley, 2008).

It is also essential to develop your awareness of nonverbal communication because a change in a client's nonverbal communication can signify a change in the client. It is important to remember that any communication is two-way, meaning that you, too, are communicating nonverbally. Thus, it is equally important to be attuned to what you may be saying to a client via your nonverbals during an interview.

REFLECTION QUESTION 6.2

Now that you have had a chance to consider oral communication, particularly related to interviewing, nonverbal, and phone-based communication in field, what are your thoughts about your ability to effectively demonstrate and use your communication skills and engage in the tasks of interviewing and telephone contact? What are your concerns, if any?

ROOM TO REFLECT

WRITTEN COMMUNICATION SKILLS

The next area of communication to consider in field is written communication. The written communication you will use requires a wide range of skills. The written documents that you produce will vary, depending on your agency and tasks as well as on whether or not you primarily work with individuals, families, groups, organizations, or communities.

At the micro-level, the work you do with individuals and families needs to be documented. This most likely consists of writing various documents that are contained in client records. The first step in familiarizing yourself with the written documents you need to produce at the micro-level is to review the client record. *Client records* are the official documents amassed in a binder or maintained electronically by the agency. These may include but are not limited to intake reports, consent to treatment forms, releases of information, case notes, assessments, incident reports, call logs, service plans, discharge reports, and transfer summaries. A client record may also contain copies of documents created by other agencies that are used when serving the client. As a student, you are responsible for documenting the work you do with clients. By maintaining accurate records, you are protecting the clients in case something happens to you and another worker needs to take over the case. Similarly, you protect yourself and your field instructor by documenting your actions on a case.

Once you have reviewed the client record, you want to discuss with your field instructor the plan for you to write your own documents. At the micro-level, the most common form of documentation to develop your written communication skills is the case note. A case note includes written text that documents what was said during the contact, your assessment and plan, and when the contact started and ended, the date, and the type of contact.

There are several different formats for a case note. For instance, in the SOAP note, S = subjective information, which includes what the client feels or perceives and is based on self-report; O = objective information, which is content obtained by direct observation; A = assessment, which refers to the conclusions drawn by the social worker, and P = plan, which is what the social worker will be doing (Sheafor & Horejsi, 2015).

Another format is the SOAIGP: S = supplemental information provided by the client, O = observations by the social worker, A = activities that will be done on behalf of the client, I = impressions and the social worker's assessment, G = goals, and P = plan of action (Kagel & Kopels, 2008).

The format that I used when I first practiced at a crisis intervention agency that provided a suicide prevention hotline was CAP: C = complaint, A = assessment, and P = plan. This format was a succinct way to document client hotline calls.

Regardless of the format of your case notes, note taking while interviewing is an important skill that is integral in your ability to write accurate case notes. In all likelihood, you will not be able to memorize all that is said during an interview, so you will want to take notes. This challenging task requires skill in that you will need to be able to simultaneously

- ask questions,

- jot down responses, and

- respond using your interviewing skills.

The best way to develop this skill is to follow these steps. First, before you begin your interview, create an outline of the questions and information you need and leave space for the client's answers. This will not only provide an easy way to keep track of your client's responses but will also keep you on track while interviewing. Second, inform your client that you need to jot down a few things while you are talking so that you don't miss anything important. By letting your client know what you need, both you and your client will be more comfortable during the interview. Last, if a form needs to be completed, bring the form with you so you can go over it with the client.

One thing to remember is that paperwork may be overwhelming to clients for a variety of reasons. It is important to be aware of this while you are working with your clients. I once had a client who needed to complete several forms, so I handed them to the client. As soon as I handed the documents to the client, the client looked at the forms and then back at me and became visibly upset—so much so that the client decided it wasn't a good time to meet. It occurred to me that perhaps the client could not read the forms, so I quickly interjected and said something about the fact that I, too, found the paperwork confusing and asked if the client would like us to go over it together. The client immediately relaxed and said yes. As a result of this experience, I have always made it a practice to ask my clients if they would like us to go over the paperwork together or if they would like to go over it for themselves. This way, a client can defer to me and not be made to feel uncomfortable about paperwork.

In addition to writing case notes, you also need to be skilled at writing assessments or social histories, discharge reports, and transfer summaries. It is important to determine the plan for you to be able to engage in these tasks and create these documents.

At the mezzo level, you need to document treatment group sessions. This type of note should indicate who attended the group and what the group covered. You may also need to document your work on task groups. The documentation for a task group could be in the form of minutes and include the date of the meeting, who attended the meeting, what was discussed, and any tasks that group members agreed to do before the next meeting.

At the macro-level, written communication may be in the form of formal reports, such as annual reports, newsletters, an article for the local paper, a manual, agency policies and procedures, forms, and any materials for various services of the agency, such as group materials. To develop and demonstrate competence in documenting client contact, complete Integrative Activity 6.3.

INTEGRATIVE ACTIVITY 6.3
WRITING A CASE NOTE

Purpose: The purpose of this activity is to develop and demonstrate your skill in documentation.

Directions: Following a client contact, write a case note documenting the contact. This can be done with your agency's format or you may select one of the following formats. Once you have written your case note documenting a client contact, submit the case note to your field instructor for review and discussion.

Competency 1: Demonstrate Ethical and Professional Behavior

- demonstrate professional demeanor in behavior; appearance; and oral, written, and electronic communication

The CAP Method:

C   (Complaint):

A   (Assessment):

P   (Plan):

The SOAP Note Method:

S   (Subjective Content):

O   (Objective Content):

(Continued)

(Continued)

A   (Assessment):

P   (Plan):

COMMUNICATION AND TECHNOLOGY

As you are well aware, we currently live in the information age, and the use of technology in social work practice has expanded greatly. This can best be seen in the countless videos of toddlers demonstrating competence and expectations of technology—for instance, a two-year-old going up to a television screen and swiping the screen, expecting something to happen; another showing great aptitude in unlocking and using her mother's cell phone, clicking on apps and playing games. In fact, in your own life, technology most likely feels like a given and—whether you want to admit it or not—a potential distraction. In all likelihood, while reading this chapter, you have already glanced at Snapchat, Instagram, or your Facebook page and are distracted by the multiple notifications of your current text messages. Cain (2011) states that "social communication is in transition from predominately telephone and face-to-face encounters to a digital public paradigm involving the use of social media" (p. 1036). This statement is so true and something that many social workers have not as of yet fully recognized. However, both the CSWE and the National Association of Social Workers (NASW) have recognized the necessity to address technology as it relates to both competent and ethical practice. The NASW code of ethics (2017a) states,

> With emergent technological advances over the last two decades, the profession could not ignore the necessity for more clarity around the complex ethical issues that arise with the use of various forms of technology. The NASW code of ethics contains 19 new standards and revisions to several longstanding standards developed to address ethical considerations when using technology. (About the Code, paragraph 1)

As I reflect on my own experience with technology and social work practice, I have a vivid memory of the day in the early 1990s that the agency I was working at installed voice mail. I thought to myself how terrible it was that a client would get a recorded message instead of speaking to a person. Today, many of my professional tasks are solely completed via e-mail and teleconferencing. I have developed strong professional relationships and completed important tasks with individuals I have not met in person. With the rise in the use of technology in social work practice, including telehealth, McCarty and Clancy (2002) state that "nearly anything a social worker does face-to-face could theoretically be done online. Counseling, home health visits, consultation with colleagues, research, supervision of interns, and social work education are now being performed through telecommunications" (p. 153). The use of telehealth has impacted social work practice and presents opportunities and challenges that need to be considered. For instance, there are concerns that telehealth interferes with the social worker–client relationship (McCarty & Clancy, 2002). On the other hand, telehealth has been acknowledged to provide important access to services that are not available face-to-face (Hall & Bierman, 2015; Jarvis-Selinger, Chan, Payne, Plohman, & Ho, 2008). But the most important considerations when using telecommunications in social work practice are related to infrastructure and, specifically, the clients', social work practitioners', and agencies' access to reliable technology and readiness to successfully use technology-based practices (Hall & Bierman, 2015; Jarvis-Selinger et al., 2008). For students, the question becomes *How best can I prepare myself for this type of practice?* Mishna, Levine, Bogo, and Van Wert (2013) developed a university-based practicum project in which graduate students offered both face-to-face and cyber counseling to undergraduate students as part of their field education program in order to begin to develop student's competence in the use of technology in practice. As exciting and specific as this field opportunity was for those students, most students will not have this opportunity in their field setting. So, back to the question, how can you begin to develop your understanding of the current and potential role of technology and its specific application for communication in your setting? The answer is two pronged: First, identify the role and use of technology for communication purposes in your agency, as well as your agency's expectations of your ability to effectively use technology to communicate in your practice in the agency, and then consider your future needs in this area and discuss those in supervision. It is important to recognize that there may be gaps in your field instructor's and agency's use of technology for communicating and yours or vice versa, so it is very important to explicitly discuss electronic communication and its many forms with your field instructor in order to effectively bridge any gaps that may be present.

Internet and E-Mail Use in Agencies

Ishizuki and Cotter (2008) found that the use of Internet and e-mail communication is increasing and that they are important tools for social workers. Communicating via these tools can take many forms. For instance, your agency and field instructor may use e-mail when communicating with the staff. Thus, it is important to determine whether you will have an agency-based e-mail account and how often you need to be checking your account. This can be particularly challenging, given that you may not turn to your e-mail first when you think about day-to-day communication with others. If you will not have an e-mail account at the agency, discuss how you will receive agency information communicated via e-mail. This can be handled by your field instructor forwarding important e-mails to you using your school e-mail account. If you will be using your personal e-mail account, first and foremost, make sure your e-mail address is appropriate. It is recommended that you check your school e-mail daily, as this is most likely how you will be officially communicated with by both the field program and your agency. Also, discuss confidentiality and any potential concerns or issues that could arise related to having client or agency-based information in your inbox. With regard to using e-mail to communicate with clients, discuss this with your field instructor and determine the agency policy before you give a client your e-mail address. Finn and Krysik (2007), in their study regarding unsolicited e-mail, found that social workers are receiving unsolicited e-mails from clients and that the growth in the use of electronic communication will necessitate "agency policies and infrastructure that promote e-mail safety and confidentiality" (p. 35). Should you receive an unsolicited e-mail from a current or potential client or anyone in the community requesting information, notify your field instructor and discuss how to handle the situation.

In addition to e-mail use, the use of the Internet to facilitate social work practice is well recognized. For instance, social workers may conduct searches for information and to locate and learn about community resources. Students can also log on to their university's library via the Internet and search for articles that can advance their and other social workers' practice in the agency. However, some agencies may monitor Internet searches and may not want employees, volunteers, and students using agency computers to do their online shopping, banking, updating their personal Facebook status, uploading photos to Snapchat or Instagram, or accessing sites that the agency considers inappropriate. Other agencies may feel that it is fine to do the above when someone is on their lunch break. That is why you need to discuss this with your field instructor and know and follow the agency's policies and procedures that govern use of the Internet at work.

Cell Phone Usage

In addition, you want to discuss the use of cell phones and determine if you will have access to a cell phone when at the agency. The use of cell phones in social work practice has many important advantages. For instance, the field instructors I work with tell me they are increasingly using cell phones to text their clients, as many of their clients have unlimited texting and do not have a landline. Texting a client has become a practice that not only protects the client's limited resources but also is efficient. Furthermore, cell phones can be useful when in field for communicating with a supervisor or being notified of changing appointments or crises. However, once you are engaged with a client system, it is an expectation that your cell phone be on silent and not checked until you are done with the contact. In the event you are waiting for an important client-related call, let your client know that if the call comes in, you will need to take it; this should only be done in true emergencies. A common question that students have about cell phone use while in field is whether they can use their own personal phone. This is an important discussion to have with your field director and field instructor and is the subject of the Frequently Experienced Situation at the end of the chapter. Last, it is not recommended that students use their personal cell phones with their clients or give out their phone number, but if this is necessary and sanctioned by your program and agency, there are ways to conceal your cell phone number. Again, as you can see, all of this is key to discuss with your field liaison, director, and field instructor.

Social Media

With regard to social media, more and more agencies are turning to Facebook and Twitter as an effective means to communicate their mission and educate others about their services. In addition, according to Fang, Mishna, Zhang, Van Wert, and Bogo (2014), "social media have transformed how individuals communicate, relate, and interact; form relationships; give and receive information; and participate in a wide range of activities" (p. 809). The authors put this reality in the context of the fact that many students and young professionals rely on social media and have never known a world without telecommunications and thus, advocate that social work educators consider this environment in the training of students. The same can be said for agencies and their use of social media. One agency director with whom I worked told me that their use of Facebook resulted from her getting a friend request from a client on her personal Facebook page. The director was understandably caught off guard and, of course, she did not "friend" the client. She later realized that the use of Facebook might be an untapped resource, so the agency established a page. With regard to the use of your personal Facebook page, Snapchat, Instagram, and Twitter and using social media as a way of making your friends aware of social issues, these forums can be an important macro-level practice tool. This was seen in the significant role Facebook and Twitter played in organizing protesters during the Arab Spring, which began in 2010. The newly revised NASW code of ethics (2017b) added a sub-standard to Standard 1.06 Conflicts of Interest, which states, "(e) Social workers should avoid communication with clients using technology (such as social networking sites, online chat, e-mail, text messages, telephone, and video) for personal or non–work-related purposes" (Ethical Standards, paragraph 23).

As you can see, in order to ensure ethical practice, you need to discuss with your field instructor if you have an interest in using social media to increase awareness of potential boundary issues and specifically how to maintain confidentiality with regard to your agency and the clients you are serving. For instance, it is not appropriate to post specific client-based situations as your status. Second, if you want to increase your social media friends' awareness of an issue or a need, do so very generally and always make sure it is okay with your agency. For instance, if your agency is having a fund-raising event that is open to the community, ask your field instructor if you can post the event on your Facebook page. With your field instructor's approval, it is okay. If your agency has its own Facebook page or Twitter account, encourage your Facebook friends and Twitter followers to like their page, follow the agency on Twitter, or even retweet the status. If you want to comment on something that is happening in the news and is impacting your agency, make sure you do not officially identify yourself as a representative of the agency. This is because many agencies have individuals who are approved for media contact, and although Facebook is not the news media, you have no idea who is friends with whom and what impact your passionate post could have on your agency. Last, and I know you have been told this many times, everything you do on social media is permanent, so make sure that anything you post can stand the test of time.

With regard to personal social media, obviously, if a client sends you a friend request (yes, this can happen), make sure you delete the request and discuss with the client why you can't be friends on Facebook. Also, reset your privacy settings to ensure that clients cannot inadvertently access your personal information. When posting photos that could link you to your agency, discuss this with your field instructor to determine if it is appropriate. I generally recommend that there are no circumstances where that would be appropriate, but there could be some gray areas, such as a community-based rally or walk in which you participated. Nonetheless, always discuss this with your field instructor ahead of time. As you can see, it is important to reflect on the potentially blurred lines between your personal and professional selves on social media. If you have not done so, google yourself and see what comes up. Fang and colleagues (2014) state that given "the nature of social media allowing for immediate updates on thoughts and experiences, and sharing with a wide range of audiences, a young professional may without thinking through the consequences, post private information onto the openly public online community for unintended audiences." (pp. 806–807). Therefore, if and when you have a bad day, you think your field agency is chaotic, your agency just lost all its funding, or your field instructor suddenly quit, pause before you Tweet or post a status that could inadvertently breach confidentiality or show a lack of professionalism on your part. Ask if your agency has a policy about communicating via social media; if so, make sure you read and follow the policy. If not, then at a minimum discuss the agency and your field instructor's practices around communication via social media. All of this relates to what has been termed *e-professionalism,* defined as "attitudes and behaviors that reflect traditional professionalism paradigms but are manifest through digital media" (Kaczmarczyk et al., 2013, p. 164).

Finally, Curington and Hitchcock (2017) developed and made available a tool kit that field directors can share with field instructors and students to assist them in developing their own social media policy. They define a social media policy as a way to "inform clients, constituents, colleagues and others about when, how, and why you use social media in a professional capacity" (p. 10). Begin to reflect on what your own policy might look like and discuss this with your field instructor. Both agency-based and worker-based policies can be very helpful for client systems. The authors offer a worksheet to assist in the process of assessing the forms of social media that are personally used and then discerning how and if that form would be used in professional practice (Curington & Hitchcock, 2017, p. 24). For example, a policy might include very straightforward guidelines, such as not friending clients on Facebook, to more complex guidelines for e-mail, including under what circumstances clients can send an e-mail, when e-mails are checked and answered, and who to contact if the e-mail is not returned as well as a reminder that e-mail is not secure so that clients do not inadvertently leave confidential information in an e-mail. This discussion reflects the expectation that "social workers use technology ethically and appropriately to facilitate practice outcomes," which is one of the component behaviors of Competency 1 in the EPAS (CSWE, 2015, p.7).

Computer Systems

Another possible use of technology in your field agency could be the use of computer-based client records and documentation. Using the computer to maintain client records and document client contacts could be used in addition to paper-based files or it could be the sole format. Whatever the case, it is important for you to discuss how this is done and develop a plan to be trained on the computer system and required databases. Most importantly, the type of access you will have regarding the computer system needs to be addressed. This is extremely important, given that a student's learning may be compromised by failing to address this issue early on in the placement. If you are not trained or do not have access to client records, this will hamper the learning process.

REFLECTION QUESTION 6.3

Now that you have had a chance to consider the use of technology in field, what are your thoughts about the appropriate use of technology in social work practice such as e-mail, cell phones, social media, and computerized records? What is your current level of competence in the use of technology, and what are any specific needs in this area?

ROOM TO REFLECT

COMMUNICATION CHALLENGES IN FIELD

From time to time, challenging situations will come up when communicating with clients that will require a more thoughtful response. For instance, you may experience a client who becomes verbally aggressive and angry and expresses intense emotions. These situations have happened to the students with whom I have worked, and these situations require skill to manage. For instance, a student who was working at a child welfare agency was supervising a visit between a mother and her children when the mother became very angry and started yelling at the student. The situation escalated to the point that the client began shouting, cursed at the student, and called her a derogatory name. The student was able to remain calm and use the verbal de-escalation skills she had learned during her training. She reflected back to the client that she could hear she was very upset and felt it would be a good idea for the client to speak to her supervisor, who would be better able to address her concerns. She asked the client to wait in the room, took the children with her, and got her supervisor. The student reported later that she was caught off guard and was scared, but she also knew that if she acknowledged the client's anger using her active listening skills and got assistance from her supervisor, she would be able to manage the situation. In another similar situation, a student reported that her client became extremely angry during an interview, and again, the student used her active listening skills, acknowledged the client's anger, and sought assistance from her supervisor. Both of these situations demonstrate that even in a situation where you may be caught off guard, it is always useful to go back to the basics and use active listening and reflecting back.

Another situation that can be challenging, particularly the first time a student experiences it, is when a client displays intense emotion, such as crying uncontrollably during an interview or in group session. Although displaying intense emotion such as crying is normal and expected, many students report that when faced with this situation, they do not know how to respond. The best plan of action is to go back to the basics, acknowledge your client's feelings, allow the client time to experience the feelings by using silence, and reflect the feelings back to the client by saying something as simple as "I can see how upsetting this is for you." All of these techniques can be very helpful to a client and let him or her know that you understand; they require the ability of the social work student to be comfortable with experiencing intense emotions. Once a client's feelings are acknowledged and understanding is established, it is more likely that you will be able to redirect the client to the task and continue your work.

Given the likelihood that you will encounter situations in which clients are upset or display strong emotions, it is important to consider your comfort level with this type of communication. If you are someone who has not been exposed to strong emotions, it will be important to prepare yourself for this eventuality. Similarly, if you have experienced intense emotional outbursts and have not processed them sufficiently, these types of situations could trigger your own personal reactions. Either way, it is advised to discuss these types of situations with your field instructor and develop a plan for how you will respond and manage them while in field.

The last challenge that students can face when communicating with clients relates to the students' desire to assist their client. This can take the form of jumping to problem solving by giving advice, monopolizing the interview by only asking questions, or doing all of the talking. All of these actions can result in the student missing opportunities for reflecting feelings or content back to a client, which is an important part of interviewing. Reflecting back what you are hearing gives the client important information and an opportunity to process their situation. It is very important to relax and allow the client to tell his or her story, to seek out opportunities for the client to engage in problem solving by reflecting back what you are hearing, and to allow for silence. Allowing for silence, particularly after you have reflected something back to a client, gives the client time to think about and process the conversation, which often will result in the client having a realization or developing a plan. By rushing to problem solving or information giving, you may inadvertently prolong the process or, worse, miss the opportunity to engage the client fully. For the social work student, this can be challenging because in all likelihood, he or she has a genuine desire to assist the client and perhaps even has excellent ideas and resources; however, if he or she has not engaged the client, the client may not be able to benefit from what the student and agency has to offer. The opposite can hold true as well; the social work student can allow the client to prolong the process and inadvertently delay the helping process. In this case, the student must develop the skill at using positive confrontation to redirect focus back to the task at hand.

The challenges discussed above become excellent sources for a process recording and analysis in supervision. Do not be afraid to bring these challenges to the attention of your field instructor, faculty field liaison, and peers if you are taking an integrative seminar course.

REFLECTION QUESTION 6.4

As you reflect on the challenges that can present themselves related to multilevel communication in field, what challenges, if any, do you face? What is your level of competence with regard to oral and written communication? What are your communication strengths and weaknesses, and what do you need to develop your competence?

ROOM TO REFLECT

FREQUENTLY EXPERIENCED SITUATIONS

The following is a frequently experienced situation that reflects the content in this chapter. Review the situation and reflect on how you might handle this, should it happen to you or be a question or concern you have in field.

Can I use my cell phone at field?

Can I use my cell phone at my field site? It would just make everything so much easier.

This is a great and very timely question. As discussed, the use of technology in social work practice has grown over the years. More and more social workers and agencies are turning to the use of technology in the form of computers, Internet, cell phones, social networking, and computerized files. When I was practicing in child welfare in the 1990s, we began to use portable phones when we went on home visits. In those days, the phones were the size of a shoebox but did provide an important safety feature to increase communication between the worker and the office. Today, almost everyone has a cell phone, and many cell phones function as one's office—people receive their e-mail and perhaps surf the Internet during the day, if they have a smartphone. But back to the question: Is it okay for a student to use a personal cell phone at field?

My answer to this question is, it depends on how and with whom you are using your phone. Giving your cell number to your field instructor, field director, and faculty liaison and using it in the course of your day to communicate with your agency, university, and other professionals is perfectly appropriate and can be very helpful if you need to discuss an issue, are lost, or are running late to a meeting.

I do not, however, recommend that you give your personal cell phone number to your clients, for several reasons. First and foremost, it is important to establish appropriate boundaries and educate your clients with regard to those boundaries. The client should have the number of the agency and your extension, if you have one; if you don't, discuss with your field instructor about giving clients your field instructor's extension. The client should also be given the emergency after-hours number and be told how to appropriately use the emergency line. This will let the client leave you messages, if necessary, and receive services in a crisis. If you need to call your client, you should use the agency phone. If your agency has portable phones that you can take with you when you do home visits, you can, of course, use that phone to call your clients. If you are out and need to use your phone to contact your client to let them know you are running a few minutes late, make sure to conceal your number by using a feature that does not display your number. There are ways to set up another number that is associated with your phone but is not your personal number.

Second, if your client has your cell phone number, they could call you unsolicited. A client could call any time of the day or night, and given that you are only in field part-time, unless you have a block placement, your clients could end up calling you when you are not at field, in class, or at work.

Third, a client could call in crisis when you are not working at your agency, and you may not have access to the information you need to assist the client or even contact your field instructor. As a student, you never want to be the sole person responsible for your client;

therefore, there should be other resources that your clients can draw on when they are in need.

I worked with a student who was at a setting where she said everyone used their cell phones, and it didn't make sense to her why she shouldn't go ahead and do the same. It is always challenging to navigate the world of the student and the world of the agency, but it is important to remember that, first and foremost, you are a student, and just because the professional social workers engage in a particular practice at the agency

does not mean that you should do so as a student. In the event that a student wants to use his or her phone, it is important to discuss the situation with the field instructor, field director, and perhaps faculty liaison. Together, make a decision that is in the best interest of all parties, taking into account the fact that the student is not an employee of the agency and is learning about professional practice and therefore may not have the same level of skill and expertise as the social workers at the agency.

Suggested Field Tasks

- Communicate with clients and at the organizational level using verbal, nonverbal, and written skills.

- Discuss the agency's use of social media and determine whether the agency has a social media policy.

- Google yourself and review your online persona.

- Evaluate your professional communication skills.

- Complete documentation and professional writing practice.

- Intake and engage individuals, families, task and treatment groups, organizations, and communities via phone and in person.

- Use empathy and effective interpersonal skills.

- Practice a wide variety of communication skills with clients.

References

Alle-Corliss, L., & Alle-Corliss, R. (1998). *Human service agencies: An orientation to fieldwork*. Pacific Grove, CA: Brooks Cole.

Beall, A. E. (2004). Body language speaks. *Communication World, 21*(2), 18–20.

Cain, J. (2011). Social media in health care: The case for organizational policy and employee education. *AJHP: Official Journal of the American Society of Health-System Pharmacists, 68*(11), 1036–1040. doi:10.2146/ajhp100589

Chang, V., Scott, S., & Decker, C. (2009). *Developing helping skills: A step-by-step approach.* Belmont, CA: Brooks/Cole.

Council on Social Work Education (CSWE). (2015). *Educational policy and accreditation standards*. Alexandria, VA: Author.

Curington, A. M., & Hitchcock, L. I. (2017). *Social media toolkit for social work field educators*. Retrieved March 17, 2018, from http://www.laureliversonhitchcock.org/2017/07/28/social-media-toolkit-for-social-work-field-educators-get-your-free-copy/

Fang, L., Mishna, F., Zhang, V. F., Van Wert, M., & Bogo, M. (2014). Social media and social work education: Understanding and dealing with the new digital world. *Social Work in Health Care, 53*(9), 800–814. doi:10.1080/00981389.2014.943455

Finn, J., & Krysik, J. (2007). Agency-based social worker's attitudes and behaviors regarding service-related unsolicited e-mail. *Journal of Technology in Human Services, 25*(3), 21–38.

Graybeal, C. T. (1995). Process recording: It's more than you think. *Journal of Social Work Education, 31*(2), 169–181.

Hall, C. M., & Bierman, K. L. (2015). Technology-assisted interventions for parents of young children: Emerging practices, current research, and future directions. *Early Childhood Research Quarterly,* 3321–3332. doi: 10.1016/j.ecresq.2015.05.003

Ishizuki, T., & Cotter, J. (2008). Social worker's use of the Internet and e-mail to help clients in Virginia. *Journal of Technology in Human Services, 27,* 127–140.

Jarvis-Selinger, S., Chan, E., Payne, R., Plohman, K., & Ho, K. (2008). Clinical telehealth across the disciplines: Lessons learned. *Telemedicine Journal and E-health: The Official Journal of the American Telemedicine Association, 14*(7), 720–725. doi: 10.1089/TMJ.2007.0108

Kaczmarczyk, J. M., Chuang, A., Dugoff, L., Abbott, J. F., Cullimore, A. J., Dalrymple, J., & Casey, P. M. (2013). e-Professionalism: A new frontier in medical education. *Teaching and Learning in Medicine, 25*(2), 165–170. doi:10.1080/10401334.2013.770741

Kagel, J., & Kopels, S. (2008). *Social work records* (3rd ed.). Long Grove, IL: Waveland Press.

McCarty, D., & Clancy, C. (2002). Telehealth: Implications for social work practice. *Social Work, 2,* 153.

Mishna, F., Levine, D., Bogo, M., & Van Wert, M. (2013). Cyber counselling: An innovative field education pilot project. *Social Work Education, 32*(4), 484–492. doi:10.1080/02615479.2012.685066

Mullin, W. J., & Canning, J. J. (2007). Process recording in supervision of students learning to practice with children. *Journal of Teaching in Social Work, 27*(3/4), 167–183.

National Association of Social Workers (NASW). (2017a). *Code of ethics.* Retrieved March 18, 2018, from https://www.socialworkers.org/About/Ethics/Code-of-Ethics

National Association of Social Workers (NASW). (2017b). *Read the code of ethics.* Retrieved March 17, 2018, from https://www.socialworkers.org/About/Ethics/Code-of-Ethics/Code-of-Ethics-English

Neuman, K. M., & Friedman, B. D. (1997). Process recordings: Fine-tuning an old instrument. *Journal of Social Work Education, 33*(2), 237–243.

Sheafor, B., & Horejsi, C. (2015). *Techniques and guidelines for social work practice* (10th ed.). Boston, MA: Pearson Education.

Sidell, N., & Smiley, D. (2008). *Professional communication skills in social work.* Boston, MA: Pearson Education.

ETHICAL PRACTICE IN FIELD

Social work practice is grounded in the values of the profession. The ethical practice demonstrated by a social worker reflects those values and is integral to competent practice. As a student in field, you will become immersed in these values and will have opportunities to demonstrate ethical decision making, particularly in the area of resolving ethical dilemmas. This chapter will explore several important content areas, such as values and ethics in field, your agency's ethical practice via the ethics audit, ethical decision making, resolving ethical dilemmas, and the role of the law in ethical decision making.

VALUES AND ETHICS IN SOCIAL WORK

The National Association of Social Workers (NASW) delegate assembly initially approved the current code of ethics in 1996, revised it in 2008, and revised it again most recently in 2017. In terms of the history of the code, according to the NASW (2017a), the first code of ethics came out in 1960 and consisted of 14 "I" statements. In 1967, the code was revised to include a 15th nondiscrimination "I" statement. The 1979 revision was a significant revision in that it dropped the 15 "I" statements and introduced six sections of standards and 82 principles. It was in this version that the social worker's ethical responsibility to clients, colleagues, employers and employing organizations, the profession, and society were explicitly laid out. Even more importantly, it was this version that called for social workers to use the code as the basis and standard for their day-to-day conduct. Other notable additions included social worker impairment and dual relationships, which were added in 1993. In 1996, there was a need to focus more specifically on ethics, and lastly, in 1999, the code clarified situations where a social worker might need to disclose confidential information even when a client does not consent. The most recent revision was in response to the rise of technology and the potential impact on practice as well as concerns with regard to potential ethical violations and thus the need to revise the standards and sub-standards (NASW, 2017b).

If you have not had a chance to read all of the versions, I encourage you to do so. What I found most interesting when reviewing all the codes is how brief the 1960 and 1967 versions were as compared to the current version. Also, the language of the first code and the first revision is written as a pledge and, most interestingly, includes "I" statements and explicit preference to professional responsibility over personal interests. The first two statements are "I regard as my primary obligation the welfare of the individual or group served, which includes action for improving social conditions," and "I give preference to my professional responsibility over my personal interests" (NASW, 1960). This is in comparison to the 1979 revision, which drops the reference to a pledge and changes the "I" to "social worker." This version also drops the explicit reference to giving preference to one's professional responsibility over personal interests and changes the language from the social worker's primary obligation to the welfare of individual and groups to promoting the general welfare of society. The 1979 version, on the one hand, is more comprehensive, but on the other hand, it may have diluted some of the focus of the profession on the welfare of individual and groups and focused more on the professional conduct of the social worker. That being said, Reamer (1998) describes the code as "the most ambitious set of ethical guidelines in social work's history" (p. 488). Congress (2002) states that the "NASW Code of Ethics with 155 ethical standards is the most comprehensive ethical code for social workers and represents a dramatic change from previous codes" (p. 162). Yet, even with a comprehensive code of ethics, engaging in ethical practice is challenging for the seasoned professional in that "today's social workers face issues involving values and ethics that their predecessor in the profession could not possibly have imagined" (Reamer, 2013a, p. ix). For students, who lack practice experience, managing values and engaging in ethical practice can be even more daunting. Thus, in order to begin the process of developing and demonstrating competence in ethical practice in field, let's first review the values and ethical principles outlined in the current code of ethics.

In the preamble, the NASW code of ethics outlines several overarching ethical principles, which are grounded in the profession's core values of

- service,
- social justice,
- dignity and worth of the person,
- importance of human relationships,
- integrity, and
- competence (NASW, 2017b, p. 1).

The ethical principles are as follows:

- Social workers' primary goal is to help people in need and address social problems.
- Social workers challenge social injustice.
- Social workers respect the inherent dignity and worth of the person.
- Social workers behave in a trustworthy manner.
- Social workers practice within their areas of competence and develop and enhance their professional expertise. (pp. 5–6)

In addition to the preceding ethical principles, the code identifies multiple ethical standards that relate to social workers' activities. The standards fall within six broad categories and reflect a social worker's responsibilities to clients, colleagues, practice settings, themselves as professionals, the profession, and the broader society. The code also identifies six purposes, which are to

- name the core values on which the profession's mission is based,
- summarize the board ethical principles that reflect the core values and establish a set of ethical standards that guide social work practice,
- help social workers identify relevant considerations when their professional obligations conflict or ethical uncertainties arise,
- provide ethical standards the general public can hold the profession accountable to,
- socialize practitioners new to the field to the mission, values, ethical principles, and ethical standards, and

- articulate standards that the social work profession itself can use to assess whether social workers have engaged in unethical conduct (NASW, 2017b).

One of the most important purposes of the NASW code of ethics is to offer "a set of values, principles, and standards to guide decision making and conduct when ethical issues arise" (NASW, 2017b, p. 2). However, the code is not prescriptive in nature. This means that the code is not going to tell a social worker what should be done in any given situation; instead, it provides direction for thinking about the context of any given practice situation and the likely conflicts that will arise even within the standards themselves. Furthermore, the code does not identify which standard is more important or which standard should outweigh another. Thus, it is critically important that social workers be competent in their ethical decision-making process and in knowing how to resolve the ethical dilemmas that present themselves when practicing.

REFLECTION QUESTION 7.1

After reviewing the NASW code of ethics, as you enter field and consider your values and the values of the profession, what stands out to you? Where do you see congruence, and where is there possible dissonance between your values and those of the profession? What are your thoughts about the history of the code of ethics and the revisions to date? Would you make any changes today?

ROOM TO REFLECT

THE AGENCY ETHICS AUDIT

A helpful activity for you to engage in to begin to develop your understanding of ethics in field and to assist you in the development of your competence as an ethical practitioner is to conduct an *ethics audit* (Reamer, 2000, 2013a) of your agency. According to Reamer (2013a), an ethics audit provides social workers with a framework to both analyze and impact the ethical practices of an agency. For students in field, the most helpful aspect of the ethics audit is the "opportunity to identify pertinent ethical issues in their practice settings that are unique to the client population, treatment approach, setting, program design, and staffing pattern" (p. 211). Reamer (2000) states that an ethics audit should focus on two main areas:

1. knowledge of social work ethics and how they relate to the practice setting and

2. assessment of risk level and engagement in ethical decision making.

Although Reamer's (2000) ethics audit primarily targets risk management, this task is extremely beneficial to you in field in that the two main areas of the audit—knowledge of ethics related to your agency and consideration of risk level and ethical decision making—are extremely important areas to consider as you develop and demonstrate competence in the area of ethical practice.

The first task of the audit is to review and develop your knowledge related to ethics, particularly ethical practice in your agency. To accomplish this goal, review the NASW code of ethics, which can be found at http://www.socialworkers.org, and any other pertinent codes of ethics specific to your agency. In the NASW code of ethics, several standards in the area of social worker's responsibility to clients are important to focus on:

- competence
- cultural competence
- conflicts of interest, particularly in the area of dual or multiple relationships
- confidentiality

In your supervision session, discuss these ethical standards in the context of your practice setting. This can be done by asking your field instructor to share some of the common ethical issues that may be inherent to the agency and that relate to each of the areas identified above.

I worked with a student who conducted a weekly review of the NASW code of ethics in her supervision session. This consisted of reviewing one of the standards each week and discussing how this standard was met in the agency, any ethical issues that might have arisen related to the standard, and how those issues were handled. Both the student and field instructor reported that this was an extremely beneficial task for field supervision.

Review the agency's policies and practices to determine the level of risk those practices present to clients, the workers and students, and the agency. Reamer (2000) identifies four risk levels that can be applied to the areas audited: (1) no risk, (2) minimal risk, (3) moderate risk, and (4) high risk. The purpose of assigning a risk level is to identify those procedures or practices within the agency that are strong and thus represent no risk and those that may increase risk to the clients and agency and thus represent a high risk. Reamer identified several areas that you can explore as you conduct this part of the audit: "clients' rights, confidentiality and privacy, informed consent, service delivery, boundary issues, conflicts of interest, documentation, defamation of character, supervision, training, consultation, referral, fraud, termination of services, and practitioner impairment" (p. 357). One additional area to add is the use of technology and the need to assess the agency's practices through this lens. According to Reamer (2013b), the current code explicitly references electronic media in the delivery of services but was written in 1996, well before the invention of what we know today to be social media. Reamer goes on to say that

> emerging forms of digital and electronic practice have unleashed a staggering array of ethical and risk management issues involving practitioner competence, client privacy and confidentiality, informed consent, conflicts of interest, boundaries and dual relationships, consultation and client referral, termination and interruption of services documentation, and research evidence. (p. 163)

In light of the explosion of social media, the NASW partnered with the Association of Social Work Boards (ASWB), Council on Social Work Education (CSWE), and Clinical Social Work Association (CSWA) to develop a set of technology standards for social workers (NASW, ASWB, CSWE, & CSWA, 2017). Again, if you have not had a chance to review those standards, then do so, as this will facilitate your assessment of the agency's practices in your ethics audits. Assessing your agency's practices should be thought of using a multilevel approach, meaning that you should, at the micro or individual client system level, assess the digital and electronic technology that is being used for direct practice. For instance, this could include online, telephone, or video counseling; self-guided web-based interventions; social networks; e-mail; or text messages. Reamer (2013b) provides an overview of these practices with clients that is helpful in better understanding which should be used with clients. Next, consider the macro or larger system level, and assess how the agency uses technology at the organizational and or societal level—for instance, using text messages to set up appointments and to communicate with clients who do not have a landline or who have phone plans with limited minutes of voice calling, or a Facebook page or Twitter account that is used to increase awareness of the service of the agencies in the community and advocate for policy initiatives. According to Gagnon and Sabus (2015), many health care organizations are relying on social media as an integral part of their services to patients and, therefore, have developed policies to provide guidance for organizational accounts and employee use, both personally and professionally. The authors go on to identify four spheres of social media use, which can be helpful to you as you reflect on your agency's practices—platform terms of service, professional standards, organizational policy, and individual best practices (p. 408). However, as you set out to examine your agency's use of technology, and particularly social media, you might be surprised to know that in a global study conducted by Manpower Inc. (2010), only 29% of the 11,000 American employers surveyed indicated that they had a formal policy (p. 3). Thus, Cain (2011) encourages health care organizations to create policies around the use of social media for the workplace and to educate employees on the proper use of social media. By exploring the practices and procedures that your agency employs and assigning a risk level, you will develop your understanding of the agency's overall ethical practice. It is important to note that not all of the preceding areas will be relevant, given your agency and practices. You may want to discuss with your field instructor the areas that you will be auditing. That being said, make sure to include use of technology and specific focus on social media in your audit, as this is a growing area of practice.

The final area that Reamer (2000) identified in the ethics audit is ethical decision making. This is a critically important competence and an important part in resolving ethical dilemmas, so this will be explored separately.

Integrative Activity 7.1 is an opportunity to apply all of the preceding information to your agency. This activity asks you to consider specific areas related to ethical practice, assess the current level of risk or successful practices of the agency in a particular area, and address any needed action within the agency to reduce risk.

INTEGRATIVE ACTIVITY 7.1
THE AGENCY ETHICS AUDIT

Purpose: The purpose of this activity is to audit key ethical practices and procedures of your agency, with a specific focus on technology.

Directions: For each of the following key ethical areas, gather information through interview or observation of the practices and procedures of your agency related specifically to that area and ask yourself the identified questions. Then give each area a rating of **1 = no risk, 2 = minimal risk, 3 = moderate risk,** or **4 = high risk** related to your assessment of the risk this area presents to clients and employees of the agency. *Risk* refers to practices or procedures that could directly or indirectly harm clients or create the potential that the ethical values and standards set forth in the NASW code of ethics may not be met by the agency. For each area, provide any comments that you would like to discuss in supervision based on the audit. Once you have looked at all relevant areas, provide an overall assessment of the ethical practice and procedures of your agency and their potential for risk.

Competency 1: Demonstrate Ethical and Professional Behavior

- demonstrate professional demeanor in behavior; appearance; and oral, written, and electronic communication

- use technology ethically and appropriately to facilitate practice outcomes

(Continued)

(Continued)

Key Ethical Areas of Potential Risk	Rating			
Use of Digital, Online, and Other Electronic Technology (online, telephone, or video counseling; cybertherapy; self-guided web-based interventions; social media; e-mail with clients; text messages): Does the agency use any of these digital and electronic practices with individual client systems? Does the agency use any of these digital and electronic practices at the organizational and societal level? Does the agency have a social media policy?:	1	2	3	4
Comments:				
Client's Rights: Does the agency have a client's rights statement? A client's rights statement typically addresses confidentiality; release of information; informed consent; access to services; access to records; service plans; service provision; and options for alternative services and referrals, the right to refuse services, potential for harm by receiving services, termination of services, and grievance procedures. Also, assess how frequently and competently the agency informs clients of their rights.	1	2	3	4
Comments:				
Confidentiality and Privacy: Does the agency have practices and procedures for releasing and obtaining information about the client? Does the agency outline the limits of confidentiality, meaning identifying when confidentiality must be breached? Assess the practice and procedures for protecting written (secure client files) and electronic information as well as use of electronic devices such as faxes, e-mail, and texting. Consider the privacy practices that prevent sharing of confidential information in public (corresponding with clients and staff maintaining confidentiality) and the practices of informing clients of the confidentiality policies.	1	2	3	4
Comments:				
Informed Consent: Does the agency have informed consent documents and procedures? Also, are clients informed of the right and procedure for withdrawing consent to receive services? Do the policies and practices of the agency ensure that clients are mentally capable of providing consent?	1	2	3	4
Comments:				
Service Delivery: How are services provided? Do social workers present as competent and practice only within their education, training, and license? Is the agency delivering the services that they say they are?	1	2	3	4
Comments:				

Boundary Issues and Conflicts of Interest: Do the social workers establish and maintain proper boundaries with respect to multiple or dual relationships, such as encounters in public, physical contact, receiving gifts, delivery to two or more clients who have a relationship (couple or family), attending social community events, social networking sites, and self-disclosure?	1	2	3	4
Comments:				

Documentation: Does the agency have established practices and procedures for documentation? Is the documentation produced by the social workers timely, accurate, and client driven? Are the social workers following the procedures for documentation? Is the documentation such that should a worker become ill or unavailable, client services would continue? Are records routinely reviewed to ensure compliance with documentation policies and procedures? Are records digital, and if so, how are they stored?	1	2	3	4
Comments:				

Supervision: Does the agency have policies and procedures for supervision? Do the social workers regularly attend and use supervision? Do the supervisors provide needed information to the social workers to serve their clients? Is there a plan for supervision in the absence of the supervisee? Does the supervisor routinely review the work of the social worker, such as documentation, assessments, service plans, and treatment summaries, to name a few?	1	2	3	4
Comments:				

Training: Does the agency provide training directly or indirectly for the social workers?	1	2	3	4
Comments:				

Referral: Does the agency have practices and procedures that address client referral when the social worker or agency cannot serve the client?	1	2	3	4
Comments:				

(Continued)

(Continued)

	1	2	3	4
Termination of Services: Does the agency have practices and procedures for when and how client services are terminated? Does the agency have practices and procedures for how clients can obtain services in the event of an emergency or if they cannot contact their social worker?				

Comments:

Overall assessment of agency's ethical practices and procedures and level of risk:

In the space below, provide your thoughts about the agency's ethical practices and procedures, include your assessment of their overall risk and any specific areas that you feel need to be addressed, and identify your plan, if any, for how to address the areas of risk.

Source: Reamer (2000).

REFLECTION QUESTION 7.2

Now that you have conducted your agency ethics audit with a specific focus on technology, what did you learn about the ethical practices of your agency? What were the areas of significant risk and of no risk? What would you recommend that the agency do to address the areas you identified as being high risk?

ROOM TO REFLECT

ETHICAL DECISION MAKING

Ethical decision making is a process that involves several important considerations. Rothman (2005) identifies several components of ethical decision making: defining the ethical problem, gathering information relevant to the problem, determining a theoretical base, exploring professional values, understanding client values, and finally, considering the impact of the personal values that are identified. Congress (1996) developed the ETHICs model: (1) *e*xamine your values, (2) *t*hink about the ethical standards, (3) *h*ypothesize different courses of action, (4) *i*dentify who may be harmed and who may be helped, and (5) *c*onsult with your supervisor or colleagues. Mattison (2000) states that "ethical decisions made by social workers are shaped by the decision maker and the process used to resolve ethical dilemmas" (p. 201), thus emphasizing the person in the process of ethical decision making. This emphasis considers both the impact of the practice setting and who the decision maker is as well as how that person makes decisions. Weinberg and Campbell (2014) challenge traditional approaches to ethical practice and advocate that social workers go beyond a focus on codes and standards to consider the practice context in which client–worker relationships occur as a way to improve the ethical practice of social work.

> We need to view ethics as a relationship in process between worker and service user. We must also recognize the structural constraints and paradoxes that are part of the everyday experience of practitioners while we conceptualize practice as a political activity that either reinforces inequities in society or moves toward social transformation. A model that emphasizes collaboration and dialogue and sees the worker not as separate but joined with a service user must be encouraged to form a truly ethical bond. (p. 48)

As you can see, engaging in ethical practice can be complex and challenging for a student. Thus, it is important for you, through reflection and supervision, to increase your understanding of how you engage in ethical practice and resolve dilemmas and how those decisions are unique to your practice setting and who you are becoming as a social worker.

As a student in field, you may experience a wide variety of ethical dilemmas that will require critical thinking, effective use of supervision, and competence in ethical decision making so that you can successfully resolve the dilemma. As a field director, I work with students who experience multiple ethical dilemmas that reflect the competing obligations that social workers have to their clients, colleagues, practice setting, themselves as professionals, the profession, and society. A dilemma can be straightforward or extremely complex and multifaceted. The following situations have come up over the years and will give you an idea of what you might encounter. As you read the various scenarios, notice what stands out to you as you think about the situation, as well as what you might do if you found yourself in a similar situation.

The first situation involved a student who was working with older adults in an apartment complex that offered social work services. One day, the student arrived at work; it happened to be his birthday. This news spread throughout the center, and he was greeted with many birthday wishes. During one of these birthday wishes, one of the residents gave him a five-dollar bill and said, "Happy birthday! Buy yourself something nice." The student replied that the gift wasn't necessary and attempted to return the five-dollar bill. To this, the resident insisted and again placed the money in the student's hand. The student walked away, knowing that he should not accept the money but also not knowing exactly how to handle the situation. The student discussed the situation with his field instructor, who recommended that he go back to the client and explain how much he appreciated the gesture, but the agency's policy is that staff cannot accept gifts from clients. The student felt very comfortable with the plan and expected it to go smoothly. However, when the student explained the policy and attempted to return the money, the client became upset, expressed feeling offended, stated that the whole situation was ridiculous, and refused to take the money. At this point, the student, too, was frustrated and went back to his supervisor. The field instructor then spoke to the client and suggested that the money be used to purchase cookies for everyone, to which the client stated that he didn't really care what they did.

This situation identifies many of the challenges discussed; for instance, the importance of the relationship and the contextual nature of setting. The social work student clearly identified the gentleman in this situation as the client, but did the gentlemen identify himself as such? And if not, how did he see his relationship with the student? Yes, the agency and profession had clear guidelines around accepting gifts, but given this context, is the policy the most important factor? Clearly, the gentleman's reaction to the decision, the fact that he no longer even cared about what "they" (the student and staff) did with the money, reflected his frustration and the loss of the genuine moment of connection when he gave the student the money. Some social workers would say that the way this was handled did damage to that client, while others would say that it was a necessary part of professional practice. What do you think?

As a result of the student and field instructor processing this ethical dilemma, it was determined that the agency would institute a birthday celebration to formalize the acknowledgment of the birthdays of both staff and residents as a way to allow celebrations to occur. This institutional change was the result of both the student and field instructor realizing that at the heart of this dilemma was the social need to acknowledge and recognize something as simple as a birthday. However, this normal social exchange was happening within a professional context that involved professional relationships and boundaries as well as a clear agency policy, hence the dilemma. In a follow up, the student reported that the birthday celebrations were going well and if a client wanted to acknowledge someone's birthday, he or she could contribute to the birthday fund, from which cookies were purchased and offered to all the residents and staff.

When the student processed the situation and dilemma, he could clearly see the competing values and ethical obligations; that is, the value of human relationships and the standard of commitment to clients versus the value of competence and the standard of the commitment to employers. It was clear to the student that he needed to adhere to the policy of the agency, which stated that staff could not accept gifts from the residents. But at the same time, he saw the need to reflect on the context and to acknowledge the importance of the value of human relationships. The agency instituted the birthday program as a way to strike a balance between the needs of the residents and staff to share in normal human experiences while also maintaining an agency policy that they felt was equally important to preserve the integrity of the agency and the professional conduct of the staff.

In addition to the preceding scenario, I have also seen students experience extremely challenging situations that have required consultation from multiple sources. For instance, students have had dilemmas arise with regard to their responsibility as mandated reporters of suspected abuse or neglect on the one hand and their commitment to their client and the standard of maintaining confidentiality on the other. In these situations, although the students involved could clearly point to their legal responsibility as a mandated reporter, the experience was nonetheless challenging for them, particularly when placed in the context of their relationship with their client and the need to breach confidentiality. Again, this dilemma generated extremely helpful discussion in class for the student involved as well as the class as a whole. For even when we, as professionals, know we are acting appropriately, it can still be challenging and require support. That is why supervision, consultation, and support are so important when dealing with ethical dilemmas.

Last, it is not uncommon for a student to observe or be exposed to the questionable conduct of a coworker or question the practices of the agency. The dilemmas that result from these kinds of situations are extremely challenging. For instance, I worked with a student who was exposed to illegal behavior on the part of a coworker. Again, although the student knew that she had to tell her field instructor what had happened, it was still stressful, as she worried about what would happen to the coworker and even questioned if she would be able to continue at the agency herself. With a great deal of support and consultation, the student informed her field instructor, the situation was handled well by the agency, and the student did not feel the need to leave the agency.

These are only a few of the many dilemmas that students with whom I have worked over the years have experienced. Before moving on to developing your competence in resolving the ethical dilemmas you will experience, consider the following reflection question.

REFLECTION QUESTION 7.3

As you reflect on the presented scenarios, how would you have handled the situations? What ethical dilemmas could you see happening in your agency?

ROOM TO REFLECT

Resolving Ethical Dilemmas

Now that you have had a chance to think about the types of dilemmas you might face as a student, the next step is to develop your competence in resolving ethical dilemmas. The first step in developing your ability to resolve an ethical dilemma is to be able to recognize the dilemma. An *ethical dilemma* is defined as a situation in which you have to choose between two arguably correct yet competing courses of action (Royse, Dhooper, & Badger, 2018). Ethical dilemmas are often those situations that stick with you or gnaw at you. A dilemma can be between you and your client, involve policies and procedures of your agency that impact your clients, or involve your obligation to uphold laws even if that potentially harms your client.

For instance, a student with whom I was working had a client who violated the safety policy of the shelter and the violation resulted in the client being removed from the shelter. The student knew that this could potentially put the client at risk, particularly if the client returned to her abuser. But the student also knew that the client, who had been informed of the policy and the consequences of violating the policy, put the other clients at risk and therefore had to be removed. This dilemma was difficult for the student to navigate because, on the one hand, it could be considered to be fairly straightforward: The policies of the shelter and the need for clients to uphold them superseded the individual needs of the client. Yet, this situation could also be considered to be more complex when factoring in safety or an analysis of the agency policies that might not accurately reflect the challenges and pressures a client in an abusive relationship may be experiencing from her abuser and even the ambivalence that the client may be experiencing with regard to being in the shelter in the first place.

The ethical dilemmas that students experience are often not as dramatic and clear as the preceding one and thus require more attention. For instance, some of my students were asked by their clients to do something that may not have been within their role, such as attending a social event. The tendency of the student is to be torn between accepting the invitation to express caring and not accepting to maintain clear boundaries. One student was working with a family, providing in-home parent education services, and the client invited her to her daughter's birthday party. At first, the student wanted to say yes because she knew that the client saw her as a support in her life. But she also wondered if it would be appropriate to do so. Thus, the student considered the situation carefully, using the steps of an ethical decision-making process to guide her examination. She determined that the request did not fall within her role and was purely social. So, she declined the invitation. She felt that had the social event been linked to the work she was doing with the client, it may have been appropriate. But given the fact that attending her client's daughter's birthday party had no relation to the work she was doing, she informed the client that she could not attend the party. In discussing the situation with her field instructor, the field instructor shared that she had once been invited by a client to attend the client's GED graduation. Given the fact that achieving a GED was one of the goals they were working on, the field instructor felt it would be appropriate to attend the graduation but not go to the reception. Thus, similar situations had very different outcomes, both of which were appropriate, given the specifics of the situation and the case.

The next step is to engage in an ethical decision-making process to resolve the dilemma. The steps are as follows:

1. *Recognize* that you are experiencing an ethical dilemma.

2. *Identify* the two competing but arguably correct courses of action.

3. *Gather* all relevant information regarding the situation. This could include agency-based policies and procedures and information specific to the case that might inform the situation.

4. *Consult* the code of ethics to determine the standards that support each course of action and your field instructor for information you may not have considered.

5. *Reflect* on your own values and the practice context and consider where you are coming from as you think about the situation with specific focus on relationships.

6. *Consider* the potential outcome of each course of action in terms of the impact on the client, on you the student and your field instructor, on the agency, and on society.

7. *Decide* the course of action you want to take, based on all of the preceding.

8. *Analyze* the decision you made, its outcome, and whether or not you would do anything differently.

Figure 7.1 illustrates the critical steps of resolving an ethical dilemma using the previous case example.

Now that you have had a chance to review ethical decision making and considered a step-by-step process in resolving ethical dilemmas, it is important in the development of your competence in resolving ethical dilemmas to engage in the process of resolving a dilemma you have directly experienced in field. Integrative Activity 7.2 will provide you with the necessary framework to engage in this process and thus demonstrate your competence.

The Role of the Law in Resolving Ethical Dilemmas

Many times during the process of resolving an ethical dilemma, you will identify a legal obligation that will supersede all other ethical obligations. For instance, your legal obligation to report suspected abuse or neglect, prevent harm or warn someone of impending harm, and report a felony will override other ethical obligations such as confidentiality and the value of human relationships. Other times, you may feel a law or policy is unjust and question whether or not it should be followed. According to Reamer (2013a), "Social workers and others sometimes

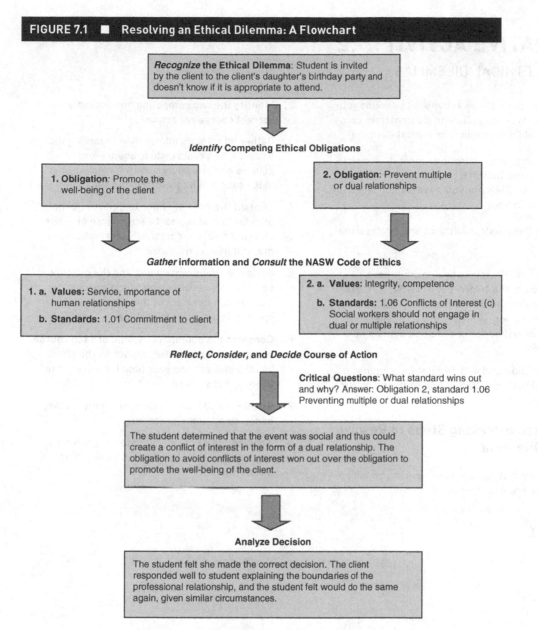

FIGURE 7.1 ■ Resolving an Ethical Dilemma: A Flowchart

Recognize the Ethical Dilemma: Student is invited by the client to the client's daughter's birthday party and doesn't know if it is appropriate to attend.

Identify Competing Ethical Obligations

1. Obligation: Promote the well-being of the client

2. Obligation: Prevent multiple or dual relationships

Gather information and *Consult* the NASW Code of Ethics

1. a. Values: Service, importance of human relationships
   b. Standards: 1.01 Commitment to client

2. a. Values: Integrity, competence
   b. Standards: 1.06 Conflicts of Interest (c) Social workers should not engage in dual or multiple relationships

Reflect, Consider, and *Decide* Course of Action

Critical Questions: What standard wins out and why? Answer: Obligation 2, standard 1.06 Preventing multiple or dual relationships

The student determined that the event was social and thus could create a conflict of interest in the form of a dual relationship. The obligation to avoid conflicts of interest won out over the obligation to promote the well-being of the client.

Analyze Decision

The student felt she made the correct decision. The client responded well to student explaining the boundaries of the professional relationship, and the student felt would do the same again, given similar circumstances.

have felt it necessary to violate laws and regulations to protest injustice or to achieve some higher-order good" (p. 161). However, the idea of violating a law should never be taken lightly, especially as a student. Thus, should you find yourself in a situation in which you are contemplating violating a law, it is very important that you consult with someone first and consider the potential impact on your educational and professional goals as well as on your program, field instructor, and agency. The first step in preparing yourself to manage the intersection of law and practice is to become aware of any laws that pertain to your agency and role, and always consult your field instructor when dilemmas that involve a legal obligation present themselves in practice.

INTEGRATIVE ACTIVITY 7.2
RESOLVING ETHICAL DILEMMAS

Purpose: The purpose of this activity is to develop your ethical decision-making skills and demonstrate competence in your ability to resolve an ethical dilemma.

Directions: Using the following ethical decision-making process and flowchart to guide your thinking, resolve an ethical dilemma you have experienced or are experiencing in field.

Competency 1: Demonstrate Ethical and Professional Behavior

- make ethical decisions by applying the standards of the NASW code of ethics, relevant laws and regulations, models for ethical decision making, ethical conduct of research, and additional codes of ethics as appropriate to context

- use reflection and self-regulation to manage personal values and maintain professionalism in practice situations

Ethical Decision-Making Steps to Resolve an Ethical Dilemma

1. **Recognize** that you are experiencing an ethical dilemma and describe the dilemma.

2. **Identify** the two competing but arguably correct courses of action.

3. **Gather** all relevant information regarding the situation, this could include agency-based policies and procedures and information specific to the case that might inform the situation.

4. **Consult** the code of ethics to determine the standards that support each course of action and your field instructor for information you may not have considered.

5. **Reflect** on your own values and the practice context and consider where you are coming from as you think about the situation with specific focus on relationships.

6. **Consider** the potential outcome of each course of action in terms of the impact on the client, you the student and your field instructor, the agency, and society.

7. **Decide** the course of action you want to take, based on all of the preceding.

8. **Analyze** the decision you made, its outcome, and whether or not you would do anything differently.

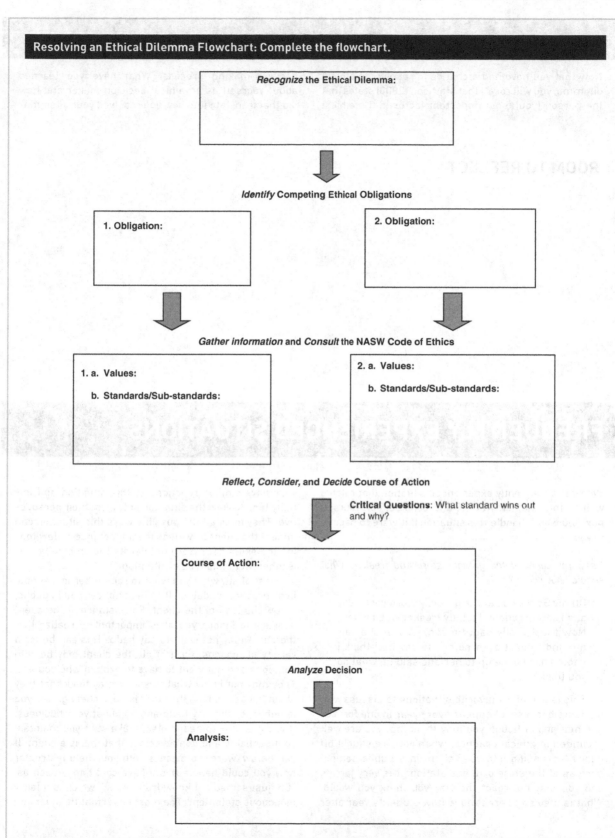

Resolving an Ethical Dilemma Flowchart: Complete the flowchart.

Recognize the Ethical Dilemma:

Identify Competing Ethical Obligations

1. Obligation:

2. Obligation:

Gather information and *Consult* the NASW Code of Ethics

1. a. Values:

   b. Standards/Sub-standards:

2. a. Values:

   b. Standards/Sub-standards:

Reflect, Consider, and *Decide* Course of Action

Critical Questions: What standard wins out and why?

Course of Action:

Analyze Decision

Analysis:

REFLECTION QUESTION 7.4

Now that you have had a chance to resolve an ethical dilemma, you will recall that Mattison (2000) states that the person (you) is an important factor in the ethical decision-making process. What have you learned about yourself as an ethical decision maker and how did that translate into how you resolved your dilemma?

ROOM TO REFLECT

FREQUENTLY EXPERIENCED SITUATIONS

Below is a frequently experienced situation that relates well to this chapter. Review and consider for yourself how you would handle this situation if it were to happen to you.

I saw my client at the grocery store and freaked. What should I have done?

Oh my God! I was at the grocery store yesterday and I saw my client. I totally freaked out and left. Now I feel really bad. I mean, what if she saw me and I didn't even bother to say hi. I think I should have gone up to her and said hi; what do you think?

This is one of my favorite situations to discuss with students because it happens every year in one form or another, and although you may think that you are well grounded in ethical practice, when you are caught off guard by running into your client in a public setting, such as at the store or a gas station, it is very jarring and you may not react the way you think you would. What is also so interesting is how students year after

year have similar reactions to this situation and initially tend to view the situation only from their perspective. They miss all the possible ways this situation can impact the client as well as the importance of developing the skills necessary to tolerate the ambiguity that is inherent in this type of situation.

First of all, what you want to remember is a simple best-practice guideline: If a client notices you in public, follow the lead of the client. For instance, if the client appears to ignore you, it is important to realize that the client may not want to say hello. This can be for a variety of reasons. First of all, the client may be with someone and not want to have to explain who you are. They may not know what to say or may think that they shouldn't say hi. If on the other hand, a client greets you in public, simply say hello and go about your business. If you are with someone else, make sure you maintain confidentiality and don't disclose that this is a client. It can be awkward, so discuss with your field instructor how you could handle this. I have said things such as, "Oh, just someone I know from work," which is a fairly innocuous statement. The most important thing for you to remember is that it is not the client's responsibility to maintain confidentiality—it is your responsibility. Therefore, if the client says hi, it's okay to say hi back. But if the client does not, do not acknowledge the client.

The part of not acknowledging a client is where students struggle the most and state that they don't want their clients to think they are rude or mean, or they think it is ridiculous that they can't say hi to a client. However, once the situation is explored in more detail and put in the context of ethical responsibility, and once they consider how the client might feel or what the client needs, most students come to realize that it is necessary to always err on the side of confidentiality.

I tell the students with whom I work that I, too, have experienced many instances of seeing clients in public, and each situation is very different. I have had clients shout my name down a grocery store aisle or make eye contact, turn around, and quickly walk away. I always follow my client's lead. Although our values may tell us to be nice to all clients in all situations, we must develop the skills necessary to allow our professional values to guide our actions.

If you are practicing in a rural or small town, I can guarantee that this will happen. You may even want to discuss this ahead of time with your clients and let them know how you plan to operate to see if that fits with what the client would like to happen. Oftentimes, how to react to each other in public can be negotiated ahead of time, particularly if you and your clients frequent the same establishments and you have no other options.

Suggested Field Tasks

- Review the related course work and discuss it in supervision.

- In supervision, identify and discuss personal values and distinguish personal and professional values.

- Read the NASW code of ethics and any agency-based code of ethics.

- Read the NASW and ASWB technology standards.

- Discuss ethical principles and standards and any agency-based ethical standards.

- Discuss state and local laws that may govern practice at your agency.

- Identify and discuss common ethical dilemmas in a practice setting.

- Conduct an agency audit regarding ethical practices and discuss this in supervision.

- Identify, analyze, and resolve ethical dilemmas using the NASW code of ethics standards as a guide.

References

Cain, J. (2011). Social media in health care: The case for organizational policy and employee education. *AJHP: Official Journal of the American Society of Health-System Pharmacists, 68*(11), 1036–1040. doi:10.2146/ajhp100589

Congress, E. (1996). *Social work values and ethics.* Chicago, IL: Nelson-Hall.

Congress, E. (2002). Social work ethics for educators: Navigating ethical change in the classroom and in the field. *Journal of Teaching in Social Work, 22*(1/2), 151–166.

Gagnon, K., & Sabus, C. (2015). Professionalism in a digital age: Opportunities and considerations for using social media in health care. *Physical Therapy, 95*(3), 406–414. doi:10.2522/ptj.20130227

Manpower Inc. (2010, January). *Employer perspectives on social networking: Global key findings*. Retrieved March 8, 2018, from https://candidate.manpower.com/wps/wcm/connect/2e3a7f80420bb0d9a9b2eda17e379a88/social_networking_key_findings.pdf?MOD=AJPERES

Mattison, M. (2000). Ethical decision making: The person in the process. *Social Work, 45*(3), 201–212.

National Association of Social Workers (NASW). (1960). *Code of ethics.* Washington, DC: Author. Retrieved March 18, 2018, from https://www.socialworkers.org/About/Ethics/Code-of-Ethics/g/LinkClick.aspx?fileticket=lPpjxmAsCTs%3d&portalid=0

National Association of Social Workers (NASW). (1979). *Code of ethics.* Silver Springs, MD: Author. Retrieved March 25, 2018, from https://www.socialworkers.org/LinkClick.aspx?fileticket=eKQXR46sasc%3d&portalid=0

National Association of Social Workers (NASW). (2017a). *The history of the NASW code of ethics.* Washington, DC: Author. Retrieved March 18, 2018, from https://www.socialworkers.org/About/Ethics/Code-of-Ethics/History

National Association of Social Workers (NASW). (2017b). *Code of ethics of the National Association of Social Workers.* Washington DC: Author. Retrieved March 18, 2018, from https://www.socialworkers.org/About/Ethics/Code-of-Ethics/Code-of-Ethics-English

National Association of Social Workers (NASW), Association of Social Work Boards (ASWB), Council on Social Work Education (CSWE), & Clinical Social Workers Association (CSWA). (2017). *NASW, ASWB, CSWE, & CSWA standards for technology in social work practice.* Washington, DC: Authors. Retrieved March 18, 2018, from https://www.socialworkers.org/LinkClick.aspx?fileticket=lcTcdsHUcng%3D&portalid=0fileticket=lcTcdsHUcng%3d&portalid=0

Reamer, F. (1998). The evolution of social work ethics. *Social Work, 43*(6), 488–500.

Reamer, F. (2000). The social work ethics audit: A risk-management strategy. *Social Work, 45*(4), 355–366.

Reamer, F. (2013a). *Social work values and ethics* (4th ed.). New York, NY: Columbia University.

Reamer, F. (2013b). Social work in the digital age: Ethical and risk management challenges. *Social Work, 58*(2), 163–172; doi:10.1093/sw/swt003

Rothman, J. (2005). *From the front lines: Student cases in social work ethics.* Boston, MA: Pearson Education.

Royse, D., Dhooper, S., & Badger, K. (2018). *Field instruction: A guide for social work students* (7th ed.). Long Grove, IL: Waveland Press.

Weinberg, M., & Campbell, C. (2014). From codes to contextual collaborations: Shifting the thinking about ethics in social work. *Journal of Progressive Human Services, 25*(1), 37–49. doi:10.1080/10428232.2014.856739

DIVERSITY AND SOCIAL, ECONOMIC, AND ENVIRONMENTAL JUSTICE IN FIELD

Developing your understanding of and competence in engaging diversity and advancing social, economic, and environmental justice in field is critical to effective practice and foundational to the generalist practice field education approach. In fact, diversity and social, economic, and environmental justice can permeate many aspects of your field education experience. For instance, you cannot sufficiently know your agency and the services you will be trained to provide and deliver competently without considering them within the context of client system diversity and social, economic, and environmental justice.

With regard to diversity and particularly cultural competence, many years ago, I and several other social workers had the opportunity to have an informal discussion with one of the members of the National Association of Social Workers (NASW) committee that was working on a major revision of the code of ethics and considering adding cultural competence to the standards. I remember a few social work practitioners expressing concern with regard to the move from cultural sensitivity to competence. Even though this discussion was more than two decades ago, it remains relevant today. In the discussion, a few social workers questioned their ability to be truly culturally competent. This is an understandable anxiety for all social workers and reflects the awesome responsibility inherent in the work we do as social workers, particularly in our increasingly diverse world. On the other hand, the same social work practitioners applauded the efforts of the committee and the NASW to advance the expectations for professional social workers to be culturally competent.

In 2001, the NASW developed standards for culturally competent practice. These standards were revised in 2015, and while they maintained a focus on cultural competence, the concepts of "cultural humility as a guiding stance vis-à-vis cultural differences, and intersectionality as a way of understanding the complexities of those at the margins of our society" (NASW, 2015, p. 8) were introduced. Each of these will be explored in more detail, along with the concepts of culture and cultural competence, particularly as they relate to the diversity competency outline by the Council on Social Work Education (CSWE). In the educational policies and accreditation standards (EPAS) put forth by CSWE in 2015, intersectionality was added in Competency 2. This addition signals an understanding of the complexity of diversity and the role that power and position play in both understanding diversity and issues of social, economic, and environmental injustice, thus the focus of this chapter.

Given the expectation of competence in both diversity and advancing social, economic, and environmental justice in field, you are most likely asking yourself, "Okay, so where do I begin?"

This chapter will provide an overview of diversity with specific emphasis on culture and cultural competence. In addition, specific attention will be paid to cultural humility and intersectionality as well as social, economic, and environmental justice. The purpose of this overview is to ground your thinking and to prepare you to apply key aspects of your knowledge, values, and skills to your practice in field. This will be accomplished through your use of the chapter's integrative activities (IAs) and your consideration of the reflection questions.

UNDERSTANDING KEY ASPECTS OF DIVERSITY

Human diversity is vast, and the client systems that you will interact with in field will reflect this vastness. In field, you will encounter clients who come from all ages, economic backgrounds, races, ethnic groups, religions, mental and physical abilities, gender identities, and sexual orientations, to name a few. Thus, it is critical that you develop your understanding of diversity as it relates to the key concepts of culture, cultural competence, cultural humility, and intersectionality. Sheafor and Horejsi (2015) state, "Diversity brings richness to the life experience. A failure to recognize and appreciate the many differences within the human family is a major obstacle in any type of helping and service delivery" (p. 57). According to the EPAS, diversity includes but is not limited to "age, class, color, culture, disability and ability, ethnicity, gender, gender identity and expression, immigration status, marital status, political ideology, race, religion/spirituality, sex, sexual orientation, and tribal sovereign status" (CSWE, 2015, p. 7). Given that culturally competent practice is grounded in an understanding and appreciation of diversity and that demonstration of effective skills is an expected outcome of both social work education and field, it is also helpful to begin by defining culture and cultural competence.

CULTURE

There are many definitions of *culture*. However, the one that provides the best context for the social work student in field says that culture is

> comprised of certain beliefs, values, ideals, customs, standards of right and wrong, symbols and language, and patterns of behavior, all of which are rooted in a people's shared history and experiences. . . . It shapes how they make sense of their experiences and cope with problems and conflicts, both within their own group and with outsiders. (Sheafor & Horejsi, 2015, p. 139)

This definition is helpful in that it places a person's behaviors, beliefs, and values at the center of his or her ability to meet needs or respond to life's challenges, which is often the point at which a social worker interacts with a client system. Thus, this definition encourages the social work student to view the client's culture as being in a dynamic relationship with their experiences and, therefore, must be considered as the social work student attempts to understand the client's needs and assist him or her in meeting those needs. In addition to the beliefs, values, and patterns of behavior that help define culture, Sheafor and Horejsi (2015) conceptualize culture as a "lens through which a people view life" (p. 139). It is important that you realize that all people have a cultural lens and that your exploration of culture and development of culturally competent practice skills begins with considering your own. This is even more important when you consider that all people tend toward *ethnocentrism*, the belief that their culture is correct; thus, self-awareness is recognized as a standard for the development of culturally competent social work practice (NASW, 2015).

What is unique to field is the fact that you will develop and demonstrate competence in engaging diversity and difference in practice in an agency. Thus, considering how that agency reflects and responds to diversity is an important consideration in your development as a social worker. As Miller and Garran (2017) state, with respect to racism and the agencies and organizations in which social workers practice, "None of these sites is immune to the many forms of racism. . . . In fact, health, human service, and educational facilities are likely to emulate the dynamics of racism in society at large" (p. 257). This means that it is important for you to simultaneously reflect on your own and your agency's way of understanding and responding to diversity. You will have an opportunity to do just that in Integrative Activity 8.1 below. But, before you do that, it is necessary to continue to explore the foundational concepts that will aid you in that exploration.

CULTURAL COMPETENCE

The next concept to discuss is cultural competence, what it means to be culturally competent, and how the concepts of cultural humility and intersectionality contribute to this expectation. In the standards and indicators for cultural competence in social work practice (NASW, 2015), the definition put forth draws from the literature and encompasses several key points. First, cultural competence is grounded in the ability of systems and practitioners, by way of behaviors, beliefs, and policies that match the needs of diverse clients, to respond in a respectful and effective manner to diverse client systems with the goal of preserving the client system's dignity and worth. Next, the definition emphasizes the ability of the social worker to transform knowledge in a way that is appropriate, given the culture of the client system. Finally, social workers need to demonstrate insight into the unique needs of diverse clients, with a particular focus on culturally relevant interventions. The challenge that this presents to new and even experienced workers is acknowledged, thus the need to engage in practices that increase the likelihood of the social worker being able to meet these expectations. Ortega and Faller (2011) offer four essential skills necessary for cultural competence, and Garran and Werkmeister Rozas (2013) emphasize self-reflection with a specific focus on identity development and one's position in a sociopolitical hierarchy while considering the constructs of power and privilege. Both of these contributions will be discussed later and offered as ways for you to develop your skills. All of this is grounded in your ethical responsibility to your clients as defined by the NASW (2017) code of ethics. Standard 1.05 Cultural Awareness and Social Diversity states that

(a) Social workers should understand culture and its function in human behavior and society, recognizing the strengths that exist in all cultures.

(b) Social workers should have a knowledge base of their clients' cultures and be able to demonstrate competence in the provision of services that are sensitive to clients' cultures and to differences among people and cultural groups.

(c) Social workers should obtain education about and seek to understand the nature of social diversity and oppression with respect to race, ethnicity, national origin, color, sex, sexual orientation, gender identity or expression, age, marital status, political belief, religion, immigration status, and mental or physical ability.

(d) Social workers who provide electronic social work services should be aware of cultural and socioeconomic difference among clients and how they may use electronic technology. Social workers should assess cultural, environmental, economic, mental or physical ability, linguistic, and other issues that may affect the delivery or use of these services. (pp. 3–4)

The last sub-standard was added in the most recent revision in 2017 to acknowledge the growth in technology-based social work practice and the inherent challenges and inequities experienced by certain diverse populations that can negatively impact their ability to receive services.

This is even more concerning, given that the Federal Communication Commission (FCC) removed the protections of net neutrality, which ensured that broadband providers couldn't block various websites or charge for higher-quality service or certain content and will no longer regulate high-speed Internet delivery. The potential outcome of this action is that there may no longer be a level playing field when it comes to Internet access and what information comes up on searches; thus potentially impacting individuals' access to information.

Cultural Humility and Intersectionality

As mentioned earlier, the concepts of cultural humility and intersectionality were added to the revised version of the standards and indicators for cultural competence in social work practice (NASW, 2015) in order to better enable social workers to meet this ethical standard. In order to appreciate the significance of these additions and what they can bring to your practice in field, each will be explored in more detail. First, within the context of cultural competence, social workers must embrace *humility*, which is defined as "a lifelong commitment to self-evaluation and self-critique, to redressing the power imbalances in the patient–physician dynamic, and to developing mutually beneficial and nonpaternalistic clinical and advocacy partnerships with communities on behalf of individuals and defined populations" (Tervalon & Murray-Garcia, 1998, p. 117). Another way to think about cultural humility is to consider Hook, Davis, Owen, Worthington, and Utsey's (2013) idea that *cultural humility* is defined as having "an interpersonal stance that is other-oriented in relation to another individual's cultural background and experience, marked by respect for and lack of superiority toward another individual's cultural background and experience" (p. 361). This stance implies the ability to demonstrate deference to the complexity of culture and the realization that even with advanced knowledge, values, and skills, we may never truly understand a person; thus, we must always use skills that enable our clients to tell their stories and not presuppose understanding based on specific categories. As Ortega and Faller (2011) state with respect to child welfare workers, "Drawing solely on their own knowledge will not sustain new insights, awareness, and relevant behavioral change" (p. 32). This means that child welfare workers must work to counter an inherent position of knowing and power to really understand their clients. This is best summed up by Hollinsworth's (2013) contention to forget about cultural competence and ask for your client's autobiography. This directive reflects the expectation, set forth by the EPAS, that social workers "present themselves as learners and engage clients and constituencies as experts of their own experience" (CSWE, 2015, p. 7) and is one of the component behaviors that demonstrates competence in engaging diversity and difference in practice.

Second, *intersectionality* is defined as "the critical insight that race, class, gender, sexuality, ethnicity, nation, ability, and age operate not as unitary, mutually exclusive entities, but as reciprocally constructing phenomena that in turn shape complex inequality" (Collins, 2015, p. 2). Intersectionality suggests that even within an understanding of a specific category of diversity, that category is impacted in unique ways by other categories, given that human beings are complex and made up of multiple overlapping identities. Thus, intersectionality is important because by looking through only one lens at a time, the picture is not as clear. It is only through multiple lenses, viewed simultaneously, that the clarity of the picture can be realized. The analogy I use to explain intersectionality is that of going to the eye doctor for an eye test. A standard part of the exam is being offered different lenses, one after the other, and being asked which is better, 1 or 2, 2 or 3, 3 or 4. What intersectionality does is bring the picture of the person into focus but only by way of looking through multiple lenses simultaneously. The contribution of Collins's (1986) work on black feminist thought was that it challenged the idea that all women's experiences were similar and demonstrated the importance of understanding that black women's experiences were significantly different from those of white women. An important concept that Collins (2015) articulates is the role of intersectionality in practice, particularly with regard to practices that address social problem. She states that the real importance of intersectionality is that it "is not simply a field of study to be mastered or an analytical strategy for understanding; rather, intersectionality as critical praxis sheds light on the doing of social justice work" (p. 16). This is important because for Collins (2015), intersectionality is not only about identity but also, particularly as it relates to black feminist thought, about oppression, inequality, and whose voices are heard.

In light of the addition of cultural humility and intersectionality to the lexicon of cultural competence, there is an expectation that social workers' development as culturally competent social workers will require lifelong learning throughout one's career, a learning that, in all likelihood, will never be complete. According to the NASW (2015), "Cultural competence is dynamic and requires frequent learning, unlearning, and relearning about diversity" (p. 25). I love the idea of "learning, unlearning, and relearning," especially as it relates to our own cultural identity. Garran and Werkmeister Rozas (2013) offer social identity theory as a way to have a deeper understanding of cultural competence and describe it as "how we see ourselves in relation to others, as well as the very ways that we position, align, differentiate, and categorize ourselves" (pp. 99–100). We are so ingrained in who we are and how our experiences shape our understanding of the world that it can be difficult to see that what we think and do is just that—what *we* think and do—and, even more important, how that impacts how we experience our clients. The authors go on to challenge students and those involved in field to redefine cultural competence to include notions of power and privilege in relationships, agency policies, and cultural competency trainings.

Hollinsworth (2013) also offers a critique of cultural competence that begins with the realization that it is often grounded in knowledge and attitudes that can result in "racialization, essentialism, and culturalism" (p. 1050). For instance, textbooks that have standalone chapters for specific racial or ethnic groups fail to acknowledge the variation within groups and thus essentialize an entire group. *Essentialism* is defined as

> the belief that categories of people share an inherent and immutable "essence" that is not subject to context or historical change. Essentialism ignores or denies the fluid and relational aspects of identities and cultures and typically fails to recognize similarities, parallels and commonalities between cultural identities. (p. 1051)

Hollinsworth (2013) goes on to say that this essentializing is even more concerning when it is considered within the context of the dominate culture, because often individuals from the dominant culture do not see their cultural backgrounds as guiding their decisions and thoughts and instead consider autonomy or rational choices to be guiding them and, even more concerning, may base their decisions and thoughts on "superior knowledge" or "universal truths." This is in stark contrast to the belief that culture is often all-encompassing for the other and is often used to criticize their actions, which Hollinsworth calls *culturalism*. This critique is very helpful as you enter field and begin to practice, given that the status of student and the novelty of practicing will enable you to see yourself, your clients, and agency policies and practices through fresh eyes. This unique role will also enable you to see your clients through the eyes of your field instructor, coworkers, and agency, which can illuminate the challenges that diverse clients may experience as they access services.

Now that you have had a chance to review the key aspects of diversity and the critiques of cultural competence, the first step is to reflect on your understanding of diversity from a multilevel perspective. The reflection will allow you to first consider who you are and, as discussed in Chapter 2, what role your field setting will play in your development of competence in engaging diversity and difference. Thus, similar to how you conducted an ethics audit of your agency prior to developing your competence in ethical decision making and resolving an ethical dilemma, you will want to consider diversity at the agency level. The standards for cultural competence in social work practice identify five elements that must be present for a system to be culturally competent; they are as follows: "(1) value diversity, (2) have the capacity for cultural self-awareness, (3) be conscious of the dynamics inherent when cultures interact, (4) institution-alize cultural knowledge, and (5) develop programs and services that reflect an understanding of diversity between and within cultures" (NASW, 2015, p. 14). When you are reflecting on your agency, make sure to consider these five elements. This reflection will include consider-ation of societal issues and structures as they relate to diversity. This focus acknowledges Gar-ran and Werkmeister Rozas's (2013) contention that intersectionality and discussions of power and privilege "expand the normally one-dimensional and static construction of an individual's identity by acknowledging the larger social structural forces that help shape it" (p. 101). As you complete Integrative Activity 8.1, consider all of the above and discuss your thoughts in class or in your field supervision sessions.

INTEGRATIVE ACTIVITY 8.1

UNDERSTANDING DIVERSITY IN FIELD: A MULTILEVEL APPROACH

Purpose: The purpose of this activity is to develop your understanding of diversity using a multilevel approach that involves both reflection and building experience.

Directions: For each area, explore the prompt state-ments and answer any questions; then discuss the activity in class or in supervision with your field instruc-tor. Then engage in any identified experiential activities.

Competency 2: Engage Diversity and Difference in Practice

- apply and communicate understanding of the importance of diversity and difference in shaping life experiences in practice at the micro, mezzo, and macro levels

- apply self-awareness and self-regulation to manage the influence of personal biases and values in working with diverse clients and constituencies

Individual and Family Level

1. Identify and reflect on the diverse categories that define you, taking into account social identity theory and intersectionality. In what ways is your cultural identity similar to and different from your family of origin and others who may identify in similar categories as you?

2. How would you describe your comfort level and personal experience with diversity? That is, consider the amount of experience you have had with diverse population groups and your comfort level when interacting with diverse population groups.

3. Identify your experiences with diverse populations. Develop a plan for increasing your exposure by attending cultural activities or interviewing individuals who represent diverse population groups, to name a few ideas.

Agency Level

1. Identify the diverse clients, including multiple and overlapping categories, served by your agency.

2. Explore the agency's policies, procedures, and practices from the standpoint of cultural competence. Consider the physical environment of the agency, diversity of staff, mission, policies and procedures, access to services, assessment tools used by the agency, models and theories used, cultural competence trainings, and availability of resources/referrals to address the needs of clients.

Community/Societal Level

1. Identify issues, strengths, and struggles at the community level that may or may not be impacting the diverse clients with whom you work.

2. Identify issues at the societal level, including social problems, policies, politics, and trends that may or may not be impacting the diverse clients with whom you work.

REFLECTION QUESTION 8.1

As you think about the definition of culture and the metaphor of culture as a lens through which an individual views the world and intersectionality explained via the eye test metaphor, what is your cultural lens?

How do you see the world? What has impacted and currently impacts your view? How do you see the problems your client systems are experiencing? How do you view helping and the helping process?

ROOM TO REFLECT

DEVELOPING CULTURALLY COMPETENT PRACTICE SKILLS

Now that you have had a chance to consider the elements that are important in your understanding of diversity from a multilevel perspective, the next step is to put that understanding into practice in field and develop and demonstrate culturally competent practice skills. According to Harper and Lantz (1996), the ability to be effective in what they term *cross-cultural practice* "depends upon the worker's ability to accept and respect human differences as well as accept and respect human similarities" (p. 3). They go on to say that a "social worker who is competent in cross-cultural practice moves beyond assessing cultural differences and develops awareness of the processes people use in meeting needs and solving problems" (p. 4). In addition, Rothman (2008) states that the commitment to cultural competence is a challenge for each worker in that it is a "commitment to personal awareness, to personal growth, to understanding, and to unlearning (as possible) any biases, stereotypes, or prejudices that may interfere with the worker's ability to assist the client toward culturally appropriate personal goals" (p. 15). A concept that is useful in the process of translating your understanding of diversity and cultural competence into culturally competent practice is to first conceptualize the worldview of your client system. This is supported by Ortega and Faller's (2011) idea of bridging perspectives and the idea that both the client and the social worker come to helping with their own history and experiences and thus view "the encounter through his or her own lens or worldview" (p. 37).

According to Coggins and Hatchett (2002), *worldview* refers to a variety of concepts that shape how people perceive their relationship to the natural environment, objects, institutions, and people. They go on to say that this worldview impacts people's beliefs, behavior, and expectations. The ability to gain an understanding of a client's worldview is critically important and grounded in many of the competencies necessary for effective practice. Examples include the ability to effectively communicate verbally and nonverbally with a client, the ability to use culturally competent assessment tools that consider the types of questions needed to elicit an understanding of the client's culture, and the ability to use intervention strategies that are culturally competent and sanctioned as such by the client.

Many models have been developed to assist the social worker in learning cultural competence skills; one such model is the *reciprocal exploration model* (Coggins & Hatchett, 2002). Coggins and Hatchett describe the model as "an approach to information gathering that has been adapted from a long established style of gaining cultural knowledge among and between different Native American groups" (p. 136). The model is grounded in the idea that it is important to engage in a process of understanding cultural differences, a tradition for thousands of years among Native Americans, where the sharing of information focuses on what is common among the participants as well as what is different. The conversation or exploration is grounded in "genuine interest and a nonjudgmental attitude on the part of participants in the discussion" (p. 136). In the context of the social worker–client relationship, through the process of sharing information about the situation at hand, the social worker and client "build a more solid understanding of the cultural values, beliefs, and problem-solving practices of each other's cultures" (p. 136). It is important to note that for the reciprocal model to work, the worker must be clear on his or her own culturally based beliefs, practices, and expectations for behavior. The idea of this model builds nicely on the development of your understanding of diversity from a multilevel perspective, which was the result of Integrative Activity 8.1.

Another tool that you can use to develop your cultural competence in field is Devore and Schlesinger's (1999) ethnic-sensitive generalist practice model, which identifies seven layers of understanding determined to support ethnic-sensitive practice. The seven layers are

1. social work values,

2. a basic knowledge of human behavior,

3. knowledge of and skill in using social welfare policies and agency policy that determines what services can be offered,

4. self-awareness, including awareness of one's own ethnicity and an understanding of how it may influence professional practice,

5. the impact of the ethnic reality upon the daily life of clients,

6. an understanding that the route taken to the social worker has considerable impact on the manner in which social services will be perceived and delivered, and

7. adaptation and modification of skills techniques in response to the ethnic reality (p. 93).

This perspective is particularly useful in field because it provides a comprehensive and integrated approach to assist you in developing your cultural competence and is grounded in generalist practice. Each layer emphasizes a core aspect of generalist social work practice, such as the values and roles of the profession, understanding of human behavior, and knowledge of social welfare policies and services with specific emphasis on the agency and the need to "become aware of the ways in which the organization may constrain as well as facilitate effective practice" (Devore & Schlesinger, 1999, p. 99). In addition, the perspective places emphasis on self-awareness of the worker's own ethnicity and how that might impact practice. But the two layers from Devore and Schlesinger's ethnic-sensitive generalist practice model that are particularly important to consider as you work toward being culturally competent in field are the impact of the ethnic reality of the client and the route the client has taken to become a client. According to Devore and Schlesinger, one's ethnic reality results in identifiable behaviors and dispositions that are the result of

(1) a group's cultural values as embodied in its history, rituals, and religion; (2) a group's migration experience or other processes through which the encounter with mainstream culture took place; and (3) the way a group organizes its family system. (p. 55)

A client's ethnic reality will impact many facets of his or her life, which may be related to the problem(s) the client is seeking assistance for, such as parenting, homelessness, and addiction. Similarly, it is important to consider how the client became a client and reflect on the fact that clients come to the attention of agency services and social workers in many ways along a continuum of voluntary to mandated, and regardless of the route, it is important for the social worker to elicit the client's understanding of the problem.

The last layer offered by Devore and Schlesinger (1999) is to adapt and modify what you do to assist your client: "Intervention must be reviewed, reconsidered, adapted, and modified in relation to the ethnic reality" (p. 169). When you are working with a client system, gaining a sense of the client's ethnic reality will be critical to understanding the problem and how to adapt the interventions that are offered by your agency. In Chapter 10, we will explore how to integrate cultural competence into the planned change process.

But first, it is necessary to gain experience in gathering and reflecting on the preceding information from the point of view of a client. To do this, complete Integrative Activity 8.2. Gather information on a client and reflect on that information particularly in the context of developing your understanding of the client's worldview and ethnic reality as well as how the client defines him or herself. Then, reflect on how the client became a client and the impact the agency's policies, particularly with regard to the possible services available to the client, may have on what you can do for your client. For the purposes of this IA and connecting cultural competence to the expectation of engaging diversity and difference, *diversity*, as a term, will refer to all possible categories that a client may use to identify who they are as a person. In order to be able to benefit fully from this IA, it is necessary to explore some specific skills that you can utilize in your interview in order to gather the information necessary to apply the

INTEGRATIVE ACTIVITY 8.2
DEVELOPING CULTURALLY COMPETENT PRACTICE SKILLS IN FIELD

Purpose: The purpose of this activity is to develop culturally competent practice skills through a process of gathering information on a client and reflecting on that information in the context of the services you hope to provide.

Directions: Select a client with whom you can gather the following information (using the skills identified above) and reflect on the information gathered. Following your reflection, consider and discuss in class or with your field instructor the impact this information may have on the services you hope to offer.

Competency: 2 Engage Diversity and Difference in Practice

- apply and communicate understanding of the importance of diversity and difference in shaping life experiences in practice at the micro, mezzo, and macro levels

- present themselves as learners and engage clients and constituencies as experts of their own experiences

- apply self-awareness and self-regulation to manage the influence of personal biases and values in working with diverse clients and constituencies

1. Identify a specific client with whom you are currently working. It is best to be specific and client centered. Describe the client in terms of his or her diversity; make sure to list all of the identities that could be used to describe the client, thus employing multiculturalism and intersectionality. What is the client's story? How does the client describe him or herself? Is this description similar or different from how you would describe him or her?

2. What is the client's worldview? How does the client see the world, and specifically, how does the client see his or her problem, the helping process, and the agency within a large system of services?

3. What is the client's "ethnic reality," that is, the impact his or her diversity is having on his or her situation and worldview?

4. How did the client become a client and what, if any, role did his or her diversity (name all aspects of diversity that apply) play in he or she becoming a client?

5. What are any issues related to agency policies and service constraints that need to be considered as you reflect on what you feel the client needs? How would you go about addressing those needs?

6. What are any biases or judgments that you hold that might impact how you work with your client and that might impact your ability to understand his or her worldview and needs?

Note: This IA is grounded in Devore and Schlesinger's (1999) ethnic-sensitive generalist practice perspective.

ethnic-sensitive generalist practice model. Five skills from a review of the literature that are helpful to employ are

1. listening and specifically listening to the client's story using interpreters when indicated (Hollinsworth, 2013; NASW, 2015; Ortega & Faller, 2011),

2. demonstrating openness and curiosity to the complexity of people using an other-oriented stance (Hook et al., 2013; NASW, 2015; Ortega & Faller, 2011),

3. moving from a knowing to a learning perspective and developing comfort in not knowing (Hollinsworth, 2013; NASW, 2015),

4. demonstrating a client-centered versus category-centered perspective on diversity that incorporates the impact of systems of oppression and power and privilege (NASW, 2015; Tervalon & Murray-Garcia, 1998), and

5. continuous self-reflection and self-awareness grounded in a nonjudgmental stance (Garran & Werkmeister Rozas, 2013; NASW, 2015; Ortega & Faller, 2011; Tervalon & Murray-Garcia, 1998).

UNDERSTANDING SOCIAL, ECONOMIC, AND ENVIRONMENTAL JUSTICE IN FIELD

The concepts of social diversity and the impact of oppression identified in Standard 1.05 (c) of the NASW code of ethics link diversity to social and economic injustice. In addition, the NASW standard for culturally competent practice identifies "empowerment and advocacy" as one of the 10 standards (NASW, 2015, p. 35). The interpretation of the standard states that culturally competent social workers

> should be aware of and take action to confront and change the deleterious effects of bias, fears, and isms . . . and other forms of oppression on client's lives. Social advocacy and social action should be directed at empowering marginalized clients and strengthening communities. (pp. 35–36)

This link is best understood in the context of the negative effects that people can experience in society solely based on their membership in a group determined by the majority to be the "other"; these people often lack sociopolitical power. Membership as the "other" is often determined by affiliation with distinct and overlapping categories of gender, race, ethnicity, creed, age, sexual orientation, socioeconomic status, and ability, to name a few categories. People who represent certain groups within the distinct and overlapping categories listed above often experience societal -*isms*, such as racism, elitism, classism, sexism, heterosexism, ageism, and ableism, as a result of their particular categorization. According to DuBois and Miley (2014),

> Societal *isms* are the prejudicial attitudes directed against groups that society identifies as "lesser"—less capable, less productive, and less normal. The *isms* provide rationalization for stratified social structures that provide fewer prospects—fewer opportunities, fewer possibilities, and fewer resources—for those with lower status. Stratified structural arrangements perpetuate exploitation and dominance of some segments of society by others. Some groups of people have access to power, prestige, and resources, and others do not. (p. 137)

In field, you want to become aware first of the diversity of your clients and second of the -*isms* that your clients may be experiencing. By doing so, you are developing your understanding of the social injustices that may be directly or indirectly impacting your clients. You will want to develop ways to challenge social, economic, and environmental injustice in your practice in field. As Cordero and Rodriguez (2009) state,

In short, the development of cultural competency is a journey of cross-cultural learning through the development of critical self-consciousness, an appreciation and respect for difference, understanding the sociopolitical context in which cross-cultural interactions take place and a commitment to advocacy for social justice. (p. 137)

Social justice is one of the core values of the profession of social work, and the NASW (2017) code of ethics defines the broad ethical principle based on this value:

Social workers challenge social injustice.

Social workers pursue social change, particularly with and on behalf of vulnerable and oppressed individuals and groups of people. Social workers' social change efforts are focused primarily on issues of poverty, unemployment, discrimination, and other forms of social injustice. These activities seek to promote sensitivity to and knowledge about oppression and cultural and ethnic diversity. Social workers strive to ensure access to needed information, services and resources; equality of opportunity; and meaningful participation in decision making for all people. (pp. 1–2)

The NASW (2017) code of ethics goes on further to identify "social workers' ethical responsibilities to the broader society" in the following standards:*

6.01 Social Welfare
Social workers should promote the general welfare of society, from local to global levels, and the development of people, their communities, and their environments. Social workers should advocate for living conditions conducive to the fulfillment of basic human needs and should promote social, economic, political, and cultural values and institutions that are compatible with the realization of social justice. (p. 18)
6.04 Social and Political Action
(a) Social workers should engage in social and political action that seeks to ensure that all people have equal access to the resources, employment, services, and opportunities they require to meet their basic human needs and to develop fully. Social workers should be aware of the impact of the political arena on practice and should advocate for changes in policy and legislation to improve social conditions in order to meet basic human needs and promote social justice.
(b) Social workers should act to expand choice and opportunity for all people, with special regard for vulnerable, disadvantaged, oppressed, and exploited people and groups.
(c) Social workers should promote conditions that encourage respect for cultural and social diversity within the United States and globally. Social workers should promote policies and practice that demonstrate respect for difference, support expansion of cultural knowledge and resources, advocate for programs and institutions that demonstrate cultural competence, and promote policies that safeguard the rights of and confirm equity and social justice for all people.
(d) Social workers should act to prevent and eliminate domination of, exploitation of, and discrimination against any person, group, or class on the basis of race, ethnicity, national origin, color, sex, sexual orientation, gender identity or expression, age, marital status, political belief, religion, immigration status, or mental or physical ability. (pp. 18–19)

Barker (2003) defines *social justice* as "an ideal condition in which all members of a society have the same basic rights, protection, opportunities, obligations, and social benefits" (pp. 404–405). As a student in field, it is very likely that you will witness instances of social injustice, which are

---

* Reprinted with permission of the National Association of Social Workers Press, 750 First Street, N.E. Suite 800 Washington, DC 20002-4241, USA. NASW Code of Ethics. No use or content can be made without written consent of the NASW Press

evident when a society denies certain population groups civil rights by excluding them from full participation in decision making, when it distributes institutional resources in deference to privilege and power, or when its members show prejudicial attitudes and discriminatory actions toward each other. (Miley, O'Melia, & Dubois, 2011, p.7)

Advancing human rights and social, economic, and environmental justice—a competency identified by CSWE (2015)—can be challenging for a variety of reasons. First, in the current societal and political environment, the views of the role of government and social welfare programs are polarized around those arguing for smaller government, lower taxes, and less funding of social welfare programs and those arguing for what they see as government's necessary role in promoting the social well-being of its members, particularly in the areas of health care, food, and affordable housing. Second, society is unable to effectively eradicate social systems and structures that directly discriminate and oppress various groups, as seen in the fact that women continue to be paid less than men for the same job and that rampant reports of sexual harassment in the work place can cripple a person's ability to be successful. Third, it is important to note that in 2015, the CSWE EPAS added environmental justice to acknowledge the significant number of people who are already negatively impacted by other forms of injustice and are also disproportionately impacted by environmental hazards (Jarvis, 2013). Fourth, there is often a lack of focus on social action and advocacy taken by agencies in their service delivery. Blundo (2010) advocates that students "learn to understand the complexity and unique ways social justice is a part of their practice and the lives of their clients" (p. 99). This expectation for students' competence in advancing social, economic, and environmental justice through social action is challenging to meet, given the overwhelming emphasis on clinical practice with individuals, families, and groups in social work, most likely fueled by students' interests. Lane and colleagues (2012) state that social work educators "have an obligation to show students the relevance and importance of social justice and teach them the strategies and skills to create change" (p. 532). Thus, when you are working with your clients in field, you want to first develop the skills necessary to identify instances of social, economic, and environmental injustice and second, identify ways in which you can intervene and advocate to redress issues of injustice. With regard to human rights and human rights practice, Steen and colleagues (2017) surveyed students and supervisors in field and found that respondents reported that they encountered issues of human rights related to poverty, discrimination, self-determination, violence, and dignity and identified advocacy as one of ways to promote human rights practice.

A first step in meeting the above expectation is to consider Integrative Activity 8.3 and to discuss your reflection in class or in supervision with your field instructor.

INTEGRATIVE ACTIVITY 8.3
IDENTIFYING SOCIAL, ECONOMIC, AND ENVIRONMENTAL INJUSTICE IN FIELD

Purpose: The purpose of this activity is to help you identify specific instances of social, economic, and environmental injustice impacting the clients with whom you work and to help you consider strategies for practices that advance social and economic justice.

Directions: Consider the following areas and discuss your thoughts in class or in supervision with your field instructor.

Competency 3: Advance Human Rights and Social, Economic, and Environmental Justice

- apply their understanding of social, economic, and environmental justice to advocate for human rights at the individual and system levels

- engage in practices that advance social, economic, and environmental justice

(Continued)

(Continued)

1. Select a client with whom you are working and identify specific instances of social, economic, and environmental injustice that are impacting them.

   and environmental injustice, what specific strategies might you engage in to address the instances of social, economic, and environmental injustice experienced by your client?

2. How are the instances of social, economic, and environmental injustice experienced by your client impacting the problem(s) they are having as well as the options for addressing those problems?

4. If your agency does not provide specific services that target social, economic, and environmental injustice, what specific strategies might you engage in to assist your client?

3. If your agency provides specific services that directly target issues of social, economic,

REFLECTION QUESTION 8.2

As you think about the clients you work with, what –*isms* do you think they experience and how do these –*isms* impact the problems they are experiencing and their ability to address these problems? What specific issues of social, economic, and environmental injustice are impacting your clients? How might you begin to address these issues?

ROOM TO REFLECT

ADVANCING SOCIAL, ECONOMIC, AND ENVIRONMENTAL JUSTICE IN FIELD

Although identifying instances of social, economic, and environmental injustice is an important first step in developing your understanding of the role that social, economic, and environmental justice will play in your practice, it is equally important to intervene to advance social, economic, and environmental justice. Interventions that target social, economic, and environmental injustice or advance social, economic, and environmental justice can happen at the individual, family, group, organization, community, and societal levels. In fact, it is important to identify all the ways in which you can address the issues of injustice that may be impacting your client's ability to meet his or her goals and needs and to realize that interventions that target various types of injustice occur at all levels of practice, not only at the macro or larger system level. The reason this is important is because only viewing interventions that address social, economic, and environmental injustice at the macro level perpetuates what Miley and colleagues (2011) identify as the division of the social work profession into two mutually exclusive practice areas, one focusing on individual or micro practice and the other on larger system or macro practice. It is critically important to develop the skills necessary to identify all forms of injustice that may be impacting clients and to target interventions at all levels of service, thus taking an inherent generalist approach.

Advocacy and Policy Practice

Two practice interventions that cut across all system levels and are effective when advancing social justice are advocacy and policy practice. The foundational professional role of advocacy was discussed in Chapter 3, and you were encouraged to identify (1) how your agency uses the role of advocacy and (2) opportunities for you to engage in advocacy with client systems. You want to consider how to use advocacy when addressing issues of injustice. Sheafor and Horejsi (2015) identify two activities a social worker might engage in as they use the role of advocacy; they are client or case advocacy and class advocacy.

Client or case advocacy is used to ensure that the client is receiving the service to which they are entitled. An example of this might be the student who accompanies a client to the social security administration office to assist the client in the application process for social security disability benefits. Class advocacy is when a social worker is serving a group of clients or a segment of the population with the goal of removing obstacles or barriers to receiving rights or services. These efforts might take the form of building a coalition of concerned citizens or organizations to effect change at the societal level. For instance, a student might become a member of a coalition of organizations that advocate for the development of affordable housing units within a neighborhood that is experiencing gentrification. Class advocacy can also involve the next intervention, which is policy practice.

Policy practice can be extremely effective in addressing issues of social, economic, and environmental injustice. Figueira-McDonough (1993) states that "progress toward social justice requires direct involvement in the formation and modification of social policy" (p. 180). Yet, the ability of social workers to directly intervene in matters of policy development can be challenging, and in fact, policy decisions that impact your clients in field are often made by those who lack a full understanding of those impacted and their unique circumstances.

The first step in developing your skills for policy practice in field is to conduct a policy analysis. Policy can be thought of in two ways: agency-based policies and social policies. During your orientation, you were asked to become proficient with regard to your agency's policies. Now you will want to consider how those policies serve your clients and reflect local, state, or federal policies directly or indirectly.

The next step is to identify opportunities for policy practice to address issues of social injustice or to advance social justice that may be available to you in your field agency. Students can engage in a variety of tasks that target policy development, such as supporting new legislation or working to ensure the continuation of current legislation.

As you consider your efforts to address all forms of injustice experienced by the client systems you work with in field, it is critical that you develop the ability to (1) identify instances of injustice that are impacting your client system and (2) consider all possible interventions that target individuals, families, groups, organizations, communities, and society through the use of advocacy and policy practice. This can be accomplished by engaging in Integrative Activity 8.4. This IA will enable you to increase your understanding of how the policies of your agency impact your clients as well as the impact of local, state, and federal policies on the policies and services offered to clients to address their problems. Finally, this activity will assist you in identifying ways to engage policy practice at your field site and thus demonstrate competence in this important area of social work practice.

INTEGRATIVE ACTIVITY 8.4
POLICY ANALYSIS AND PRACTICE

Purpose: The purpose of this activity is to guide you in (1) conducting an analysis of an agency policy within the context of state or federal policy in order to better understand the link between policy and practice and (2) identifying opportunities for policy practice in your field agency. Both of these will contribute to the development of competence in policy analysis and practice.

Directions: Address each of the following areas by providing a brief description of the requested information, and discuss your findings in supervision with your field instructor.

Competency 5: Engage in Policy Practice

- identify social policy at the local, state, and federal level that impacts well-being, service delivery, and access to social services

- assess how social welfare and economic policies impact the delivery of and access to social services

- apply critical thinking to analyze, formulate, and advocate for policies that advance human rights and social, economic, and environmental justice

1. Identify and explain an agency policy that directly impacts your clients and is grounded in or reflects a state or federal policy (attach a copy of the policy).

2. Identify the state and or federal policy that relates to the agency policy identified in Question 1 (include the name and number of the policy).

3. Explain the history and basic tenets of the state or federal policy.

4. Explain how the state or federal policy led to the agency policy or how the agency policy reflects the state or federal policy.

5. Identify a specific client system and explain how the policy impacts your client system and your agency (be specific and use examples).

6. Analyze the agency policy in general and state whether or not it serves your client system and supports your work.

7. What changes would you recommend to the policy?

8. What would you do to engage in policy practice and enact your recommended changes?

9. What are the specific opportunity(ies) for policy practice at your agency? (This could involve the development of new policy or efforts to maintain current policy both at the agency level and state or federal level.)

10. Identify any specific policy needs of your agency or client systems and how you would address them through policy practice.

REFLECTION QUESTION 8.3

Now that you have had an opportunity to analyze a policy and consider both advocacy and policy practice to address social and economic injustice, what do you see as the key issues of social, economic, and environmental justice in your practice in field and in the lives of the client systems with which you work? What specifically can you do in your agency to address issues of social, economic, or environmental injustice and advance social and economic justice?

ROOM TO REFLECT

Suggested Field Tasks

- Attend agency-based, community, or campus diversity trainings and events.

- Present and analyze client system information through the lens of diversity and social, economic, and environmental justice.

- Review related course work on diversity and social, economic, and environmental justice.

- Identify diversity at the agency and client system levels.

- Increase your knowledge of diverse population(s) served by the agency.

- Identify value-based issues related to diversity.

- Review the standards of cultural competence as set forth by NASW.

- Identify how the agency trains workers in cultural competence.

- Develop and practice cultural competence skills.

- Design and implement cultural competence practice interventions.

- Identify and discuss issues of oppression and discrimination that directly impact clients in the agency at all levels.

- Analyze agency and larger-system policies to determine their impact on client systems.

- Identify how advocacy is used at the placement site to advance social, economic, and environmental justice.

- Design and implement interventions that target advocacy to address oppression and discrimination and issues of human rights and social, economic, and environmental justice.

References

Barker, R. L. (2003). *The social work dictionary* (4th ed.). Washington, DC: NASW Press.

Blundo, R. R. (2010). Social justice becomes a living experience for students, faculty, and community. *Journal of Teaching in Social Work, 30*(1), 90–100.

Coggins, K., & Hatchett, B. (2002). *Field practicum: Skill building from a multicultural perspective*. Peosta, IA: Eddie Bowers.

Collins, P. H. (1986). Learning from the outsider within: The sociological significance of Black feminist thought. *Social Problems, 33*(6), S14–S32. Retrieved March 19, 2018, from http://users.clas.ufl.edu/marilynm/Theorizing_Black_America_Syllabus_files/Learning_from_the_Outsider_Within.pdf

Collins, P. H. (2015). Intersectionality's definitional dilemmas. *Annual Review of Sociology, 41*, 1–20.

Cordero, A., & Rodriguez, L. (2009). Fostering cross-cultural learning and advocacy for social justice through an immersion experience in Puerto Rico. *Journal of Teaching in Social Work, 29*(2), 134–152.

Council on Social Work Education (CSWE). (2015). *Educational policy and accreditation standards*. Alexandria, VA: Author.

Devore, W., & Schlesinger, E. (1999). *Ethnic-sensitive social work practice* (5th ed.). Boston, MA: Allyn and Bacon.

DuBois, B., & Miley, K. (2014). *Social work: An empowering profession* (8th ed.). Boston, MA: Pearson Education.

Figueira-McDonough, J. (1993). Policy practice: The neglected side of social work intervention. *Social Work, 38*(2), 179–188.

Garran, A. M., & Werkmeister Rozas, L. (2013). Cultural competence revisited. *Journal of Ethnic & Cultural Diversity in Social Work, 22*(2), 97–111. doi:10.1080/15313204.2013.785337

Harper, K., & Lantz, J. (1996). *Cross-cultural practice: Social work with diverse populations.* Chicago, IL: Lyceum Books.

Hollinsworth, D. (2013). Forget cultural competence; ask for an autobiography. *Social Work Education, 32*(8), 1048–1060. doi:10.1080/02615479.2012.730513

Hook, J. N., Davis, D. E., Owen, J., Worthington, E. J., & Utsey, S. O. (2013). Cultural humility: Measuring openness to culturally diverse clients. *Journal of Counseling Psychology, 60*(3), 353–366.

Jarvis, D. (2013). Environmental justice and social work: A call to expand the social work profession to include environmental justice. *Columbia University School of Social Work*, 436–445.

Lane, S., Altman, J., Goldberg, G., Kagotho, N., Palley, E., & Paul, M. (2012). Inspiring and training students for social action: Renewing a needed tradition. *Journal of Teaching in Social Work, 32*(5), 532–549.

Miley, K., O'Melia, M., & DuBois, B. (2011). *Generalist social work practice: An empowering approach* (6th ed.). Boston, MA: Allyn and Bacon.

Miller, J., & Garran, A. (2017). *Racism in the United States: Implications for the helping professions.* New York, NY: Springer.

National Association of Social Workers (NASW). (2015). *National standards for cultural competence in social work practice.* Washington, DC: Author.

National Association of Social Workers (NASW). (2017). *Code of ethics.* Retrieved March 19, 2018, from https://www.socialworkers.org/About/Ethics/Code-of-Ethics

Ortega, R. M., & Faller, K. C. (2011). Training child welfare workers from an intersectional cultural humility perspective: A paradigm shift. *Child Welfare, 90*(5), 27–49.

Rothman, J. (2008). *Cultural competence in process and practice building bridges.* Boston, MA: Allyn and Bacon.

Sheafor, B., & Horejsi, C. (2015). *Techniques and guidelines for social work practice* (10th ed.). Boston, MA: Pearson Education.

Steen, J. J., Mann, M., Restivo, N., Mazany, S., & Chapple, R. (2017). Human rights: Its meaning and practice in social work field settings. *Social Work, 62*(1), 9–17.

Tervalon, M., & Murray-Garcia, J. (1998). Cultural humility versus cultural competence: A critical distinction in defining physician training outcomes in multicultural education. *Journal of Health Care for the Poor and Underserved, 9*(2), 117–125.

CRITICAL THINKING IN FIELD

Critical thinking is at the heart of liberal arts education, is foundational to social work education and practice, and is identified as an important element of the generalist practice field education approach outlined in Chapter 1. According to Gambrill (2013),

> Critical thinking encourages us to reflect on how we think and why we hold certain beliefs. It requires an acceptance of well-reasoned conclusions, even when they are not our preferred ones. Critical thinkers question what others take for granted. They challenge accepted beliefs and ways of acting. (p. 111)

Although critical thinking was dropped as a standalone competence in the 2015 version of the educational policies and accreditation standards (EPAS), it is still recognized as a foundational aspect of competent practice. According to the Council on Social Work Education (2015), competence is recognized as holistic, "that is, the demonstration of competence is informed by knowledge, values, skills, and cognitive and affective processes that include the social worker's critical thinking, affective reactions, and exercise of judgment in regard to unique practice situations" (p. 6). Mathias (2015) set out to answer the question of how social workers should think by exploring the literature on critical thinking to determine what social work scholars identify as important. The findings indicated a definition that focuses on correct action of the practitioner and illuminated two predominate orientations for critical thinking from the literature, one that focuses on scientific reasoning and the other that considers values. Mathias (2015) states that the

> contrast between scientific reasoning and social constructionist versions of critical thinking is clearly linked to debates about the role of science in social work and the relation between research and social work practice, but it should not be conflated with those debates. Although the latter have been concerned primarily with the epistemological foundations of theoretical reasoning in social work—that is, how we know what is—the focus of the critical thinking literature is on how we know what we ought to do. These concerns are certainly not unrelated, but the relation between them should itself be a topic for discussion. (p. 470)

Critical thinking is the ability to analyze information, make a determination about a situation, and engage in problem solving. Critical thinking is an important skill for being able to practice effectively in field and learn from your practice experiences. Several activities will develop your critical-thinking skills:

1. developing knowledge, values, and skill through coursework

2. observing practice tasks in field

3. writing reflection journals

4. discussing practice tasks in supervision

5. linking course work and academic assignments with practice experiences of field

6. consulting with peers in field and in the classroom

7. engaging in focused task analysis

Many of the preceding activities have already been discussed in previous chapters. This chapter will focus specifically on task analysis and linking course work with the practice tasks of field and will provide an overview of evidenced-based practice.

TASK ANALYSIS

Critical thinking is linked with experiential learning (Gibbons & Gray, 2004), provides the foundation for your learning in field, and is distinct from training. With regard to experiential learning, Kolb and Kolb (2005) state that is not sufficient for students to only have experiences; those experiences have to be transformed through reflection and analysis. Chapter 2 discussed your training and identified it as an essential part of orientation. However, being trained to complete a task is only one part of learning in field. In fact, Rogers (1995) advocates for a paradigm shift in field from training to learning and states,

> Requiring students to simply engage in the experience of the practicum is not enough for quality learning to be realized. To transform *doing*, that is, the acts or skills of practice, into learning, that is, the understanding and critique of the accumulated experiences, requires a process of dialogue and reflection. This is the paradigm that quality field education encompasses. (pp. 529–530)

This paradigm shift advocated by Rogers (1995) is best exemplified by an experience a student shared in a seminar class. This particular student was working at a neighborhood-based social service agency that provided a variety of services. The primary work the student was engaged in was running the youth program. One day, the student arrived at field and learned that the agency was to be audited the next day and the computers were down. Everyone in the agency was hand-counting intake information to include in the report. The student was asked to assist and was trained on how to count the data and tally the results on the data sheets. At first, the student reported being irritated by having to conduct such a mundane task and being pulled away from her normal tasks. But then the student reported that as she was counting each client served and placing hash marks in the various demographic area boxes, she began to realize that each hash mark represented a person who had sought out the services of the agency.

She began to focus on whom these hash marks represented and noticed that the majority were African American males between the ages of 18 and 24. She reflected on this data and developed several questions. Why were there so many clients in this demographic group? What were the particular needs of this demographic group? Was the agency adequately serving this group? And last, was there anything the agency could do to reduce the needs of this demographic group? The student took her observation and questions to her next supervision session and engaged in a focused discussion targeting this demographic group. As a result, the agency began to focus on this demographic group and provide services that targeted their specific needs. The student reported that what had started out as a mundane and bothersome task became an excellent learning experience and one that was grounded in critical thinking. This experience exemplifies the need for students to differentiate between learning and simply performing a task. This is not to say that every task or experience you engage in while in field will result in significant learning, but it is important to lay the foundation such that you will be able to discern the tasks that can provide excellent learning and engage in a process that will increase your ability to elicit learning from a task.

To assist you in the process of meeting the goal of learning versus doing, see Integrative Activity 9.1. Engaging in this activity while in field will provide you with an opportunity to develop, demonstrate, and use your critical-thinking skills so that you can learn from your practice experiences. The activity identifies several steps to follow to analyze a task. Each step offers suggested activities or questions to consider as well as an identified goal.

As you can see, the first step is to identify a task to analyze. This involves three activities: first, select a task; then, set the stage—that is, provide the necessary background; and finally, based on your observations, share any and all information that will be helpful in the analysis. When conducting the task analysis in supervision, these three activities are particularly important for two reasons. First of all, it is helpful for your field instructor to gain a sense of the task from your perspective and for you to begin to develop your skill in verbally presenting your

INTEGRATIVE ACTIVITY 9.1
TASK ANALYSIS

Purpose: The purpose of this activity is to guide you in the process of analyzing a field task you are engaging in, both to develop and demonstrate your critical thinking skills and to increase your overall learning.

Directions: Identify a task of field that you would like to analyze on your own or in supervision, and address each distinct area (1–7). Each area has specific suggestions or questions for you to consider as well as an identified goal. The worksheet is grounded in Bogo and Vayda's (1998) integrative processing loop and Kiser's (2008) integrated processing model. You may find that you want to analyze several tasks throughout your field experience. If this is the case, make copies or use a separate sheet of paper on which you can take notes.

Note: Although the EPAS (CSWE, 2015) does not include a designated competency of critical thinking, critical thinking is included in several competencies' component behaviors.

Competency 4: Engage in Practice-Informed Research and Research-Informed Practice

- apply critical thinking to engage in analysis of quantitative and qualitative research methods and research findings

Competency 5: Engage in Policy Practice

- apply critical thinking to analyze, formulate, and advocate for policies that advance human rights and social, economic, and environmental justice

Competency 7: Assess Individuals, Families, Groups, Organizations, and Communities

- collect and organize data and apply critical thinking to interpret information from clients and constituencies

Competency 8: Intervene with Individuals, Families, Groups, Organizations, and Communities

- critically choose and implement interventions to achieve practice goals and enhance capacities of clients and constituencies

Competency 9: Evaluate Practice with Individuals, Families, Groups, Organizations, and Communities

- critically analyze, monitor, and evaluate intervention and program processes and outcomes

1. Task
  a. Select a specific task to analyze.
  b. Set the stage.
  c. Based on your observations, share any and all information that will be helpful in the discussion.
Goal: Increase your observation skills.
	Notes:

2. Link Task to Competencies a. Identify the competency the task best reflects. Goal: Increase your ability to link specific tasks of field to the expected competencies identified in EPAS (CSWE, 2015).	Notes:

3. Reflection
  a. Share your thoughts about and reactions to the task, then answer the following questions:
  1. How did it go?
  2. What went well?
  3. What was difficult or uncomfortable?
  4. What specifically did the client do?
  5. What did you do?
  6. What assumptions, based on your knowledge, did you make about the situation, the client, and anyone involved in the experience, including yourself?
  7. What values and beliefs were challenged or supported while engaging in the task?
Goal: Increase your awareness of what is going on for you in relation to the task and develop the ability to explore both your values and beliefs and actions.
	Notes:

4. Linking Curriculum to Task
  a. What knowledge, values, and skills did you draw on when engaging in the task?
  b. Were there any gaps in your knowledge, values, and skills as you attempted to complete this task?
  c. What do you currently know about this task or experience?
  d. What knowledge, values, and skills do you need to acquire for the next time you complete this task?
Goal: Increase your ability to integrate the curriculum with the task and to identify gaps.
	Notes:

5. Review and Process Learning Tools a. Look over any and all learning tools, such as case notes, interview check list, process recording, assessment tools (ecomap, genogram, social history), and interventions that were used when conducting the tasks. Goal: Develop your ability to use learning tools effectively.	Notes:

6. Verbalize Learning
  a. What, if anything, stood out to you while you were engaged in the task?
  b. What specifically did you do?
  c. What is one specific thing you learned?
  d. What was your primary role in the task?
  e. How did you execute that role?
	Notes:

(Continued)

(Continued)

	Notes
f. What, if any, personal reactions, such as challenging or confirming values and beliefs, did you have while you were engaged in the tasks? g. As you look back on the task, what would you do differently, if anything? Goal: Develop your ability to verbalize learning.	
7. Next Steps/Plan a. Identify a specific plan targeting the following: 1. the client system 2. the task 3. the role the task is playing in your overall learning b. Ask yourself what needs to happen next. c. What do you need to know to execute your plan? Goal: Develop your ability to design a plan specific to the analysis of the task.	Notes

work. Second, once you are practicing independently, or if you are in a setting where you don't work closely with your field instructor, providing the overview will give your field instructor the necessary background information to assist you in your analysis. The goal of this step is to increase your observation and task presentation skills.

When considering a task to analyze, remember that a task can also be an experience, something significant that happened in field that requires analysis. Furthermore, not all the tasks and experiences will require the use of your critical thinking skills or garner significant learning, but without developing a structure and format for processing the tasks of field, you may miss important learning opportunities. It is often the unexpected tasks, as in the previous example, that garner the most significant learning.

The second step is to link the task to the expected competencies identified in the EPAS (CSWE, 2015). Once you have selected the task you want to analyze, refer to Integrative Activity 1.1 in Chapter 1 to identify which competency the task reflects. Remember, the task list in Integrative Activity 1.1 is not inclusive, so if your task is not included, you may need to review the characteristic knowledge, values, skills, and cognitive and affective processes as well as the component behaviors for each specific competence to determine which competency is best reflected in the task. For additional assistance, reach out to your field instructor or field faculty.

The third step is reflection and sharing of your reaction to the task. In your reflection, consider several questions, such as how the task went, what went well, what was difficult or uncomfortable, what the client did or did not do, what you did or did not do, what values or beliefs were challenged or supported, and any assumptions you made about the situation, the client, and anyone involved in the task, including yourself. The goal of this step is to increase your awareness of what is going on for you in relation to the task and your reactions and to evaluate the role your values and beliefs play in both your actions and your analysis of the task.

The fourth step is to link the task to your curriculum. This step is at the heart of both field education and generalist practice in two ways. First, the purpose of field is the integration of the knowledge, values, and skills acquired in the classroom with the practice tasks experienced in field. Second, generalist practice is grounded in the knowledge, values, and skills acquired in the classroom. This step is accomplished by referring to the Integrative Activity 2.3 and identifying the knowledge, values, and skills from your curriculum that you drew on when engaging in the task. It is equally important to identify whether there were any gaps in your knowledge, values, and skills as you attempted to complete this task. The last activity in this step is to identify what knowledge, values, and skills you will apply or need to acquire to take the next step in the task or to complete this task in the future. The goal of this step is to increase your ability to integrate your curriculum with the tasks of field and to identify gaps. A useful question to ask is, *what do I currently know about this task or experience?* For instance, if you are cofacilitating a group, identify your current knowledge base about running groups. By doing so, you are applying critical thinking skills to task analysis. We will say more about knowledge and focus specifically on evidence-based practice later in the chapter.

The fifth step is to review and process any learning tools used when completing the task. This can be accomplished by reviewing your case notes; an interview check list or process recording; any assessment tools, such as an ecomap, genogram, or social history completed during the task; or an intervention you used, such as an anger management activity. The goal of this step is to develop your ability to use learning tools to enhance your analysis as well as see how the various learning tools relate to the tasks of field.

The sixth step is to identify your learning from the analysis of the task. This may be done while thinking, in writing, or verbally. As Kiser (2008) states,

> Using words to explain and describe what you have learned pushes you to conceptualize your learning. . . . You then have a greater command over this learning as a more tangible, concrete, and lasting "possession" that you can retrieve and use as needed. (p. 79)

To articulate your learning in supervision or other settings such as the classroom, ask the following questions: What, if anything, stood out to you while you were engaged in the task? What specifically did you do? What was one specific thing you learned as a result of conducting this task? What was your primary role in the task? How did you execute that role? What, if any, personal reactions did you have while you were engaged in the task? And as you look back on the task, what would you do differently, if anything? The goal of this step is to develop your ability to verbalize and explain your learning. This skill will become extremely important in your professional development and will be a useful tool as you prepare for your professional or academic life after field.

The last step in the task-analysis process is to identify a specific plan for what to do next. The plan you develop should be grounded in the outcome of the first five steps and should take into consideration three specific entities:

1. the client system
2. the task
3. the role the task is playing in your overall learning

In terms of the plan for the client system, this will vary, depending on the client system. For instance, if the client system includes the members of the social skills–building group you are cofacilitating, you will want to consider the plan for those group members. If your client system is an individual, you can determine what you need to do next on behalf of that person. Last, if your client system is the agency (and, specifically, the client satisfaction survey you conducted), you will want to determine the next step in how to address the agency's needs. As you can see, the plan will vary, depending on the client.

Next, focus on the task itself and consider what your plan is for the task, what you need to do next in relation to the task. Using the example of the group, the plan would be to develop the next group session, taking into consideration the members of the group and your knowledge, values, and skills related to cofacilitation of a group. You may determine, as a result of exploring the earlier steps in the process, that you need to develop your skill in managing the group's session time and keeping the participants on task. You may decide to develop a time line to follow and to identify specific things you can say to group members who go off task in order to redirect the group back to the task at hand.

Finally, consider the role the task is playing in your overall learning. This is important in that it can assist in the process of refining your activities while in field. You may determine that you have maximized your learning with regard to a particular task and plan to not engage in that task anymore so that you can engage in other tasks. Or, conversely, you may determine that you have much to learn and will continue to focus your attention and time on this particular task. Considering the role the task plays in your learning provides that necessary pause you may need, particularly in a hectic agency or one that offers many exciting learning opportunities. The task or experience you identified may have been a onetime task or experience, and therefore, there is no specific next step in relation to the task. The plan for this task is to articulate the learning and identify the role the task played in your overall learning; once that is completed, your focus on that task is done.

The goal of this final step is to develop and demonstrate your ability to develop plans related to the tasks you are engaging in while in field.

EVIDENCE-BASED PRACTICE IN FIELD

Critical thinking is grounded in knowledge; as Gibbons and Gray (2004) state, "Knowledge is a social construction; where the limits of knowledge are recognized; and where knowledge is seen as ever changing, even shifting and unstable" (p. 19). They go on to state that students "are 'constructing' their own knowledge by testing ideas and approaches based on their prior knowledge and experience, sharing these with one another, applying them to a new situation, and integrating the new knowledge gained with preexisting intellectual constructors" (p. 27). Hutchison (2017) states, "We *know* for the purpose of *doing*" (p. 18) and identifies the four things that social workers need to know to practice effectively: "knowledge about the case, knowledge about the self, values and ethics, and scientific knowledge" (p. 19). In the day and age of claims of fake news and the potential impact of your personal experiences with how you determine what is true, consideration of scientific evidence is even more important. In this text thus far, we have touched on the first three, so let's turn our attention to scientific knowledge. Hutchison states that scientific knowledge comes from *scientific inquiry*, which is defined as "a set of logical, systematic, documented methods for answering questions about the world" (p. 21). Two important types of scientific knowledge undergird your practice in field; they are *theory* and *empirical research*. A theory is an "interrelated set of concepts and propositions, organized into a deductive system that explains relationships among aspects of our world" (p. 21). Although the idea of applying a theory to your practice in field can seem overwhelming, in all likelihood, you have already done so but may not have identified it as such.

For instance, you may have immediately known to prioritize the issues and needs of your client who is in crisis by assessing his or her safety and by helping the client draw on his or her resources, thus using a tenet of the crisis intervention model and its underlying theory. Or you may notice that you have developed your own thoughts as to why your client is experiencing his or her difficulties and what you think your client should or should not do, thus developing your own theory about the case. However, it is important to take the happenstance and make it systematic. This can be accomplished through a critical thinking process directed at reflection and analysis that will enable you to systematically apply what you know and seek out the information that is necessary to practice effectively in field.

Empirical research is associated with science and is widely held as the most rigorous and systematic way of understanding something. There are two predominant types of empirical research. First, quantitative research, which emphasizes quantifiable measures of a concept, systematically collects data, focuses on identified variables, and uses statistics to draw conclusions. The significance of the findings is often determined by the p value established for the study. What this is determining is the percentage that you, as the researcher, are comfortable with being wrong. Most social science studies set a p value at .05, which means that if the results are significant, then there is a chance of being incorrect 5% of the time, which most social scientists feel is a reasonable margin of error. There are some studies, such as in medical research, that set a much higher p value at .01 or even .001, establishing a 1% or .01% margin of error. When evaluating quantitative research, it is important to also assess the study design, sample, and what statistical analysis was used to answer the question. Knowledge of research and developing the skills necessary to evaluate research findings is critical to your ability to transfer research findings to your practice in field.

Qualitative research is more experiential and flexible and attempts to gather the participant's understanding or experience of something through interviewing or observation, as opposed to responding to the researchers' predetermined criteria (Hutchison, 2017). Mixed methods studies use both of these foundational research methods to explore research questions, and this methodology is often thought to be a more comprehensive approach. Both of these types of research are important and useful to you in your practice in field and reflect what is meant by evidence-based practice (EBP). As Gambrill (2016) states,

> A concern for helping and not harming clients obliges us to critically evaluate assumptions about what is true and what is false. Relying on scientific criteria offers a way to do so. The essence of science is both guessing and rigorous testing. (p. 5115)

EBP can be defined as practice that is grounded in the "strongest documented information to guide practice-related judgments and decisions" (Sheafor & Horejsi, 2015, p. 100). EBP states that social workers will use the most effective interventions and discontinue the use of interventions that don't work. Furthermore, EBP reflects the value of competence and the ethical practice of using knowledge that is empirically based, as identified in the National Association of Social Workers code of ethics. Rubin and Parrish (2007) define EBP as

> a process in which practitioners attempt to maximize the likelihood that their clients will receive the most effective interventions possible by engaging in the following five steps:
>
> 1. Formulating an answerable question regarding practice needs
>
> 2. Tracking down the best evidence available to answer that question
>
> 3. Critically appraising the scientific validity and usefulness of the evidence
>
> 4. Integrating the appraisal with one's clinical expertise and client values and circumstances and then applying it to practice decisions
>
> 5. Evaluating outcome (with the use of single-case designs if feasible) (p. 407)

It is also important to note that EBP, like all sound practice interventions, must be "adapted to the client's unique or particular circumstances" (Thomlison & Corcoran, 2008, p. 12). The skill of adapting and applying EBP interventions to client systems will be discussed more specifically in Chapter 10, which reviews the phase of implementing plans.

In light of the emphasis placed on EBP in the literature, it is important to note that there are possible limitations to adopting a purely EBP model, particularly given the complexity of the problems clients experience and the concern that EBP alone cannot adequately prepare practitioners to address their clients' needs (Adams, Matto, & LeCroy, 2009). That being said, Adams and colleagues (2009) state that the

> skills in finding and interpreting research evidence are among many other very important skills for students of social work. . . . Good social work practice, and by extension, good social work education for future practitioners, needs to be grounded in theory and practice skills overlaid with in-depth training in selected intervention approaches. (p. 180)

So, you might ask yourself, *Where do I go from here?* The answer is to first build your EBP knowledge specific to your field site and develop your skill in evaluating research. Do not be surprised if your agency does not have a global approach to evidence-based interventions. Wiechelt and Ting (2012) surveyed 17 Bachelor in Social Work–level field instructors on their beliefs, experience, and self-efficacy with regard to EBP and found that although field instructors had moderate levels of perceived self-efficacy with regard to EBP, implementation of EBP at the agency tended to be piecemeal, given agency-based barriers. The authors go on to say that "to affiliate students' exposure to EBP in their settings, social work programs must work collaboratively with field instructors and provide them with necessary academic resources" (p. 589). Integrative Activity 9.2 is a place to start by conducting a review of the literature to identify EBPs that reflect the work you are doing in field. Before you complete Integrative Activity 9.2, ask your field instructor about his or her use of EBP and how he or she sees it being used in the agency.

INTEGRATIVE ACTIVITY 9.2
THE LITERATURE REVIEW

Purpose: The purpose of this activity is threefold. First, it will develop your ability to conduct a literature review that is grounded in your practice experiences, which will develop your understanding of how practice informs research. Second, by reflecting on the types of research findings your literature review generated (e.g., qualitative or quantitative), you will increase your understanding of evidenced-based practice. Third, by applying your findings from the research to your practice in field, you are demonstrating your ability to engage in research-informed practice.

Directions: Identify a practice-based research question and write it down. Then conduct a literature review that relates to your question. After you have developed a bibliography, select, read, and analyze several peer-reviewed scholarly research articles and books or book chapters, and discuss their applicability to your practice in field with your field instructor.

Competency 4: Engage in Practice-Informed Research and Research-Informed Practice

- use practice experience and theory to inform scientific inquiry and research

- apply critical thinking to engage in analysis of quantitative and qualitative research methods and research findings

- use and translate research evidence to inform and improve practice, policy, and service delivery

Steps to Conducting a Literature Review

1. Using your library's website, conduct a search using the general search feature following the guidelines suggested in the chapter and create a bibliography of the results.

   Note: Many programs' library websites have features that can assist you in creating a bibliography.

2. After reviewing the results and reading the abstracts, select at least three research articles from your search and read the entire study.

3. Write a brief review of the article, identifying the type of research, the findings, and their applicability to your practice setting.

4. Discuss your findings in supervision and in class. Share the results with the agency.

Practice-Based Research Question:

Research Article: Cite your literature sources using the APA style guide.	Summarize the article; include the type of research and identify the major finding(s).	Identify how the article informed your practice and what questions have arisen as a result of the article.

ROOM TO REFLECT

After you have had this discussion, begin your review of the literature. This is done by conducting a search through your university's library website. It is recommended to start with the overall search feature, using general terms that relate to your population, the context of the agency services, the type of service, or specific interventions, and then get more specific. It is also recommended to select the dates of publication within the last five years to obtain the most current research. Start with the subject as the search term to get the most comprehensive results. If these guidelines produce an overwhelming number of results, then your terms and setting may be too general; it might be helpful to refine the search terms or set the term guidelines as *title*, which will only identify those research studies that have your search terms in the title. However, this may be too narrow, as sometimes authors use creative titles versus using the specific variables of the study. You may want to do a few searches going from the general to the specific to identify the array of studies in your area of interest.

Next, do a preliminary review of all the suggested studies, paying close attention to the type of study—quantitative, qualitative, mixed methods, conceptual, or theoretical—by doing a quick review of the abstracts. From that, develop a bibliography of those you want to keep for a full review. Finally, read at least three articles and critique them in supervision or present them in class to determine those that will be most useful for you in field. For those that are applicable, identify in supervision how the research informed your practice. Integrative Activity 9.2 will provide an overview to help you complete this field task.

CASE PRESENTATION

A way to complement the aspects of critical thinking in field emphasized in the chapter thus far—task analysis and the literature review—is to develop your competency in case presentation. Presenting cases in field can serve several important purposes and can enable you to develop and demonstrate the competencies that relate specifically to this chapter.

In terms of the purpose, case presentation can assist you and the clients you work with in many ways. First, gathering needed information from multiple sources and presenting a case will help you gain a better understanding of that case. This is done at the agency or practice level when a case is presented in individual or group supervision, grand rounds, peer supervision, or ethics review boards or with the agency clinical consultant. At the program or academic level, this is done when a student presents a case in the integrative seminar course or incorporates case-based practice experiences in their other classes and course work. Another purpose of the case presentation is to present the outcome of your case work. At the agency or practice level, this might happen in supervision as you are reviewing your caseload or in a meeting where you are presenting the outcome of your research or the findings of the client satisfaction surveys you conducted. At the program or academic level, this might happen in the integrative seminar course or in a capstone assignment, such as in a case analysis.

Whether you are presenting a case to gather more information or presenting the outcome of work you have completed, case presentation is a necessary task that can help you develop and demonstrate your competence in critical thinking, as seen by your

- ability to present information in an organized and thought-out manner, drawing from multiple sources;

- ability to formulate a question based on the synthesis of the information you have gathered; and

- assessment of the outcome of your work and perhaps recommendations for next steps.

To develop a case presentation, complete Integrative Activity 9.3. This activity will assist you in preparing your presentation, organizing the information you plan to share, and identifying any specific questions you need answered.

INTEGRATIVE ACTIVITY 9.3
CASE PRESENTATION

Purpose: The purpose of this activity is to guide you in a process of preparing and conducting a case presentation and to assist you in developing and demonstrating competence in critical thinking. (Remember, a *case* can be an individual, a family, a treatment or task group, or a program you are developing, a policy you are writing, or research and evaluation you are conducting on behalf of the agency.)

Directions: For each area, jot down notes to prepare your case presentation. In the sections for recommendations and next steps, write down suggestions received and your next step with regard to the case. After you have presented your case in supervision or in your team or staff meeting or seminar class, assess your skill at presenting a case.

Competency 1: Demonstrate Ethical and Professional Behavior

- demonstrate professional demeanor in behavior; appearance; and oral, written, and electronic communication

- use supervision and consultation to guide professional judgment and behavior

Competency 9: Evaluate Practice with Individuals, Families, Groups, Organizations, and Communities

- critically analyze, monitor, and evaluate intervention and program processes and outcomes

- apply evaluation findings to improve practice effectiveness at the micro, mezzo, and macro levels.

(Continued)

(Continued)

---

1. Describe the case you are presenting. (Provide necessary background; identify if this is a micro-, mezzo-, or macro-level case; identify how long you have worked on the case, your role, the goals, etc.)

   Micro: (an individual and/or family you are working with)

   Mezzo: (a task or treatment group you are facilitating)

   Macro: (a program, community, policy, or research or evaluation you are developing or conducting)

---

2. Identify why you are presenting this case (i.e., your goal in the case presentation, whether you are presenting the outcome of the case or gathering needed information, etc.).

   Goal:

   Outcome: (if you are presenting the outcome, include your analysis of the outcome)

   Gathering information: (What do you need?)

---

3. If you are gathering information, identify the information needed and any specific question(s) you would like answered as a result of the presentation:

---

4. Write down what information you have received, including any recommendations:

---

5. List the next steps based on the presentation:

6. Assess your case presentation skills:

Suggested Field Tasks

- Review related course work.

- Analyze multilevel field tasks.

- Review Integrative Activity 1.1 to assist in linking specific field tasks to the identified competency(ies).

- In supervision, describe and explain your practice tasks.

- Analyze and present client system information.

- Demonstrate your ability to conceptualize practice.

- Use reflection to explore your role, tasks, and experiences of field.

- Articulate your learning from the tasks.

- Explain what knowledge, skills, and values you have developed as a result of your field experiences.

- Identify and discuss how research is used by the agency to support the activities of the organization.

- Identify at least one research question that relates to your placement setting.

- Conduct a literature review on a practice area, identifying the database searched and the search parameters.

- Read and discuss an article, and present your findings

References

Adams, K., Matto, H., & LeCroy, C. (2009). Limitations of evidence-based practice for social work education: Unpacking the complexity. *Journal of Social Work Education, 45*(2), 165–186.

Bogo, M., & Vayda, E. (1998). *The practice of field instruction in social work: Theory and process* (2nd ed.). Toronto, Ontario, Canada: University of Toronto Press and Columbia University Press.

Council on Social Work Education (CSWE). (2015). *Educational policy and accreditation standards.* Alexandria, VA: Author.

Gambrill, E. (2013). *Social work practice: A critical thinker's guide* (3rd ed.). New York, NY: Oxford University Press.

Gambrill, E. (2016). Is social work evidence-based? Does saying so make it so? Ongoing challenges in integrating research, practice and policy. *Journal of Social Work Education, 52*(S1), S110–S125. doi:10.1080/10437797.2016.1174642

Gibbons, J., & Gray, M. (2004). Critical thinking as integral to social work practice. *Journal of Teaching in Social Work, 24*(1/2), 19–38.

Hutchison, E. (2017). *Essentials of human behavior: Integrating person, environment, and the life course* (2nd ed.). Thousand Oaks, CA: SAGE.

Kiser, P. (2008). *The human services internship: Getting the most from your experience* (2nd ed.). Belmont, CA: Thomson Brooks/Cole.

Kolb, A. Y., & Kolb, D. A. (2005). Learning styles and learning spaces: Enhancing experiential learning in higher education. *Academy of Management Learning & Education, 4*(2), 193–212. doi:10.5465/AMLE.2005.17268566

Mathias, J. (2015). Thinking like a social worker: Examining the meaning of critical thinking in social work. *Journal of Social Work Education, 51*(3), 457–474. doi:10.1080/10437797.2015.1043196

Rogers, G. (Ed.). (1995). *Field education: A pedagogy of its own in social work education views and visions.* Dubuque, IA: Kendall Hunt.

Rubin, A., & Parrish, D. (2007). Challenges to the future of evidence-based practice in social work education. *Journal of Social Work Education, 43*(3), 405–428.

Sheafor, B., & Horejsi, C. (2015). *Techniques and guidelines for social work practice* (10th ed.). Boston, MA: Pearson Education.

Thomlison, B., & Corcoran, K. (2008). *The evidence-based internship: A field manual.* Oxford, UK: Oxford University Press.

Wiechelt, S. A., & Ting, L. (2012). Field instructors' perceptions of evidence-based practice in BSW field placement sites. *Journal of Social Work Education, 48*(3), 577–593.

THE PLANNED CHANGE PROCESS IN FIELD

Knowledge of and ability to effectively use the *planned change process*, also identified as the *helping, problem-solving,* or *empowering process,* is central to competent social work practice. There is much in the literature that defines this important process and identifies it as a significant part of generalist practice (Johnson & Yanca, 2007; Kirst-Ashman & Hull, 2018; Miley, O'Melia, & DuBois, 2011; Sheafor & Horejsi, 2015).

This chapter provides the necessary content to increase your knowledge of the planned change process, particularly as it relates to your field work. Furthermore, the chapter provides resources that will assist you in the process of using the phases of engagement, assessment, contracting, intervention, monitoring, evaluation, and termination as you work with client systems.

The ability to effectively use the planned change, helping, problem-solving, or empowerment process can be daunting for the student in field. The chapter content and integrative activities are designed to be used in a step-by-step fashion throughout your field experience. The purpose is to make the planned change process more manageable while also bringing to life the best of what generalist social work practice can offer, which is to competently assist your client systems in meeting their goals or resolving issues. For a breakdown of each of the five steps in using the planned change process in field, see Table 10.1.

TABLE 10.1 ■ Five-Step Process of Using the Planned Change Process in Field	
Step 1	Review the phases of the planned change process.
	Identify what each phase looks like in your agency.
	Develop common language.
	Integrate an understanding of contexts that shape practice.
	Complete Integrative Activity 10.1.
Step 2	Shadow and practice each phase at agency.
	Complete Integrative Activity 10.1.
Step 3	Conduct a multilevel assessment.
	Complete Integrative Activity 10.2.
Step 4	Develop and implement a multilevel plan based on the multilevel assessment.
	Complete Integrative Activities 10.3 and 10.4.
Step 5	Conduct the planned change case analysis.
	Complete Integrative Activity 10.5.

THE PHASES OF THE PLANNED CHANGE PROCESS

The first step in developing your ability to effectively use the planned change process in your practice with client systems at your field site is to review your knowledge base with respect to the phases of the planned change process. Although there are many names for the planned change process and various conceptualizations of the phases, to allow for consistency and understanding, this chapter refers to the phases defined by Kirst-Ashman and Hull (2018).

Kirst-Ashman and Hull (2018) define *planned change* as "a process whereby social workers engage a client; assess issues, strengths and problems; and establish a plan of action, implement that plan, evaluate its effects, terminate the process, and do subsequent follow-up to monitor the client's ongoing status" (p. 38). The phases of the planned change process are

- engagement,
- assessment,
- planning,
- implementation,
- evaluation,
- termination, and
- follow up (p. 41).

It is important to first review your knowledge base of each of these phases as well as to identify what each phase of the planned change process looks like in your field agency. Integrative Activity 10.1 will assist you in this learning task.

Furthermore, as you are developing your knowledge of what the planned change process looks like in your agency, make sure you develop common language for what you, your field instructor, and program faculty call each phase. This is important for supervision and integrating your course work with your practice experiences in the field, as well as for determining how the tasks you engage in relate to the various phases of the planned change process.

Finally, as you are conceptualizing the planned change process in your agency, reflect on the agency as a whole, its history, and the larger system-level issues that may be impacting the agency, such as funding, legislation, political, and societal issues. Much of the information will come from the agency analysis you engaged in, and it will assist you in developing competence in understanding the contexts that shape practice and how that impacts the planned change process at your agency.

Integrative Activity 10.1 first defines each phase of the planned change process and then provides an opportunity for you to discuss with your field instructor or agency designee how that phase is accomplished at your agency. For instance, the first phase is engagement. This phase includes how you begin to develop your understanding of the client system and the problem. Engagement is also important to establishing the working relationship. For example, when working with an individual, in order to engage your client, you must consider your preparation and effective use of empathy and interpersonal skills. This effective use of engagement is critical to developing an accurate understanding of the focus of the work and what both you and your client are hoping to accomplish.

An important part of engagement is intake. *Intake* refers to how a client system accesses the services of the agency, or more simply, it answers the question, *how did this client system become a client system?* A client system can access the services of your agency in many different ways.

For instance, an individual client may walk into the agency during hours of operation, call a hotline, schedule an appointment for an intake session with an agency representative, or be referred to attend a group being run at the client's school. Or a client system might be a community that has identified a need that can be met by your agency. In fact, sometimes the client system is the organization itself, as in the example of the need to establish a new program or policy. So, the client system can be many things. Therefore, it is critically important to always ask yourself, *who is my client?*

As you consider the phase of intake, it is also important to determine the following:

- whether or not the intake is done over the phone or in person

- whether a referral is called in or faxed to the agency by a referring agency

- whether the social worker does the intake at your agency office or if the intake is done at another location

- whether the client system, as in the case of a community or the agency itself, is determined to be a client by the agency itself and, if so, who makes that determination

All of this information is important to ascertain, particularly in the context of the second step of the five-step process of using the planned change process in field, which is to identify specific opportunities that you will have to practice each step of the planned change process through shadowing and practice. This is the purpose of the last column in Integrative Activity 10.1; in that column, list the specific tasks that you will conduct to practice each phase. Again, focusing on engagement and particularly emphasizing intake, identify how you will intake a client system at your agency. If for some reason this is not possible, I recommend that you, at a minimum, educate yourself with regard to the process and shadow that process.

For instance, say you are working at your county's children's protective services and have been placed in the ongoing unit (i.e., you will be working with families that already have a substantiated allegation of abuse or neglect). You will at least want to shadow and learn about the intake process, which most likely would be a central hotline where allegations of abuse or neglect are called in. In the best-case scenario, you will be able to work in intake, take calls, gather information, and go out with the case worker to do the investigation. As in the previous example, if the official intake process is not available for you to conduct yourself, for some reason, focus on your first contact with your client system. Your first contact is an intake and an important part of the engagement phase. The first contact you have with the client system can be very rewarding as well as provide you with an opportunity to practice your communication skills of introducing yourself, explaining your role, demonstrating warmth and empathy, and establishing the working relationship. All of these lay the foundation for the subsequent steps of the planned change process that follow.

As you are familiarizing yourself with each phase of the planned change process, think critically about how the planned change process unfolds in your agency. It is important to realize that all social work practice, regardless of the setting and the client systems served, has a beginning, middle, and end with distinct phases. This realization will provide you with the necessary structural framework to conceptualize the bigger picture of what your agency does as well as help you identify the skills that are necessary to become an effective practitioner.

As you reflect on the planned change process in your agency, ask yourself if the planned change process is long term or short term. For instance, if you are in an agency that provides social services to walk-in clients, you may use the planned change process several times a day with multiple clients. If, on the other hand, you are a social work student at an agency that provides ongoing case management services, the planned change process may take several months, with you revisiting certain phases multiple times to complete the entire process. I always tell students that it doesn't matter what the planned change process looks like or how long it takes to complete all the phases. What does matter, however, is that you develop an understanding of

- what the phases of the planned change process are,

- what each phase looks like in your agency,

- how each phase is completed,

- what each phase is called,

- who does each phase and where,

- how the planned change process is impacted by organizational and societal issues, and

- your opportunities to practice each phase.

As you are familiarizing yourself with the planned change process as it relates specifically to your agency and role, ask yourself if all the phases are equally emphasized or if some are missing or condensed. In all likelihood, the process will look different in every agency. Year after year, when I discuss and review the planned change process in class with my students, several students tell me that the process does not look like how it is laid out in their book. This will probably be the case for you as well. However, regardless of how the planned change process at your agency may be similar to or different from what is spelled out in your textbook, all the phases should somehow be present, and you need to develop your understanding of what the process entails in your field site.

INTEGRATIVE ACTIVITY 10.1
THE PHASES OF THE PLANNED CHANGE PROCESS IN FIELD

Purpose: The purpose of this activity is to (1) assist you in developing your understanding of the phases of the planned change process as they relate specifically to your agency; (2) identify the specific field-based learning tasks that you will engage in to develop the ability to complete each phase; and (3) analyze the planned change process at your agency.

Directions: In supervision, review each phase of the planned change process, and discuss what each phase looks like at the agency. Next, identify the various field-based learning tasks associated with each phase that you will be able to complete to develop competence. Remember, a client system can be an individual, family, task or treatment group,

organization, or community. Last, provide an overall analysis of the planned change process at your agency.

Competency 6: Engage with Individuals, Families, Groups, Organizations, and Communities

Competency 7: Assess Individuals, Families, Groups, Organizations, and Communities

Competency 8: Intervene with Individuals, Families, Groups, Organizations, and Communities

Competency 9: Evaluate Practice with Individuals, Families, Groups, Organizations, and Communities

Phases of the Planned Change Process	Agency Practice: Discuss the phase and identify how the agency completes that phase.	Field-Based Learning Task(s): List the specific learning task(s) to practice the phase.
Engagement: This phase is defined as either the first contact the client system has with the agency or the first contact the student has with the client system. It is a period of orientation to the situation and establishing communication and the foundations of the helping relationship.	Discuss and identify how a client system becomes a client of the agency. Identify the agency's intake process.	Identify the specific tasks you will complete to engage client systems.
Assessment: This includes all the information that the student gathers about the client system so that decisions can be made about how to assist the client in solving the problem. This also includes the ability of the student to make a determination about the situation.	Discuss and identify how the agency gathers information; that is, identify the assessment process. Also, identify the assessment tool(s) that the agency uses to gather information. In this step, also define your client system. Note: If your agency does not use structure assessment tools, you may want to develop an outline of the information that you will gather from your client systems or identify tools, such as an ecomap or genogram, for your own use with client systems.	Identify the specific task(s) you will complete to assess your client systems, identifying any and all tools you will use in the assessment process.
Planning/Contracting: This phase involves the student together with the client system deciding what is to be done, based on the determination of the assessment. The critical steps of this process involve 1. prioritizing the problems or issues, 2. turning problems into needs, 3. determining the level of the need (micro, mezzo, macro), 4. developing goals and objectives to address the needs, and 5. formalizing a contract.	Discuss how the agency determines the needs of the clients. Discuss common needs, goals, and objectives identified by clients and how the agency develops a contract with a client (i.e., verbal or written).	Identify the specific task(s) you will complete to engage in planning/contracting with your client system.

(Continued)

(Continued)

Phases of the Planned Change Process	Agency Practice: Discuss the phase and identify how the agency completes that phase.	Field-Based Learning Task(s): List the specific learning task(s) to practice the phase.
Implementation: This is the phase where the student fulfills the plan (contract) by doing (intervention) various things to meet the determined goals and objectives. In this phase, the student will also monitor the progress to determine if anything has changed. It is often during the doing that students use the roles of social work practice: counselor, broker, advocate, case manager, facilitator, and mediator.	Discuss and identify how the agency implements the plan and contracts that are developed with clients. Also identify and discuss the agency-based interventions, meaning what the agency does to assist client systems to meet their goals.	Identify the specific task(s) you will complete to implement your client system's plans.
Evaluation: In this phase, the student considers two important things: (1) how effective the student was in meeting client needs—Did the plan work?—and (2) the agency's effectiveness through program or client satisfaction evaluation measures.	Discuss and identify agency- and worker-based evaluation measures and tools.	Identify the specific task(s) you will complete to evaluate your client system interventions and the agency's level of effectiveness.
Termination: This is the final phase, in which the student ends the working relationship with the client system. Termination involves specific skills and planning. In the GIM, follow-up is the final stage, which involves checking up on the client system to determine if the client is still making progress.	Discuss how client systems usually terminate contact with the agency. Identify the agency-based tools involved in the termination process, such as a termination summary, discharge report, or other. Discuss how the agency gathers follow-up information on the clients served by the agency.	Identify the specific task(s) you will complete to terminate with your client systems.

Documentation/Record Keeping: A critical part of the planned change process is the documentation and record keeping that may coincide with each step. *Documentation and record keeping* refers to what the student writes and maintains officially, in client or agency records, about the client system and work.	Discuss and list all documentation and record keeping maintained by the agency according to each step of the planned change process. Intake: Assessment: Contracting: Implementation: Evaluation: Termination:	Identify the specific task(s) you will complete to document your work with client systems. Note: If you identify a step that does not have documentation/record keeping maintained by the agency, you may want to develop your own way of documenting that step.

Overall Analysis of the Planned Change Process: Identify your thoughts about how the planned change process plays out in your agency. What steps flow seamlessly, and what steps are either absent or vary?

Source: This worksheet is grounded in the generalist intervention model (GIM) by Kirst-Ashman and Hull, 2018.

THE PLANNED CHANGE PROCESS: MULTILEVEL

For most students in field, the planned change process is most readily conceptualized within the context of micro-level practice or work with individuals and families. The tasks involved in engaging an individual or family as a client, gathering information necessary to assist the client, establishing goals, agreeing on a plan of action, implementing the plan by conducting various interventions, monitoring the client's progress, evaluating the work, and ending the helping relationship (and sometimes providing follow-up) is what most students think about when they consider social work practice. Furthermore, it is often easier to identify and practice the phases when working with individuals and families.

However, the planned change process is also used in mezzo-level practice when working with task or treatment groups. In fact, practicing at the mezzo level is an excellent learning opportunity to deepen your understanding of the planned change process, because not only does a group have a beginning, middle, and end (for example, the eight-week anger management group has a beginning session Week 1, a midpoint Week 4, and a last session Week 8) but each session for the group also has a beginning, middle, and end. For instance, if the group is an hour long, it has

- a beginning: the start time of group at 3:00 in the afternoon;

- a middle: the midpoint, perhaps where you are implementing the plan for that week's session around 3:30; and

- an ending: with the group ending for that day at 4:00, reviewing what happened and identifying what will be happening the next week.

In this example, the student really gets to develop a comprehensive understanding of the planned change process at the mezzo level.

In terms of ongoing groups, such as those that are run at a hospital that are open, where members rotate in and out, it is helpful to develop a sense of the planned change process as it relates to the group's purpose. Even though the group is ongoing and structured such that it repeats various exercises and content on a cycle so the clients can benefit, regardless of when they start or end their involvement in the group, it is still important for the student to conceptualize how the goals of the group and the planned change process relate to the overall purpose of the group. Conceptualizing the planned change process as it relates to this type of group can be challenging for a student because the group will not have a specific beginning, middle, and end as in a time-limited group. However, it is still necessary for the student to gain an understanding of what the group is trying to accomplish and how best to achieve that by using the planned change process. With ongoing groups, the student can focus on how the phases of the planned change process play themselves out in each session, given each session has a beginning, middle, and an end.

Similarly, when working on task groups, using the planned change process can be helpful to (1) develop your understanding of each phase of the planned change process in a task group and (2) improve the overall functioning of the task group by increasing the likelihood that the group will meet its goals. I have found that students often miss important learning opportunities when serving on a task group and would benefit from introducing the idea of using the planned change process while serving on the task group. In the case where a student does not have control over the functioning of the group, the student can reflect on the phases of the planned change process, determine if the group is using a planned change process, and discuss his or her observations and recommendations in supervision. In order to engage a task group, it is helpful to get an understanding of the membership, meaning who each member is; what agency, organization, or community they represent; and what they do. If the task group member is from an outside agency, research that agency or organization so that you have a better understanding of who everyone is. If the person is from the community and is not officially representing an agency or organization, introduce yourself and tell them that you need to learn about the members and ask them to share with you how they became a member of the task group.

Last, in macro-level practice, work with organizations, communities, and at the societal level, the planned change process is equally important and necessary to accomplish goals. According to Kirst-Ashman and Hull (2015), the process that one goes through to target change at the organization and community levels may be more complex, and because many system levels are involved and the goals are often outside of the social worker's job responsibilities, the phases of the planned change process are still present and need to be used.

For instance, a student was working at an agency and recognized an unmet need of their clients. She had the opportunity to address this need and develop and implement a plan of action. The need was for a food pantry. The student developed a multifaceted process to engage the agency as a whole, assess the clients' needs as well as the agency's resources and needs, set the goal of developing a new program, develop and implement a plan, monitor and evaluate the process and the program, and, once the program was established and sustainable, terminate her involvement in the program. By using the planned change process, and planning for and reflecting on each phase, the student could integrate her knowledge of the planned change process at the macro level. The student also realized that by engaging in program development, she was shaping the agency to better respond to the needs of its clients. In addition, the student was able to integrate policy practice, as she needed to write a policies and procedures manual for the food pantry, thus integrating and demonstrating many different competencies within one learning task. It is often the case that when you use the planned change process, you will also be integrating and developing other competencies. It is important to identify and reflect on these additional competencies as you work through the planned change process.

The educational policies and accreditation standards (EPAS; Council on Social Work Education, 2015) integrate knowledge of human behavior and the social environment with each phase of the planned change process, stating that "social workers understand theories of human behavior and the social environment, and critically evaluate and apply this knowledge . . . with clients and constituencies, including individuals, families, groups, organizations, and communities" and specifically develop competence in the ability to "apply knowledge of human behavior and the social environment, person-in-environment, and other multidisciplinary theoretical frameworks . . . with clients and constituencies" (p. 9). Thus, you will want to first consider what theories of human behavior and the social environment will inform each phase and then effectively apply that knowledge to engage, assess, intervene, and evaluate client systems. With regard to engaging clients and constituencies, and specifically a group for individuals struggling with addiction, the ability to successfully engage the group members will be dependent on your ability to demonstrate your understanding of addiction and how it impacts individuals as well as their phase of development, such as if the group members are adolescents or adults. If the group members are adolescents, you may want to let them know that recovery is very challenging, particularly if their friends use drugs and alcohol, as you know how important their friends are to them at this phase of development.

REFLECTION QUESTION 10.1

Now that you have had a chance to review the steps of the planned change process and analyze how the planned change process plays itself out in your agency, do you feel that your agency is effectively using the planned change process? What are the areas of strength? What, if anything, would you recommend that the agency do differently to more effectively use the planned change process?

ROOM TO REFLECT

MULTILEVEL ASSESSMENT AND IMPLEMENTATION OF MULTILEVEL PLANS

A conceptualization of generalist practice or the generalist approach that should ground you as you apply your generalist training in field is the notion that multilevel assessment dictates multilevel intervention (Johnson & Yanca, 2007; Kirst-Ashman & Hull, 2018; Schatz, Jenkins, & Sheafor, 1990). Specifically, Kirst-Ashman and Hull's (2018) GIM focuses on a generalist approach, which emphasizes the need to view a problem from a multilevel perspective as well as to consider micro-, mezzo-, and macro-level systems as the target of change. Similarly, Johnson and Yanca (2007) define a *generalist approach* as being one that "requires that the social worker assess the situation with the client and decide which systems are the appropriate *units of attention,* or focus of the work, for the change effort" (p. 1). Schatz and colleagues (1990) state,

> Rather than beginning with methodological commitments or preconceived notions of the interventions that will be used, the generalist approaches the assessment process with attention to the social and cultural context of each practice situation; determines if intervention is most appropriate at the individual, family, group, organization, or community level; and selects and applies skills from a range of social work methods. (p. 224)

To effectively apply your generalist training to your field agency, consider two important and necessary learning tasks:

1. engage in multilevel assessment
2. develop multilevel plans that are grounded in your multilevel assessment

The ability to meet this expectation can be challenging in field, for a number of reasons. First, students often enter the planned change process at the point of implementation or the delivery of a service provided by the agency. For instance, a student is placed in an agency that provides a social skills–building group at a school and is assigned to cofacilitate one of the groups. Although cofacilitating a social skills group is an excellent mezzo-level learning task, more often than not, the student's first encounter with the client system (the group) is going to be when the student goes with the cofacilitator the first day of group to run the group. When this is the case, the student has already missed several important phases of the planned change process that may or may not have happened prior to delivering the service (the group), namely engagement, assessment, and contracting. The steps of engagement, assessment, and contracting are necessary to determine that for these clients, based on their needs, attending a social skills group is identified as the appropriate intervention. So, although the student may be meeting the competency of developing group facilitation skills, in the context of the planned change process, the student may be missing important information necessary to consider the best way to assist each client to meet his or her goals.

We already discussed the fact that the planned change process will play itself out in the context of the group, and therefore, the student can focus on applying the phases of the planned change process to the group as a whole (in the case of a time-limited group) or during each session of the group (if the group is ongoing). Developing mezzo-level practice skills is necessary to one's development as a generalist practitioner and is an important learning task. However, if the student is focusing only on the planned change process as it relates to the running of the group, he or she may be missing the bigger picture of each individual client's situation and the need to consider all possible interventions that may be helpful for each member of the group (not only attending the group) and most importantly, why the interventions are indicated. Therefore, the way to make running the group the most effective learning experience is for the student to become involved in the entire process of the group: interviewing and determining who would best benefit from participation in the group, following the clients through the group process to ultimately evaluate if the group was an effective intervention, and identifying all other interventions that may be indicated for the client. Again, if this is not possible due to agency constraints, at a minimum, the student should be able to conceptualize and articulate an understanding of the preceding process and, prior to beginning to cofacilitate the group, learn about how and why that particular service (the group) was developed, who the clients are and why they were referred, and whether the group is effective. If the group is a task group, apply the preceding process as well.

As you can see, it is important for you to be able to link the various tasks you are engaging in with the phases of the planned changed process and, whenever possible, to engage in all steps of the planned change process with client systems. By doing so, you will develop a comprehensive understanding of how the planned change process is used by your agency to assist your client systems in meeting their goals. To ground you in the two critical steps of conducting multidimensional/ multilevel assessments and implementing multilevel plans, we will review each individually and discuss the integrative activities that will assist you in these learning tasks.

CONDUCTING MULTIDIMENSIONAL/ MULTILEVEL ASSESSMENTS

As a field director for over 20 years who also teaches two courses in the curricular area of human behavior and the social environment, I regularly see a gap between the specific application of the content taught in these two courses with what most of my students do in field to assess their client systems. In other words, I am aware of the time spent teaching and helping students integrate their knowledge of the multidimensional, multitheoretical framework for assessing human behavior and development across the life span, yet I rarely, if ever, hear students talk specifically about their ability to apply that framework at their field agency and conduct a comprehensive biopsychosocial assessment. In fact, although all agencies utilize assessment, the form and process of the phase of assessment varies greatly and tends to reflect the services the agency provides. As a result, from agency to agency, there is not a consistent understanding of assessment and how best to train a student to be able to competently assess a client system. In fact, there tend to be two distinct trends; one is where an agency representative says, "Oh, we don't do assessments," and the second includes the agencies that do conduct detailed, comprehensive, diagnostic assessments but often don't include this as a task for the student. Both of these are concerning and reflect the need to focus specifically on defining this phase and providing students with the opportunity to conduct their own assessments, regardless of how the agency operationalizes this phase of planned change. The fact that agencies do not have a consistent way of operationalizing assessment is understandable, given the wide array of services provided by agencies. And, from the agencies' perspective, one could argue that it is not their responsibility to consistently ensure that a specific curriculum content area be applied in a specific way. Assessment at its core is information gathering, and all agencies gather information in order to serve their client systems. But the variation that exists in what is considered an assessment can be problematic and may hamper students' education and socialization as a generalist practitioner if they do not have the opportunity to conduct (or, at a minimum, conceptualize) a multidimensional/multilevel assessment.

Thus, the third step in the process of using the planned change process in field is to conduct a multidimensional, multilevel assessment of a client system in your agency. Integrative Activity 10.2 provides the guidance for you to complete this step. Conducting a multidimensional/ multilevel assessment is important because you need a way to both understand your client's story and to help the client address the issues that he or she is bringing to you. Social work has historically paid attention to the interplay between the person and environment and considers many dimensions when it comes to assessment. The activity is grounded in Hutchison's (2017) bio/ psycho/psychosocial/spiritual/environmental assessment and will guide you in a comprehensive assessment process that will let you develop a rich understanding of your client.

The multidimensional approach to understanding human behavior and the social environment across the life span using theory is grounded in three important concepts—consideration of the person, the environment, and time (Hutchison, 2017)—and demands that you be able to integrate all of these concepts in your understanding of the client and his or her situation. The relevant aspects of the person are the "biological, psychological, and spiritual dimensions" and the environment considers "the physical environment, culture, social structure and social institutions, dyads, families, small groups, formal organizations, communities, and social movements" (p. 9). Time is important in that it asks you to consider a specific question—Why now?—as well as the relationship between time and the client system's problem or need. *Time* can be defined in several ways; Hutchison (2017) identifies "linear time, historical era, and chronological age" (p. 10). Linear time considers the past, the present, and the future, which complements the biopsychosocial approach by grounding you in considering the role that the past, present, and future have and will play in your understanding of the client.

For instance, as a part of your multidimensional assessment of an eight-year-old boy who is failing school, you will want to know about the client's past growth and development (possibly as early as conception), learn about his mother's pregnancy and prenatal care, and determine whether or not he met important developmental milestones as he was growing up. You also want to determine what specifically is going on in the present (such as the fact that his grandmother, who had been a major parental figure in his life, has just died) and in the future (such as where you hope this child is headed and what the future concerns are, particularly if he gets expelled due to his behavior).

Time is also relevant when we consider implementing plans and delivering an intervention, particularly when considered in the context of crisis intervention theory. Crisis intervention theory states that providing services immediately when a client system is in crisis—that is, focusing on the present—can be effective because client systems are often more open to change in the height of a crisis.

Integrative Activity 10.2 provides you with the opportunity to analyze the assessment conducted at your agency and then either conceptualize or conduct a multilevel assessment on a client system in your agency. The assessment considers three dimensions of the client—the person, environment, and time—and asks you to engage in two important tasks. First, for each dimension and

INTEGRATIVE ACTIVITY 10.2
THE MULTIDIMENSIONAL/MULTILEVEL ASSESSMENT

Purpose: The purpose of this activity is to develop and conduct a multidimensional assessment of a client system in your field agency. This will help you develop your assessment skills as well as assist you as you consider developing multilevel plans and finally implement those plans.

Directions: First, go through the assessment and identify what information your agency gathers as part of their assessment. Then, identify additional information in each section that you think would be helpful to gather to assess your client. Last, discuss with your field instructor if there is a client system with which you can complete a multidimensional assessment. If not, have a theoretical discussion about the questions you identified and how you think clients would respond and how this information would inform your understanding of the client system.

Competency 7: Assess Individuals, Families, Groups, Organizations, and Communities

- collect and organize data and apply critical thinking to interpret information from clients and constituencies

- apply knowledge of human behavior and the social environment, person-in-environment,

and other multidisciplinary theoretical frameworks in the analysis of assessment data from clients and constituencies

Multidimensional/Multilevel Assessment Outline
The Person:

1. Who is your client system? Do you have more than one client? What is your role within the agency in relation to the client system?

    Demographic: (age, sex, race, socioeconomic status)

    Presenting problem: (from the perspective of you, the referral source, and the client)

2. Biological dimension: Identify information that is gathered by your agency that

Chapter 10 ■ The Planned Change Process in Field **187**

targets this dimension and any additional information you think would be helpful by identifying the specific question(s) below. If your agency does not gather information about this dimension, identify any questions or information you think would be helpful to gather. Questions might be about a client's specific medical history, basic growth and development, biologically based diagnoses (remember there is strong evidence of the connection between physical and psychological health and external environmental conditions), and biophysical risks or protective factors.

Agency assessment questions:

a.

b.

c.

Added questions:

a.

b.

3. Psychological dimension: Identify information that is gathered by your agency that targets this dimension and any additional information you think would be helpful by identifying the specific question(s) below. Questions might target (1) cognition (thinking): whether the client is oriented to person, time, and place; how the client is thinking; if there is confusion; if there are thinking errors; (2) emotion (feeling): how the client expresses and manages emotions; what the client is feeling;

and (3) identity (sense of self): how the client sees himself or herself in the world; what his or her relationships are like; how the client manages stress; and coping, communication, and personality. Consider whether or not there are any mental health issues, needs, and possible diagnoses; psychological risks; and protective factors.

Agency assessment questions:

a.

b.

c.

Added questions:

a.

b.

4. Spiritual dimension: Identify information that is gathered by your agency that targets this dimension and any additional information you think would be helpful by identifying the specific question(s) below. Questions might target the client's sense of meaning and purpose, themes of good and bad and right and wrong, forgiveness, gratefulness, spiritual or religious affiliation, the role that religion and spirituality may or may not play in their life, and spiritual or religious practices that may be helpful.

Agency assessment questions:

a.

(Continued)

(Continued)

    b.

    c.

Added questions:

a.

b.

The Environment:

Identify information that is gathered by your agency that targets this dimension and any additional information you think would be helpful by identifying the specific question(s) below. For the added question, based on your understanding of the client, identify which of the following six aspects of the environment should be assessed, and then identify the questions you would ask. This dimension could include questions about where the client lives, their worldview, pertinent family information, whether they are involved in a community groups, involvement with various social institution, and services.

1.   Physical environment: Consider where the client lives; if the client has a home; the location of the neighborhood; if the client has water, heat, electricity, lead paint, environmental toxins, or overcrowding.

    Agency assessment questions:

    a.

    b.

    c.

Added questions:

a.

b.

2.   Culture: Consider the client's cultural background, including race, ethnicity, social class, gender, sexual orientation, and disability; consider what needs to be known about the client's cultural values, customs, practices, and beliefs that may be important to the current situation; consider any language barriers, family structure and roles, and ideas about helpers and the helping process.

    Agency assessment questions:

    a.

    b.

    c.

    Added questions:

    a.

    b.

3. Social structure and social institutions: Identify and answer one to three questions that consider the social institutions that may be impacting the client, such as government and politics, economy, education, health care, social welfare, religion, mass media, and family. Complete an ecomap.

   Agency assessment questions:

   a.

   b.

   c.

   Added questions:

   a.

   b.

4. Families: Identify and answer one to three questions that consider who is in the family, consider diverse families, complete a genogram, and identify relationships, rules, norms, roles, and issues.

   Agency assessment questions:

   a.

   b.

   c.

Added questions:

a.

b.

5. Small groups and formal organizations: Identify and answer one to three questions that consider groups and organizations that the client is a member of or affiliated with that may be impacting the situation; also consider groups or organizations that may be helpful.

   Agency assessment questions:

   a.

   b.

   c.

Added questions:

a.

b.

6. Communities: Identify and answer one to three questions that consider the client's membership in a community, physical or conceptual (i.e., the gay and lesbian community, their neighborhood, community issues, violence, poverty, crime, easy access to resources, and social movements).

(Continued)

(Continued)

Agency assessment questions:

a.

b.

c.

Added questions:

a.

b.

Time:

Identify any issues related to past, present, and future; consider the question, *Why now?* Consider the role of time in the context of the problem, how long the issue has been going on, and ideas of off-time and on-time life events.

Agency assessment questions:

a.

b.

c.

Added questions:

a.

b.

Strengths and Limitations:

Identify all the current and past strengths of the client and the limitations impacting the situation.

Agency assessment questions:

a.

b.

c.

Added questions:

a.

b.

Include other questions and content that are not listed in this outline but are important to the client. Ask your client if there is anything you missed or need to know to assist him or her.

Agency assessment questions:

a.

b.

c.

Added questions:

a.

b.

Overall Assessment: Identify your determination, based on the information gathered, of what you think is going on for your client. What are the client's protective factors, strengths, and resources? What are the risk factors and deficits? Considering problems from a multilevel perspective, what level do you consider the problem to be most focused at; that is, is this primarily a problem of an individual, a family, a group, an organization, a community, or a combination of several of these?

corresponding aspect of that dimension, identify what information is gathered by your agency, then, based on that, identify what other questions you want answered or the information you feel you need to gather to better understand your client system. Second, once you have identified the questions, if possible, gather that information and apply that information to your understanding of the client. If that is not possible, reflect on the questions and what you know about the client and consider how the client might answer. Last, specifically identify the client's strengths and limitations that are impacting the current situation. A sound understanding of the client's strengths and limitations, including risk and protective factors, is critical when you move toward identifying interventions, as interventions are often more successful when they take this information into consideration.

As you set out to develop your assessment, first and foremost, consider your role within the agency and discuss with your field instructor the information that is regularly gathered by the agency. You may want to revisit the assessment phase of the planned change process (see Integrative Activity 10.1). Then, look at the gaps. For instance, you may be in an agency that gathers only current information focused primarily on assessing if the client qualifies for the services offered. From here, discuss the questions you have identified and determine if there is a client who would benefit from a more in-depth assessment. The assessment might focus on questions that consider the past, the client's family, past services the client has accessed, the client's environment, and what the client hopes or feels needs to happen to improve his or her situation.

This was precisely the case for one student who was working at a social service agency that provided food assistance. The student discussed the desire to get to know a client more deeply and gather information along the lines of a biopsychosocial assessment. The student was concerned she was not developing her assessment skills, because the agency gathered minimal information on the clients—in fact, just enough to see if the client qualified to be referred to the food pantry. The student's field instructor identified a client who came in on a regular basis and discussed with the client the concern that he was not progressing to the point of creating enough stability and thus regularly needed services. This was of particular concern because the client was often denied services when he came to the agency too frequently.

The field instructor, who knew the client, asked if the client would like to sit down with the social work student and discuss the bigger picture of his current situation and determine if the client could do additional things to address the issue that seemed to be recurring. The client agreed, and the student, after meeting with his field instructor to identify all the questions he was going to ask, conducted a multidimensional assessment. The student reported that this became a wonderful learning experience and that the client easily shared information about his life and engaged in a process of looking at additional interventions that might be helpful beyond the services offered by the agency.

The learning task of conducting a multidimensional/multilevel assessment is best when applied to an individual or family; however, it can be applied to groups and organizational and community-based practice. With regard to group practice, it is important to remember that groups develop an identity and group members can take on various roles, both of which can be assessed. Similarly, organizations are known to develop a distinct culture and way of functioning similar to communities and thus have a history and way of seeing themselves in relation to others, all of which can and should be assessed. Last, it is important to consider the fact that a group, an organization, or a community is made up of individuals and to reflect on who those individuals are and how they are impacted by each other.

For instance, if one of your tasks is to be the agency representative at the monthly homeless coalition meeting, which is both a mezzo-level task (working on a task group) and a macro-level task (working to improve services at the larger system level), you could conduct a multilevel assessment of the coalition task group. Assessing the task group can prove to be a useful and interesting learning experience as you first identify what it is you need to know about the task group. Prior to conducting an assessment, you will have conducted the phase of *engagement*, in which you identify who each member of the group is, their history with regard to membership in the group, and their personal stake or interest in the coalition.

Next, you will want to learn about the agencies that are represented and the services that each agency provides as well as the current societal issues impacting the various services (environmental). For instance, you may learn that one of the members is a representative of the for-profit housing company that is developing mixed-income housing and reflect on the goals that are shared as well as those that conflict with the goals of the not-for-profit agency representative, who is concerned that the community is losing too many affordable housing units.

Last, gather information about the history of the coalition in terms of the past and present membership and the hopes of the coalition for the future (time). By conducting a multidimensional assessment of the task group that is engaged in macro-level practice, you are taking an often-straightforward task and placing it in a context that will ultimately improve your understanding of the task group as well as potentially impact the overall functioning of the group.

Developing and Implementing Multilevel Plans

Once you have completed the multidimensional assessment and determined the goals with the client system, the next step in the process is to identify and implement a multilevel plan. The plan should be grounded in the multidimensional/multilevel assessment and focus on all the ways you can assist the client in achieving the agreed-upon goal(s). This is done to determine the intervention that fits the assessment, rather than provide a particular intervention simply because it is what the agency does.

With regard to intervention or intervening, it is helpful to demystify this phase. Often when students hear the word *intervention*, they get this deer-caught-in-the-headlights look and report feeling overwhelmed with the prospective of naming and implementing an intervention.

To reduce the anxiety that can go along with the idea of intervention, it is useful to review what intervention means and place intervention in the context of the planned change process.

Sheafor and Horejsi (2015) define *intervention* or *action phase* as "the time when the client, the social worker, and possibly others implement the plan they believe will bring about the desired outcome" (p. 309). I like to refer to the phase of implementation as the time you will be doing what needs to be done to assist your client in meeting his or her goals—the intervention. An intervention can be when you use the role of brokering and refer your client to the jobs program to assist the client in getting a job so he or she has the income necessary to pay the rent. Another intervention might be when you refer the client to the social skills group to improve the client's social skills in the hopes of reducing the client's social isolation.

An intervention can be grounded in the roles of social work, as discussed in Chapter 2, or in various theoretical perspectives. In the context of theory, the conventional wisdom with regard to social work practice is that theory directs practice. That is, the social worker should be grounded in an understanding of theory and implement plans through the use of various interventions that are grounded in that theory.

For instance, in the case of the student who is working at an agency that provides services to individuals who are experiencing domestic violence, an understanding of crisis intervention theory would be extremely helpful as the student conceptualizes a plan and implements that plan by using an intervention. As mentioned in an example earlier, crisis intervention theory tells us that the client is more open to change in the height of the crisis. Thus, supporting the fact that the client is seeking services, facilitating her admission into the shelter becomes the most important plan to implement. Furthermore, crisis intervention theory tells us that it is important to prioritize the needs of the client and address the most important one first. In the case of a client experiencing domestic violence, safety is the most important need, so the intervention used to implement the plan to meet the goal of increasing safety is to develop a safety plan. Although the student is also aware that educating the client with regard to the cycle of violence is important, it is more important to address safety first. Only after the client's safety needs have been met will the client be able to benefit from a session in which the student, in the role of educator, provides information on the cycle of violence, yet another important intervention.

Thus, review your knowledge of the various theoretical perspectives, practice theories, and models that ground social work practice (Hutchison, 2011; Johnson & Yanca, 2007; Kirst-Ashman & Hull, 2018; Miley et al., 2011; Sheafor & Horejsi, 2015) and identify those that are useful to your practice in field. Table 10.2 provides a list of several theoretical perspectives, practice theories, and models that a student may find applicable to their practice in field as well as a list of interventions that students can use that are grounded in the various perspectives, theories, and models. The list is in no particular order of importance and is not meant to be exhaustive. In fact, you may find additional theories, models, and interventions used in your agency. For instance, I worked with an agency that trained all their students to use motivational interviewing as an important part of service delivery. That particular agency found motivational interviewing to be an effective intervention grounded in a strengths perspective and empowerment model.

Integrative Activity 10.3 will assist you in the process of analyzing and identifying the interventions that are used at your agency and the theoretical perspective(s) your agency or field instructor may be grounded in. It is useful for you to begin to

- clarify if your agency has an overarching theoretical perspective,

- identify the theoretical perspectives and models of practice in which your field instructor and agency workers are trained, and

- identify the interventions that are commonly used by the agency when delivering services.

All of these will help you begin to identify your theoretical perspective, the practice models that you find beneficial, and appropriate interventions that you can provide for your client systems.

To develop and implement a multilevel plan, identify all the possible interventions that could be used with and on behalf of the client system at the micro, mezzo, and macro levels. The plan should consider what may need to happen at the individual and family level; how task or

TABLE 10.2 ■ Theoretical Perspectives and Practice Theories and Models		
Theoretical Perspectives	**Practice Theories and Models**	**Interventions for Field**
Generalist	The generalist intervention model	Identify and implement multilevel plans.
Psychodynamic	Psychodynamic theory	Explore the impact of childhood experiences on current issues.
Social constructionist	Behavioral theory	Have a client complete an Adverse Childhood Experiences (ACE) assessment.
Social behavioral	Cognitive-behavioral theory	
Humanist	Person-centered theory	Set up a behavior chart.
Systems	Crisis intervention model	Refer the client to a mentoring program.
Ecosystems	Task-centered model	Affirm the dignity and worth of the client.
Strengths	Problem-solving model	Express positive regard.
Feminist	Psychoeducational model	Develop a safety plan.
Conflict	Addictions model	Prioritize goals/needs.
Rational choice	Solution-focused model	Provide parent education.
Developmental	Narrative therapy model	Educate the client about the cycle of violence.
	Family therapies	Discuss the disease model of addiction.
	Small group theories	Identify exceptions to the problem.
	Models for changing organizations	Conduct a family session to set family rules.
	Models for changing communities	Facilitate a group.
	Case management model	Conduct an agency retreat.
	Family preservation model	Review the agency intake process.
	Self-help model	Develop a new program.
	Empowerment-based practice model	Conduct a needs assessment of a community.
	Social network theory	Convene a meeting of community members.
		Monitor the progress of the case plan.
		Conduct an interdisciplinary treatment meeting to identify needs.
		Complete a genogram.
		Advocate for the client's access to services.
		Refer the client to Alcoholics Anonymous, a bereavement support group, or other group.
		Complete an ecomap.
		Conduct a spiritual assessment.

treatment groups work; and what needs to happen at the organization, community, or larger system level. By considering all possible multilevel interventions, you can begin to conceptualize a comprehensive plan that, when implemented, will be more effective than if you were to target only one system level. To develop a multilevel plan, start with the interventions commonly used by the agency (see Integrative Activity 10.3) and identify the level that the intervention targets. For example, if the agency offers a parent education group and you determine that the client would benefit from the group, then that would be the intervention you would identify that targets the mezzo level. Once you have identified an intervention at the mezzo level, you will also want to identify interventions at the micro level (those that target individuals and families) and at the macro level (those that target the organization, community, or larger system).

The importance of implementing multilevel plans can best be illustrated in the following situation. Many years ago, I was working with a student who was doing her field placement at a mental health hospital. One of the clients she was working with was due to be discharged, and the student was working on the discharge plan with the client (micro-level intervention). The student, however, began to encounter difficulties, as the client stated that he had nowhere to go. As the student began to develop the discharge plan, she learned that the client was dually diagnosed and was also being served by the developmental disabilities (DD) system. The DD case manager was stating that the mental health system had to secure housing, and the mental health case manager was stating that the client needed to return to the DD community placement. The

INTEGRATIVE ACTIVITY 10.3
IDENTIFYING THEORETICAL PERSPECTIVES, PRACTICE MODELS, AND COMMONLY USED INTERVENTIONS IN FIELD

Purpose: The purpose of this activity is to assist you in developing your understanding of the theoretical perspectives and practice models used by your field instructor, peers, and agency and how those relate to the interventions commonly used at your agency. This develops your ability to link theory to practice and analyze interventions. This will also help you begin to identify the theoretical perspectives and practice models that you are using or drawn to in your practice in field.

Competency 7: Assess Individuals, Families, Groups, Organizations, and Communities

- select appropriate intervention strategies based on the assessment, research knowledge, and values and preferences of clients and constituencies.

Directions: After reviewing Table 10.2 with your field instructor, discuss the theoretical perspective and practice models that are used in the agency as a whole as well as those that the field instructor may use. Identify any specific trainings or certifications obtained by the field instructor. Do the same with the other agency staff.

1. Does the agency have a theoretical perspective or practice model that it uses in direct practice with client systems? If yes, please describe and state how this model gets translated into agency services.

2. What models or theories has your field instructor been trained in or exposed to? How was this accomplished (i.e., through reading, trainings, workshops)?

3. How would your field instructor describe her or his theoretical orientation?

4. How does this get translated into your field instructor's practice and, more specifically, into the interventions he or she uses when working with client systems?

5. Ask similar questions of coworkers.

6. What interventions of the agency are commonly used to assist client systems in meeting their goals and needs? What do the agency and the social workers at the agency do to assist their clients?

7. How would you describe your beginning theoretical orientation? What theoretical perspectives and practice models are you drawn to?

8. How do these get translated into your practice in field and the interventions you use with client systems?

student became very frustrated with the client and unsuccessfully attempted on several occasions to develop a plan with the client. Finally, after taking a step back, the student determined that intervention at the micro level, targeting only the individual client, was not going to work, because the core issue was at the macro level. The student brought this to the attention of the field instructor, who agreed with the student's assessment of the situation and set up a meeting with the community mental health and DD case managers to negotiate a discharge plan. As soon as it was determined who would handle the client's placement, after much discussion and negotiation, the client's discharge plan fell into place. This is an excellent example of the need to determine the appropriate level of intervention based on the assessment. What also made this intervention exciting was the fact that the student was very proud and surprised because she never considered that she would do macro social work and yet she had, in fact, engaged in a macro-level intervention on behalf of her individual client.

REFLECTION QUESTION 10.2

Now that you have had a chance to consider the role of intervention in implementing a plan, what are all the types of interventions (the things that the social worker and agency do to assist clients) provided by your agency? How do these interventions reflect the foundational roles of social work? How are the inter- ventions grounded in theory? Are there any theoretical perspectives or practice models that you think would be helpful for your agency to use in their practice with client systems?

ROOM TO REFLECT

Integrative Activity 10.4 will assist you in developing a multilevel plan by identifying the possible multilevel interventions that you can implement based on the multidimensional assessment you conducted. The activity will help you consider what needs to happen at the individual, family, group, organization, community, and larger system levels to assist your client system in meeting their goals and needs. What is important to remember is that your client system may be an individual, a family, a group, an organization, or a community. So, it is always important to first and foremost identify your client system, determine the problem from the perspective of your primary client, and when it comes to developing a plan, consider all the possible interventions that could be implemented at all levels. Furthermore, sometimes social workers determine that the agency needs to change to better serve the client. By considering and implementing a multilevel plan, it is more likely that you will identify if and when the agency needs to be the target of the change effort. This exact thing happened as a result of a student completing this integrative activity. The student was working in foster care and one of the goals was for reunification; however, when the student spoke to the foster family about the progress of the parent and the plan, the foster family expressed concern and ambivalence with regard to the plan, to the point of interfering with parental visits. As the student explored the situation with the foster family, it was determined that many of the foster families held conflicting beliefs about the biological parents and reunification. Thus, it was determined that this topic needed to be added to the foster parent training in order to better prepare foster parents to manage this challenging aspect of their role and their own feelings about reunification.

In order to develop your skills in developing multiple plans, I encourage you to consider what I like to call the *accordion approach*. When you play the accordion, you must be able to continuously open and close the bellows in order to create a sound. The opening and closing of the bellows can represent moving from the smaller system of the individual through the mid-system to the largest system of the organization—community and society—and back again. Playing the accordion also requires the ability to play the notes, which represent the various theories and interventions utilized to assist clients. When you put these together, you can visualize what is necessary for effective generalist practice—developing the skill of seamlessly moving back and forth from the individual to a dyad, a family, a group, the organization, communities, and society (regardless of your primary client system) as you use the necessary interventions to help your client system achieve their goals or meet their needs. Also, when identifying your client system, you may realize that you have multiple clients, such as in the case of adoption services that are contracted by the local county children's services. When determining the plan, you may need to consider what your referring agency expects to happen and factor that into the plan as much as what your identified client hopes will happen.

Finally, it is essential to discuss the role that research plays in the development of multilevel plans. Clearly, developing your knowledge of what the research generally says about your area of practice is an important overall competence that relates to evidence-based practice discussed in Chapter 9. However, when you are developing a plan, you want to consider what the research specifically says are the most effective interventions to include in your plan. This develops your competence in the area of research-informed practice. As you are developing your plan, you may want to engage in a review of the literature specific to your client and the identified goals and needs so you can incorporate that information into your plan.

INTEGRATIVE ACTIVITY 10.4
DEVELOPING AND IMPLEMENTING MULTILEVEL PLANS

Purpose: The purpose of this activity is to assist you in developing and implementing a multilevel plan that is grounded in your multidimensional/multilevel assessment, to identify needed interventions, and to link those interventions to various theoretical perspectives and practice models.

Directions: Develop a multilevel plan by identifying specific interventions that could be used to assist your client and discuss the plan in supervision. Once you have developed the plan, implement the plan.

Competency 7: Assess Individuals, Families, Groups, Organizations, and Communities

- select appropriate intervention strategies based on the assessment, research knowledge, and values and preferences of clients and constituencies

Competency 8: Intervene with Individuals, Families, Groups, Organizations, and Communities

- critically choose and implement interventions to achieve practice goals and enhance capacities of clients and constituencies

(Continued)

(Continued)

- apply knowledge of human behavior and the social environment, person-in-environment, and other multidisciplinary theoretical frameworks in interventions with clients and constituencies

- use interprofessional collaboration as appropriate to achieve beneficial practice outcomes

- negotiate, mediate, and advocate with and on behalf of diverse clients and constituencies

Competency 9: Evaluate Practice with Individuals, Families, Groups, Organizations, and Communities

- select and use appropriate methods for evaluation of outcomes

- apply knowledge of human behavior and the social environment, person-in-environment, and other multidisciplinary theoretical frameworks in the evaluation of outcomes

- critically analyze, monitor, and evaluate intervention and program processes and outcomes

- apply evaluation findings to improve practice effectiveness at the micro, mezzo, and macro levels

1. Identify the client system: Who is your client? Do you have multiple clients? Remember, a client system can be an individual, a family, a group, an organization, or a community.

2. Identify your assessment of the client system's problem: Provide your determination of what you think is the problem and the important factors contributing to the problem, using the results of your multidimensional/multilevel assessment (Integrative Activity 10.2), and specifically address whether this is a problem of the individual, a family, a group, an organization, the community, a larger social system, or a combination, applying your knowledge of human behavior and the social

environment, person-in-environment, and other multidisciplinary theoretical frameworks.

3. Identify the needs and goals (i.e., what needs to happen for the client system to meet their goals).

4. Identify the client system's strengths, resources, and protective factors.

5. Identify the client system's risks, deficits, or barriers.

6. Identify multilevel interventions (e.g., evaluate the pros and cons, consider if an intervention is doable, if it will succeed, and the time frame needed to succeed).

   a. Micro: What does the individual and family need to do and or have done on their behalf? List all the possible interventions that could be implemented at the micro level, applying your knowledge of human behavior and the social environment, person-in-environment, and other multidisciplinary theoretical frameworks and link each intervention to a theoretical perspective, practice model, or both.

b. Mezzo: What needs to happen at the group level, either considering treatment or task groups, to assist the client? List all possible interventions that could be implemented at the mezzo level, applying your knowledge of human behavior and the social environment, person-in-environment, and other multidisciplinary theoretical frameworks, and link each intervention to a theoretical perspective, practice model, or both.

c. Macro: What needs to happen at the organization, community, and larger system level to help the client meet his or her goals? List all possible interventions that could be implemented at the macro level, applying your knowledge of human behavior and the social

environment, person-in-environment, and other multidisciplinary theoretical frameworks and link each intervention to a theoretical perspective, practice model, or both.

7. Evaluate the multilevel plan: What were you able to implement and how did you go about doing that? Was your intervention effective?

A final word about developing a multilevel plan: It is my hope that you will be able to implement your plan in its entirety; however, if for whatever reason, you cannot, that is understandable. This may be due to the constraints of your agency, and if this is the case, implement those interventions that you are able to do within your agency. For those that you cannot directly implement, discuss them in supervision and in your classes. In this discussion, include your thoughts about your plan, how your plan relates to your assessment, and how you would go about implementing the plan. This in and of itself will be a rich and valuable learning experience.

THE PLANNED CHANGE CASE ANALYSIS

The last step in the process of integrating and developing competence in effectively using the planned change process in field is to conduct a planned change case analysis. This activity will provide you with an opportunity to pull all the steps identified in Table 10.1 together and analyze the planned change process. By taking the time to engage in a comprehensive reflection and case analysis, you will develop a better understanding of the big picture of the process in your field site as well as have an opportunity to identify and critique specifically what you did during each phase. In addition, you will have an opportunity to consider both the multilevel assessment and the multilevel plan you developed and implemented based on your assessment, both of which are critical to generalist practice or the generalist approach. Integrative Activity 10.5 will assist you in conducting your case analysis. As in most of the activities of field, once you have completed this activity, it is important to discuss your analysis in supervision and in your course work.

INTEGRATIVE ACTIVITY 10.5
THE PLANNED CHANGE CASE ANALYSIS

Purpose: The purpose of this activity is to (1) integrate your understanding of the planned change process with a client system case you have had direct involvement with while in field and (2) analyze how the process went.

Directions:

1. Read Chapter 10 and complete all integrative activities. For additional information, review the phases of the planned change or helping process in your practice textbook(s).

2. Select a client system case; remember, a client system can be an individual, family, group, organization, community, or society you have had/are having direct involvement with. The emphasis is on the specific client system, not the general roles or functions of the agency. When selecting a case, choose one you have had or are having extensive involvement with, where you were able to conduct all phases of the planned change process. Remember, this could be a onetime contact or an ongoing experience.

3. In writing, follow the outline and, in Part D below, address each phase of the planned change process and specifically describe what you did to accomplish that phase.

Competency 9: Evaluate Practice with Individuals, Families, Groups, Organizations, and Communities

- critically analyze, monitor, and evaluate intervention and program processes and outcomes

- apply evaluation findings to improve practice effectiveness at the micro, mezzo, and macro levels

The Analysis Outline

A. Briefly describe the client system case you are going to analyze (i.e., an individual client or family, a task or treatment group—this could either be one specific session or an entire group), or an organization, community, or society.

B. Identify why you chose this client system case to analyze.

C. Given the emphasis on knowledge and the fact that the generalist field education approach is grounded in curriculum, demonstrate the knowledge you applied to your understanding of the client system case through the linkage of specific courses (revisit Integrative Activity 2.3). For instance, if your client is a child and you are working in a child welfare agency, you would describe your knowledge of both child development and the child welfare system gained in your human behavior or child welfare course. If you are selecting an organization and program that you designed as your client system case, you would draw on your macro practice course. You might also include your diversity course if you are working primarily with an African American population or your human development course if the primary population is adolescents.

D. Describe what you did in each phase of the planned change process and how the client system responded to each phase. In addition, identify any specific stage that stood out in terms of something you felt good about or found particularly challenging. In addition, given the varying nature of the settings, identify any phase(s) that differed from the book definition and discuss how your agency achieves the overall goal(s) of the planned change process in light of this difference:

1. Engagement:

2. Assessment:

3. Planning and contracting (in planning, identify a plan that targets the micro-, mezzo-, and macro-level system):

4. Implementation:

5. Monitoring:

6. Evaluation:

7. Termination:

E. Identify and describe any value-driven, legal, and ethical program or systemic issues that impacted the case and your work with the client system.

F. Identify how you used culturally competent practice skills and how you integrated your understanding of social and economic justice when working on the case.

G. For the implementation phase, consider the linkage of theory to practice (revisit Integrative Activity 10.3) and identify three theoretical perspectives or practice models that you

applied to the case. Briefly describe the theory, and identify at least one intervention you could use, based on the theory. Then identify at least one specific intervention you implemented and the theory that guided the intervention. Last, analyze the intervention's effectiveness in assisting the client in meeting his or her goal.

4. Do an overall analysis of the process, answering the following questions: How did I do? What were my strengths, and what are my growth areas? How did the planned change process flow? Did I achieve the desired result? How would the client system say they experienced the process? Is there anything I would recommend to improve the process?

FREQUENTLY EXPERIENCED SITUATIONS

Here are two situations that many students experience when practicing. The first can occur at any phase of the planned change process and thus requires specific focus. The second is specific to intervening and is particularly relevant if you are in a setting in which you cowork. Review each situation and discuss your analysis in class or with your field instructor.

My client stated that he would be better off dead and I didn't know what to say.

In group today, my client mentioned to me that he was thinking about suicide and I had no idea what to say. Fortunately, the other social worker talked with the client, but, I mean, I kind of froze and just didn't know what to say.

Suicide assessment and intervention in field is a scary and real part of your professional development and something you may encounter at any point of the planned change process. Therefore, it should be given extra time in supervision, where you can review what you learned in your practice classes prior to entering

field and determine how best to respond. Anyone at any time could have thoughts of suicide. What becomes important for you in field is developing a consistent plan of action of what to do should a client express suicidal ideation. Even the most prepared student can become nervous and anxious and stumble when working with a client who indicates suicidal ideation. That being said, should this happen, put the needs of the client first and ensure that the client is served. In the preceding situation, fortunately, the student was not alone. Even though the student froze, a worker was present who could assist the client. But what if the student had been alone? How should the student have handled the situation?

This happened when I was a field instructor. The student I was supervising went out on a routine visit to update releases of information, and in the course of the meeting, the client expressed suicidal ideation. The student was alone and handled it well by first, acknowledging what the client said; second, informing the client that she needed to call her supervisor; third, calling me; and fourth, staying with the client until I arrived. Together, the student and I assessed the level

(Continued)

(Continued)

of risk and discussed options with the client to ensure the client's safety.

To ensure that you are prepared to manage a situation of suicide risk, let's review a few important recommendations. Incidentally, many of the recommendations that relate to your duty to prevent harm (suicide risk) can apply to situations of mandated reporting or duty to warn, so make sure you are prepared for those situations as well. First, discuss in supervision specifically what your field instructor wants you to do should a client express suicidal ideation. Educate yourself with regard to the statistics and warning signs. Always maintain the possibility that any client during any contact could disclose information that would require you to act to ensure their safety. Review any tools that your agency uses to assess the level of risk. The SAD PERSONS acronym developed by Patterson, Dohn, Bird, and Patterson (1983) organizes the risk factors in a manageable way to allow for assessment of level of risk. Furthermore, Sheafor and Horejsi (2015) offer several areas of consideration to assess a person's potential for suicide. They are

- talking about harming self;

- focusing on pain, hopelessness, and helplessness;

- having a plan and access to the means; and

- lacking social support.

A helpful learning tool is to role-play with your field instructor a client experiencing suicidal ideation and to practice asking assessment questions and developing a plan of action if you have not done this thus far in your coursework.

When I worked on a suicide prevention hotline, we assessed callers to be at one of three risk levels: low, moderate, or high. If we assessed a client to be at high risk, we intervened with the goal of safety and treatment. If we assessed the client to be at low or moderate risk, we utilized contracts, linked the client with services, and often requested to speak to another person, with the permission of the client, to inform that person that the client was in distress.

Assessing the suicide risk of a client as a student can be a scary learning experience; thus, it is important to process the situation with your field instructor and always inform your field instructor if you are concerned about a client.

My group cofacilitator won't let me say anything. What should I do?

I was so excited because I was finally going to be able to run a group, but the person I was working with did all the talking. I didn't know what to do. There were so many times during the session that I wanted to say something, but I couldn't. I just don't know what to do. Now I'm dreading the next group session.

This situation can be frustrating and challenging to address as a student in field, but it is important to both your generalist training and your professional development. Two different issues are brought to light in this situation. One, the challenges of coworking when you have an identified task and two, the importance of being able to intervene with client systems. The two are actually related and illuminate the need to develop a strong coworking relationship so that you can intervene. Cofacilitating anything is challenging, due to the fact that you have to manage the task as well as your working relationship with the cofacilitator, which can often be the greater challenge of the two. It is important to negotiate and discuss your role and to plan for how you and your cofacilitator will function. I am speaking from experience.

One of my greatest professional practice challenges was cofacilitating an incest survivor group, where my working relationship with my cofacilitator became problematic to the point that it threatened our ability to continue to offer the group and required significant intervention with our supervisor. What I found most interesting was how my cofacilitator experienced my style of processing. To process a session, I would passionately discuss what happened and state my observations, concerns, and even shock with some of the content. This was the process that I would go through to debrief and figure out what to do next for the group. My cofacilitator interpreted my style and the information I shared as me not being able to handle the group, to the point that my cofacilitator reported feeling responsible for taking care of me and felt that this was not appropriate. Even though I reassured my cofacilitator that I was fine and that I enjoyed the challenge of working with this population in a group, this was not enough, and my cofacilitator discontinued working on the group. As an interesting side note, the new cofacilitator and I developed a strong and effective working relationship. So, this example shows that the working relationship of the cofacilitators is critical and is an important dynamic to consider in terms of the group process.

To develop a strong working relationship with your cofacilitator, the first thing you want to do is have a planning session. Planning for group or other tasks is an area that students tell me is often lacking in their placements. Given that you will be simultaneously developing your group skills while managing a cofacilitation relationship, it is critical that you request a planning session. During the session, review the structure of the group and the materials, and discuss the plan for your training and eventual independence as a group facilitator. The plan could be structured as in Week 1, you will observe; in Week 2, you will do one part of the group; and by Week 5, you will be able to run the entire group. Or it can flow more freely, where you will have the freedom to interject whenever you see fit. The latter, in my experience, is more challenging, but the former can feel too structured. I suggest a hybrid—allow for some structure and some spontaneity. Ask your cofacilitator to periodically ask you for feedback or sit back and allow for pauses to give you a chance to interject; have at least one thing per session that you are responsible for. After a group session, it is equally important to process the session, share your thoughts, ask for feedback, and plan for the next session. Wayne and Cohen (2001) state that "Co-leaders can help each other achieve greater self-awareness by providing feedback about their performance in the group. Through joint problem solving, they can be helped to sharpen their assessment and interventive skills" (p. 51).

Another technique to assist in this kind of situation is to develop a group session on your own that includes a planned intervention. This will give you the freedom and space to intervene while also allowing your cofacilitator an opportunity to observe you. For instance, if the group identifies issues around lacking in assertiveness, you might research that topic and develop a group session with the goal of increasing the participants' assertiveness skills. By designing the group's session, you will have a strong understanding of the content and will be able to demonstrate your skills while also improving your working relationship with your cofacilitator.

If and when issues between you and your cofacilitator come up, it is important to be assertive and discuss them, even if this causes anxiety. Remember, you can always discuss your concerns first with your field instructor, field director, faculty field liaison, or other students to gather suggestions for how to handle the situation and what to say. What is most important to remember is that if you feel your training and education are being hampered, it is critical to address the issue.

Suggested Field Tasks

- Present and analyze client system information.

- Review related course work.

- Discuss agency's practice for how students should handle situations that present risk to clients, such as suicidal ideation, child maltreatment, or harm to self or others.

- Develop and conduct a bio/psycho/psychosocial/spiritual/environmental assessment.

- Use your knowledge of development when assessing a client.

- Demonstrate your understanding of how behavior relates to and is impacted by social systems.

- Demonstrate your knowledge of theories by defining and explaining at least three theories that help you understand development and behavior and guide intervention.

- Discuss how the planned change process looks at agency.

- Intake and engage individuals, families, task and treatment groups, organizations, and communities via phone and in person.

- Prepare for client system contacts.

- Gather information on client systems.

- Identify client system goals.

- Identify formal assessments used by the agency.

- Conduct agency-based assessments (intakes, social histories, ecomaps, genograms, or other agency-based assessments) on client systems.

- Identify the client system's strengths and limitations.

- Identify the multilevel plans that help client systems resolve problems.

- Engage in interventions (implement plans) that demonstrate the roles of negotiation, mediation, and advocacy.

References

Council on Social Work Education. (2015). *Educational policy and accreditation standards*. Alexandria, VA: Author.

Hutchison, E. (2017). *Essentials of human behavior: Integrating person, environment, and the life course*. Thousand Oaks, CA: SAGE.

Johnson, L., & Yanca, S. (2007). *Social work practice: A generalist approach*. Boston, MA: Allyn and Bacon.

Kirst-Ashman, K., & Hull Jr., G. (2015). *Generalist practice with organizations and communities*. Stamford, CT: Cengage Learning.

Kirst-Ashman, K., & Hull Jr., G. (2018). *Understanding generalist practice* (8th ed.). Boston, MA: Cengage Learning.

Miley, K., O'Melia, M., & DuBois, B. (2011). *Generalist social work practice: An empowering approach*. Boston, MA: Allyn and Bacon.

Patterson, W., Dohn, H., Bird, J., & Patterson, G. (1983). Evaluation of suicidal patients: The SAD PERSONS scale. *Psychosomatics, 24*, 343–349.

Schatz, M. S., Jenkins, L. E., & Sheafor, B. W. (1990). Milford redefined: A model of initial and advanced generalist social work. *Journal of Social Work Education, 26*(3), 217.

Sheafor, B., & Horejsi, C. (2015). *Techniques and guidelines for social work practice*. Boston, MA: Pearson Education.

Wayne, J., & Cohen, C. (2001). *Group work in field education*. Alexandria, VA: Council on Social Work Education.

PROFESSIONAL DEVELOPMENT OF SELF IN FIELD

Chapter 1 introduced you to one of the important goals of field education: socialization to the profession. Throughout your field experience and socialization to the profession, you have had opportunities to experience and reflect on the various positions social workers hold and roles they use, the different types of agencies, and the different services offered by those agencies. You have also had an opportunity to specifically apply your generalist training to your practice at your field site.

The purpose of this chapter is to provide an opportunity for you to reflect on your professional development. Recall that Reflection Question 1.4, at the start of your field experience, asked you to consider what being a professional meant to you, what you saw as the advantages of being a professional versus an employee, and if there were any disadvantages. It also asked you to consider what excited you or created anxiety for you as you thought about being a professional social worker. As you reflect on the answer you gave at the time, consider Reflection Question 11.1.

As a field director, professional development of self, in the context of field education, is an interest of mine and one that I have focused on over the years. One experience in particular that stands out to me and exemplifies the transformation that students go through while in field happened to a student toward the end of her field experience. The student was working in a shelter, and one of her clients violated the confidentiality of location policy. The consequence of the violation was that the client had to leave the shelter. The student shared that this was a challenging situation, but she also knew she had to (1) uphold the policy of the agency, as the client was very aware of both the policy and the consequence of violating the policy and (2) adhere to her professional responsibility to all the clients and staff of the shelter; she understood why the confidentiality of location policy was so important.

Although this situation was not easy to manage, the student handled it well and was able to inform the client that she had to leave the shelter. At the end of the student sharing this situation, what really stood out to me was that the student stated she was glad the situation had

REFLECTION QUESTION 11.1

Would you answer that reflection question the same or differently, based on the experiences you have had in field? Do new things come to you about being a pro-

fessional social worker that did not occur to you at the beginning of your field experience? If so, what are those?

happened toward the end of her field experience versus the beginning. She went on to explain that the professional experience she gained through her field experience made it easier for her to do something that was very difficult. She even stated that she didn't know if she could have handled the situation if it had happened at the beginning of field. Thus, this situation reflects how important time and experience are to a student's professional development. It is the culmination of all the experiences of field that contributes to the development of the professional skills and enables a student to handle complex client situations. But what does it mean to be a professional? This chapter will explore many commonly understood aspects of professionalism as well as what students need to consider as they reflect on their own professional development.

THE PROFESSIONAL DEFINED

A *professional* is defined as "a person whose actions are thoughtful, purposeful, competent, responsible and ethical" (Sheafor & Horejsi, 2015, p. 47). The Council on Social Work Education (CSWE, 2015) states,

Social workers

- make ethical decisions by applying the standards of the National Association of Social Workers (NASW) code of ethics, relevant laws and regulations, models for ethical decision making, ethical conduct of research, and additional codes of ethics as appropriate to context;

- use reflection and self-regulation to manage personal values and maintain professionalism in practice situations;

- demonstrate professional demeanor in behavior; appearance; and oral, written, and electronic communication;

- use technology ethically and appropriately to facilitate practice outcomes; and

- use supervision and consultation to guide professional judgment and behavior. (p. 7)

Barker (2003) defines a *professional* as "an individual who qualifies for membership in a specific profession and uses its practices, knowledge, and skills to provide services to client systems, and in doing so, always adheres to its *values* and *code of ethics*" (p. 341). As a soon-to-be professional social worker, it is important to consider what the preceding definitions mean to you. Consider Reflection Question 11.2.

In all likelihood, this transition has been and will continue to be exciting, rewarding, and challenging.

REFLECTION QUESTION 11.2

What do you think it means to be a professional social worker? How would you assess your level of competence in demonstrating the behaviors of a professional as outlined by the CSWE (2015), and how are you transitioning from the role of a student to the role of a social worker?

ROOM TO REFLECT

At the end of every year, I ask the students what they got out of field and if field was worthwhile. Year after year, students overwhelmingly agree that they are significantly different because of their experience in field, that the field experience was worth the stress and hard work, and that they truly believe they got things out of the experience that they could not have gotten from the classroom. Over the years, several common themes have appeared as students described their professional development. For instance, students report feeling that they are

- confident in their ability to assert their knowledge, values, and skills in practice;

- able to respond effectively to complex and challenging client situations, as evidenced in the story at the beginning of the chapter;

- excited and relieved about ending or advancing their education and getting closer to becoming a "real" social worker;

- anxious about licensure and job seeking, graduate school, or advanced field; and

- able to manage the complex problems faced by client systems.

Finally, one student recently told me, on the last day of class, that field had helped him solidify his belief that he had made the right choice to become a social worker. Although the preceding sentiments are only a few of the themes related to professional development and are in no way exhaustive, they do speak to the unique contribution that field makes in the professional development of the student.

ETHICAL RESPONSIBILITIES OF THE PROFESSIONAL

The NASW code of ethics (2017) addresses social workers' ethical responsibilities as professionals and puts forth standards that address competence; discrimination; private conduct; dishonesty, fraud, and deception; impairment; misrepresentation; solicitations; and acknowledging credit (pp. 25–26). A few of these are helpful to specifically discuss.

First, in terms of the social worker's responsibility of *competence*, this ethical standard speaks to the responsibility of social workers to work within their area(s) of expertise and engage in lifelong learning. This is accomplished by keeping abreast of the knowledge through routine review of the literature and attendance at continuing education trainings.

The standards that address *private conduct* and *impairment* state that (1) social workers should not let their private lives interfere with their ability to practice as social workers and (2) when a social worker's personal conduct is interfering, that person should seek immediate action. This speaks to self-care, self-reflection, and the need of social workers to be acutely aware of how they are doing as a person first and their responsibility in knowing when they need assistance. Self-care will be addressed in more detail later in the chapter.

Another standard that needs to be highlighted is *misrepresentation*, which addresses the fact that social workers have an ethical responsibility to accurately represent themselves to their clients and claim only accurate information regarding their education, credentials, and expertise and practice accordingly. Although the code does not explicitly state that a social worker should be licensed, licensure is important for several reasons. First, it protects client systems through a governing body, a licensing board that monitors the actions of licensees and investigates issues of wrongdoing. Second, it advances the status of the social worker and allows for reimbursement of services. Third, it distinguishes you as a social worker who thus has a specific body of knowledge base, values, and skills to use in the practice of assisting client systems.

PROFESSIONAL DEVELOPMENT

Now that we have defined a professional and discussed the ethical responsibilities of a professional social worker, let's turn our attention to how one becomes a professional social worker, or the professional development of self. Barretti (2004) states that the development of a professional self is more a process than an acquired set of behaviors or values and found that development begins before students enter a social work program. Barretti states,

> Because students hold well-defined conceptualizations of social workers and of the profession through previous experiences with both, it behooves social work programs to start where the "client" is by building upon students' breadth of experience rather than assuming they are blank slates on which only they will write. (p. 22)

When considering professional development of self, it is useful to take a holistic perspective, considering who you are and your background, how you define yourself as a social worker, what it means to you to be a social worker, the experiences you have had in field and in the classroom, and how these experiences have impacted your professional development.

For the past several years, I have been exploring all of the preceding points and have expanded the discussion of professional development to include a spiritually sensitive perspective (Larkin, 2010). Now before you stop reading, let me explain.

Professional Development: A Spiritually Sensitive Perspective

Spirituality in social work practice has been written about extensively for over two decades. Derezotes (2006) identifies what he calls a second phase of spirituality that is not only concerned with personal spiritual growth but also with a transformation that leads to a deeper understanding of our responsibility to care for each other. The author states that "there is a growing awareness that spiritual development brings with it an increased responsibility to serve, and that personal spirituality and service are themselves interconnected and interrelated" (p. 2). In light of this, it is becoming increasingly important for students to have the opportunity to reflect on their own spiritual development and the role that spirituality may or may not play in their development as a social worker. This is supported by Barretti (2004), who found that some students "do not entirely credit social work training for their transformation and instead viewed their training as a complement to other developmental or spiritual changes already occurring" (p. 20).

Canda and Furman (1999) provide a definition of spirituality that is helpful as you consider your professional development of self from a spiritually sensitive perspective. They state that "spirituality relates to a universal and fundamental aspect of what it is to be human—to search for a sense of meaning, purpose, and moral framework for relating with self, others and the ultimate reality" (p. 370). They go on to say that "spiritually sensitive social workers address clients as whole persons, applying professional roles, rules and assessment labels in a flexible way that is responsive to the values of the client and his or her community" (p. 32). Derezotes (2006) distinguishes spirituality from religion by stating that

> spirituality can be seen as the *individual's* sense of connectedness, meaning, peace, consciousness, purpose, and service that develops across the life span. In contrast, religiosity can be seen as *socially* shared rituals, doctrines, and beliefs that may or may not support and enhance the individual's spiritual development. (p. 3)

An exploration of professional development of self from a spiritually sensitive perspective is grounded in spirituality, not religion. This is done with the intent to be inclusive and to provide a wider lens for your consideration. I do, however, realize that for some students, religion and spirituality are conceptually and experientially joined, and for others, any notion of spirituality may be irrelevant. Thus, I have broken down the concept of spiritually sensitive professional development into three specific areas that can be explored regardless of one's particular personal identification with spirituality or religion. Considering professional development of self from a spiritually sensitive perspective was important to students, regardless of their religious or spiritual or nonreligious or nonspiritual orientation (Larkin, 2010):

> Spiritually Sensitive Professional Development is defined as professional development that considers the whole student, is grounded in an understanding of meaning and purpose in one's work, utilizes a process of reflection and discernment for ethical practice and emphasizes spiritually based self-care. (p. 446)

To ground your thinking and reflection, each of the three grounding components of this definition will be discussed separately.

Meaning and Purpose in Work

The first aspect of spiritually sensitive professional development to consider is meaning and purpose in work. This component asks you to consider what it is about your work that brings you meaning and how does that relate to its purpose.

From a personal perspective, I don't think my work as a social worker is necessarily more important than other types of work, but I do feel that my work is meaningful to me and significant in the lives of the client systems with whom I work. As you have seen throughout your field experience, social workers often become intricately involved in the lives of their clients. It is in these moments of deep connection that recognizing and drawing on meaning can be beneficial to both the client and the worker. The same may hold true for you. During your field experience, in all likelihood, you too were confronted with deep questions of life in which the meaning and purpose of your work as well as your beliefs and values may have been both challenged and confirmed.

Use Reflection Question 11.3 below to consider your practice experiences in the field and what stands out to you.

REFLECTION QUESTION 11.3

As you think about your field experience, what direct or indirect client system experiences have you had that you would consider as having meaning? How did you handle these experiences? Was it challenging, or did it come naturally? What meaning did these experiences hold for you as a social work student?

ROOM TO REFLECT

Finding meaning in one's work is an idea conceptualized by Fox (1994). The author states,

> Good living and good working go together. Life and livelihood ought not to be separated but to flow from the same source, which is Spirit, for both life and livelihood are about Spirit. Spirit means life, and both life and livelihood are about living in depth, living with meaning, purpose, joy, and a sense of contributing to the greater community. A spirituality of work is about bringing life and livelihood back together again. And Spirit with them. (pp. 1–2)

Developing clarity about the meaning and purpose your work holds for you can also be a part of both your professional development and your ability to sustain a professional life, what Thomas (2005) calls *composing a life in the day to day*. Considering the impact of your day-to-day experiences in field is important in your ability to gain a sense of meaning and purpose. These experiences have become the foundation of your understanding of what it is to be a social worker and who you are becoming as a social worker. Reflecting on these experiences, discussed in more detail next, will help you gain a better understanding of what it means to you to be a social worker and thus to determine your purpose. On the surface, a sense of meaning and purpose in work should go beyond your job description and focus more on what it means to be a professional social worker. To begin to articulate your understanding of meaning and purpose in your work, consider Reflection Question 11.4.

REFLECTION QUESTION 11.4

What drove you to want to be a social worker, and what does being a social worker mean to you? Where did your desire to be a social worker come from? What do you see as your purpose as a social worker? Another way to look at this is to ask yourself, *What kind of social worker do I want to be?*

ROOM TO REFLECT

Reflection and Discernment for Ethical Practice

The next aspect of spiritually sensitive professional development is reflection and discernment for professional practice (Larkin, 2010). To *discern* is to develop the ability to more fully understand and make a determination about something within its context. Reflection is an important part of the process that leads to discernment. Engaging in reflection and discernment is important for you to more clearly define and articulate your professional development as a social worker and to meet the expectation of professional practice. Three aspects of professional development that are key to reflect on are

1. your professional identity—who you are as a social worker,

2. your role within the profession—what are you called to do, and

3. your professional behavior—how will you do social work in the day to day.

It is through a process of reflection that you will be able to discern these three parts of your professional development.

As you reflect, specifically on your role within the profession, I think it is helpful to mention that social workers can experience conflict related to the professional role they choose. This conflict seems to center around the following questions: Am I doing the right work? Am I doing enough? Just asking these questions can diminish the good work one is doing. Remember, according to the NASW, there are some several hundred thousand social workers in the United States who are doing all kinds of important work. Thus, you are one of many and your professional role is also one of many. There is no right or wrong professional role. Thus, as you think about your professional identity, role, and behavior, consider Reflection Question 11.5.

Ethical practice is mentioned in all three of the previously cited definitions of a professional; thus, developing the skills necessary to engage in ethical practice as a professional is critical. Reflection and discernment are two important tools to assist you in this process. Staral (2003) emphasizes self-reflection, ethical decision making, and self-care and relates them specifically

REFLECTION QUESTION 11.5

How would you describe your professional identity? What is/are the professional role(s) that you want to take on as a social worker? How would you describe the professional behavior you want to exhibit in your day-to-day life as a social worker?

ROOM TO REFLECT

ROOM TO REFLECT

to her experiences with Ignatian Spirituality. Staral exposed her students to the examen of consciousness, a Jesuit spirituality practice, which encouraged students to reflect on their daily lives. As a result of the reflection, students were better able to gain insight and resolution. So, the reflection and discernment the students engaged in helped them *discern* (see, detect, or make clearer) what they needed to do. As you will recall, reflection is a critical part of ethical decision making, resolving ethical dilemmas and understanding how your "personal experiences and affective reactions influence . . . professional judgment and behavior" (CSWE, 2015, p. 7). It is often the thing that nags at us and demands our attention that we later define as a dilemma; thus, reflection and discernment become important tools in resolving ethical dilemmas.

As you consider your experiences in field and develop your skill of reflection and discernment, you will be better able to understand who you are becoming as a social worker and manage the challenges of a professional life as well as uphold the ethical responsibilities of a professional as identified by the NASW. Canda and Furman (1999) state, "When we realize that spirituality encompasses the wholeness of what it is to be human, we become aware of the precious and wonderful nature of every moment and interaction" (p. 217).

Spiritually Based Self-Care

The last aspect of spiritually sensitive professional development is spiritually based self-care (Larkin, 2010). This refers to those things you can do to take care of yourself and expands the options to include relevant spiritually based practices. Staral (2003) also makes this link between spirituality and self-care. Thus, consider what role spirituality can play, if any, in your self-care. Barton (2006) articulates the concept of *a rule of life* as an important part of the process of spiritual transformation and states,

> A rule of life seeks to respond to two questions: Who do I want to be? How do I want to live? Actually, it might be more accurate to say that a rule of life seeks to address the interplay between these two questions: How do I want to live so I can be who I want to be? (p. 147)

Take a few minutes to reflect on the preceding quote as it relates to your professional development, particularly in light of the idea of spiritually based self-care. As you may notice, the interplay, referenced above, between who you want to be and how you want to live also relates to the three parts of professional development identified earlier: professional identity, professional role, and professional behaviors (Larkin, 2010). As you look back at your responses to Reflection Question 11.5, how do you see the idea of *rule of life* relating to how you conceptualized your professional development?

A rule of life (Barton, 2006) relates to spiritually based self-care in that it suggests that social workers identify what they need to do daily, weekly, monthly, and yearly to sustain themselves as professionals and have long careers. Spiritually based self-care practices go beyond the obvious things such as time management, making lists, attending supervision, getting enough rest, and eating right and considers practices that transcend the surface and delve more deeply into social workers' understanding of who they are, where they come from, and what they need to be social workers. For some individuals, they may draw directly from religious and or spiritual practices, such as prayer or use of scripture; others may focus on existential practices that consider questions of human suffering and our responsibility to one another; still others may turn to nature as a way to replenish their resources; and others may use their creativity in the form of art or music for self-care. Regardless of the particular practice, it is important to accept and embrace self-care, particularly in light of the fact that social work is a helping profession grounded in the care of others. To guide you in this exploration, consider Reflection Question 11.6.

REFLECTION QUESTION 11.6

What do you see as your needs related to self-care? What spiritually based practices can you draw on? What spiritually based practices might you develop?

ROOM TO REFLECT

PROFESSIONAL DEVELOPMENT OF SELF CAPSTONE PAPER

Now that you have had a chance to consider your professional development of self in general and from a spiritually sensitive perspective, it can be helpful to pull your thoughts and ideas together in the form of a capstone paper. I have been having the students I work with write professional development of self capstone papers for years. Every year, students share how they find it a useful activity in that it forces them to think more critically about the big picture of their field experience as opposed to only focusing on their work with clients or their agency. More recently, as I have added the spiritually sensitive perspective to the paper, students have reported getting even more out of the activity. In fact, one student stated, "If the capstone paper had not had the spiritual focus, I don't think I could have written it. I mean I would have, but I don't think it would have been as helpful or meaningful to me" (Larkin, 2010, p. 457).

To write your capstone paper, see Integrative Activity 11.1. This activity provides an opportunity to synthesize the responses to the reflection questions in this chapter. It allows you to integrate your understanding of your professional development from a holistic perspective, considering all aspects of yourself, even if some aspects are still not completely apparent. As you will recall, professional development is a process that involves lifelong learning. You will spend your entire career refining and learning about who you are as a social worker and how you want to put your identity into practice.

INTEGRATIVE ACTIVITY 11.1
PROFESSIONAL DEVELOPMENT OF SELF CAPSTONE PAPER

Purpose: The purpose of this activity is to provide the foundation and direction for writing a capstone paper in which you explore your development as an emerging professional social worker, incorporating a spiritually sensitive perspective.

Competency 1: Demonstrate Ethical and Professional Behavior

- make ethical decisions by applying the standards of the NASW code of ethics, relevant laws and regulations, models for ethical decision making, ethical conduct of research, and additional codes of ethics as appropriate to context

- use reflection and self-regulation to manage personal values and maintain professionalism in practice situations

- demonstrate professional demeanor in behavior; appearance; and oral, written, and electronic communication

Directions:

1. To prepare to write the capstone reflection paper, use the following directions:

   - Reflect on the three areas of the definition of spiritually sensitive professional development—meaning and purpose in work, reflection and discernment for ethical practice, and spiritually sensitive self-care (Larkin, 2010)—as they specifically relate to you and your experiences.

   - Consider your own spiritual and religious development and the role that spirituality

and religion have or have not played in your development as a professional social worker.

   - Reflect on how you would describe your professional identity, professional role, and professional behavior.

   - Reflect on spiritually based practice issues, including ethical dilemmas or any spiritually based practice interventions you may have used in field.

   - Discuss spiritually based social work practice and professional development with your field instructor.

2. Once you have reflected on the preceding items, consider these additional areas:

   - your professional strengths, weaknesses, and greatest successes and challenges

   - any value-driven ethical issues or dilemmas related to your professional development that you encountered in the field and what you learned from them

   - how you are coming to define yourself as a professional from a spiritually sensitive perspective, including what has been easy for you and what has been challenging

   - any observations of or lapses of professionalism in your field instructor, coworkers, peers, agency, and profession as a whole and the impact each has or has not had on your development

FREQUENTLY EXPERIENCED SITUATION

Below is a situation that many students experience and one that can be jarring to their understanding of social workers, who they are, and how they act. This relates to this chapter, given that a key aspect of professional identity is the appraisal of other social workers' professional behavior or lack thereof and how to understand and integrate that into one's own identity.

My coworker was really rude to a client and I don't know what to do about it.

> I went on a home visit the other day with one of the social workers in the agency. During the visit, the social worker was very short with the client and at one point, I mean in my opinion, was rude. I couldn't believe it. Then when we got in the car, she proceeded to tell me how much she dislikes this client. I honestly didn't know what to say. I still couldn't believe that the social worker spoke to the client the way she did. It really upset me because I really like and respect this worker and now I don't know what to do. One thing I do know is that I would never speak to a client like that.

This is a jarring but not uncommon experience for a student. As stated in Chapter 1, as a student in field, you will be exposed to the good, the bad, and the ugly. In my opinion, this particular situation, at least on the surface, may fall in the *ugly* category, but let's examine the situation in more detail.

First of all, one of the best things about field, as far as I am concerned, is that you get a chance to be exposed to so many different clients, workers, and situations. Along with that, you will, at times, observe things that you either don't understand or disagree with completely. Even if it is sometimes challenging, it is an important part of professional development because you will develop your own sense of yourself as a professional social worker through the process of observing a wide variety of professional behaviors.

I remember that when I was working in family preservation, my supervisor would come up with these amazing interventions, and half the time, I would state that I didn't think I could pull them off. Or I would observe a coworker working with a client in a way that I knew I couldn't, but for some reason, it worked with that particular client. I have also witnessed completely inappropriate conduct on the part of a worker that fell under the category of my ethical responsibility of protecting clients, and I reported the conduct to a supervisor. As you can see, it is expected that from time to time, you will witness practices that you will question and perhaps even feel the need to discuss with your supervisor.

With regard to the given situation, any number of things could be going on. First, this could be the style of the worker, which happens to be extremely different from your style. There could be issues on the case that the worker has had to deal with that necessitates the worker be stern—although I don't think there is ever a reason to be rude. Even if the worker states that she dislikes the client, that doesn't mean that the worker won't provide the necessary service. It is not uncommon to have clients whom you struggle with or who really challenge your skills. I suggested that the student process the session with her field instructor to get some perspective and share her concerns. The student was worried and didn't want to appear as if she was telling on the other worker. This is an understandable concern, but it is so important that as a student, you share with your field instructor what you are observing and how you are reacting to what you observe. Remember, if your field instructor is concerned, he or she will handle the situation, maintain your confidentiality, and ultimately appreciate your observations.

Suggested Field Tasks

- Engage a mentor.

- Engage in self-care activities, and monitor stress and burnout levels.

- Explore your professional development of self.

- In supervision, identify and discuss your personal values and distinguish between personal and professional values.

- Use reflection to explore your role, tasks, and experiences of field.

- Explain the knowledge, skills, and values you have developed as a result of your field experiences.

- Join your department's social work club.

- Join NASW or another professional organization.

References

Barker, R. (2003). *The social work dictionary* (4th ed.). Washington, DC: NASW Press.

Barretti, M. (2004). The professional socialization of undergraduate social work students. *The Journal of Baccalaureate Social Work, 9*(2), 9–30.

Barton, R. (2006). *Sacred rhythms: Arranging our lives for spiritual transformation*. Downers Grove, IL: Inter-varsity Press.

Canda, E. R., & Furman, L. D. (1999). *Spiritual diversity in social work practice: The heart of helping*. New York, NY: The Free Press.

Council on Social Work Education. (2015). *Educational policy and accreditation standards*. Alexandria, VA: Author.

Derezotes, D. (2006). *Spiritually oriented social work practice*. Boston, MA: Allyn and Bacon.

Fox, M. (1994). *The reinvention of work*. New York, NY: Harper Collins.

Larkin, S. (2010). Spiritually sensitive professional development of self: A curricular module for field education. *Social Work & Christianity, 37*(4), 446–466.

National Association of Social Workers (NASW). (2017). *Code of ethics of the National Association of Social Workers*. Washington DC: Author. Retrieved March 9, 2018, from https://www.socialworkers.org/LinkClick .aspx?fileticket=ms_ArtLqzel%3d&portalid=0

Sheafor, B., & Horejsi, C. (2015). *Techniques and guidelines for social work practice* (10th ed.). Boston, MA: Pearson Education.

Staral, J. M. (2003). Introducing Ignatian spirituality: Linking self-reflection with social work ethics. *Social Work & Christianity, 30*(1), 38–51.

Thomas, T. (2005). *Spirituality in the mother zone: Staying centered, finding God*. Mahwah, NJ: Paulist.

ENDINGS IN FIELD EDUCATION

I f you are reading this chapter, it means either you are the kind of person who likes to read the last chapter first to see how the book ends or you are approaching the end of your field experience. I suspect it is the latter. Completing your field experience is a wonderful accomplishment and one that is multifaceted. Every year, as the students I work with get toward the end of field, I tell them I am big on endings. This means I think it is critically important for you to

1. develop your understanding of the role endings play in social work practice and field education and

2. be present with and experience your endings.

In this chapter, we will provide and discuss reflection questions and integrative activities for you to use while in field.

ENDINGS IN SOCIAL WORK PRACTICE

As you will recall, termination is the final phase of the planned change process and is defined as "the time when the worker guides concluding activities of the process in a manner that is sensitive to issues surrounding the ending of a relationship" (Sheafor & Horejsi, 2015, p. 382). Let's look more closely at this definition and discuss the two aspects of the definition.

First, the definition states that termination involves the worker guiding the activities; that is, the worker is doing something or having a role in the process and experience of the ending. In micro-level practice, with individuals or families, this might include a final session in which the worker reviews the accomplishments of the client, acknowledges that the work is ending, and provides any final recommendations. In mezzo-level practice with a treatment group, the worker may use a ritual or activity to mark the final group session. One such activity could be having each member of the group identify one thing that he or she got out of the group that the member will continue to use in day-to-day life. Last, when it comes to macro-level practice with an organization (and, more specifically, program development), the worker may write a final report documenting that the program is up and running, that all agreed-upon tasks with regard to developing the program are completed, and who or what entity is taking over the running of the program.

As you can see in the preceding examples, the worker was active and engaged in a specific activity to mark the ending, and the ending often reflected the role the social worker played in the client's service. So, consideration of your professional role and the boundaries inherent in that role are also important when considering endings. For instance, some students state that they do not have an ongoing relationship with clients, so individually informing clients that they are leaving the agency may not be necessary. If that is the case, then it may only be important for the agency staff to be made aware that the student is leaving. That way, if anyone asked about the student, the staff could let that person know the student was no longer with the agency.

With regard to the second part of the definition, you will want to develop the skills necessary to ensure that the ending activity reflects the relationship and is responsive to how the client system may experience the ending. This is most apparent when working with individuals and families. It is very important that you develop an understanding of the endings that the clients you work with have experienced; then make sure your activities take that into consideration. A common anxiety that students express, particularly when working with children, is the fear that they will be letting the child down or become yet another person who is walking out of the child's life. This anxiety is even greater when the student is initiating the ending due to their field placement ending. This situation is common; it requires planning and discussion in supervision and can be handled well.

For instance, one student I worked with had this exact concern and, in fact, the client expressed this as well. To address this concern, the student was very direct and honest with the client. The student stated that the client was indeed correct that the student would be ending their work together soon because his field placement was ending. The student even stated his concern about this fact and questioned in supervision whether or not they should work together at this time. By first acknowledging the reality of the ending, affirming the concern of the client, and expressing his own concern, the student was able to engage the client and actually address termination in the first meeting. Thinking about the ending really should start at the beginning of the work. The client and student together were able to negotiate what they felt they could accomplish in the time they had and planned ahead for the ending. By the time the last meeting occurred, both the client and student were well prepared; the student emphasized how the client could use the relationship to accomplish the goal, even with a short time frame. This turned into the client's successful use of the helping relationship. The student asked the client how he could use what he learned in future relationships with other social workers. The client was able to identify his success and translate what he did with the student into future relationships.

This is exactly what I encourage the students I work with to do—to help clients focus on what they did and how they were able to use the helping relationship and the planned change process to successfully address their needs and problems. By doing so, this de-emphasizes the worker and, in turn, emphasizes the process and the client's ability to effectively use the process. Finally, one thing I always did when I ended work with children was to reframe the ending to help them see that by working with different people, even if it seems overwhelming, they are gaining valuable experience and skills and that each person who comes into their life brings something different that the client can use. Again, the goal is to acknowledge the fact that helping relationships end and to create an experience that honors the needs of the client and maximizes the potential outcome of the ending.

When considering how best to terminate contact with client systems, discuss all the possible ways this can be handled in supervision with your field instructor. Effective use of supervision and consultation can make a difference in how well-thought-out the termination is and how that ending will impact clients.

However, before you can adequately assess the role of endings in the lives of your clients and then ensure that your termination activities reflect that understanding, you must first reflect on how you experience endings in your life currently and in the past. As you have most likely been told in your social work program, strong social work practice skills begin with self-awareness; thus, consider Reflection Question 12.1 below.

Types of Endings in Practice

Gelman (2009) identifies three types of endings with clients that are helpful to review. They are "natural terminations, . . . client-initiated, . . . and forced" (p. 183). In a study of 54 Master of Social Work (MSW) students, Gelman found that forced termination, or a termination that occurs as the result of field ending, was experienced by 93% of students; 24% of students experienced natural termination, when the work ended because goals were met; and 35% of students

REFLECTION QUESTION 12.1

How have you handled endings in your life? As you think about ending field, what does that bring up for you? As you think about ending your work with your clients, your agency, and your program, how do you feel about that? What do you need when you experience an ending, and how can you translate that into your practice with your clients, agency, and field program?

ROOM TO REFLECT

experienced the conclusion of the relationship when the client initiated the ending (p. 183). It is interesting to note that for 44% of the students surveyed, forced endings were the only type of termination experienced (p. 183). Gelman also found that although the students had received training in their course work, they would have benefited from earlier discussion of termination in their supervision session and emphasis on planning for termination. Baum (2006) also found that students experienced distress due to "untimeliness of the end-of-year treatment termination" (p. 649) or what the author defined as a "forced termination" (p. 639). So, considering the types of endings you are likely to experience and the impact these endings will have on you and your clients is a useful part of the termination process.

REFLECTION QUESTION 12.2

As you begin to think about termination, specifically the client systems with whom you are working, what are the possible activities that you could use to facilitate the ending? Next, what are the specific needs of your client systems that you should take into consideration as you plan for the ending? Last, what are the types of endings you are likely to experience at your field site, and what impact will these endings have on you?

ROOM TO REFLECT

ENDINGS IN FIELD EDUCATION

For some students, the previous reflection question may illuminate the fact that, due to the nature of their work at their field site, the impact of the student ending field will be minimal on the clients they serve. For example, for the student who works at the local social services agency that provides primarily emergency-based service, such as rent or utility assistance and referrals to the food pantry, he or she has not established ongoing working relationships with clients; in fact, he or she may see many different clients each day. For this student, the focus on termination will be more on the field experience as a whole, which is the second area of consideration and is important for all students to consider.

Ending Your Relationship With Your Agency

As you approach ending your field experience, the first thing to reflect on is the fact that you are ending your working relationship with your agency. This involves acknowledging all of the contributions the agency has made in your development as a social worker as well as the contributions you have made to the agency. The latter is what I call your *legacy*. Thus, reflect on the contributions you have made to your agency and acknowledge them as a part of the termination process.

Next, acknowledge the impact the relationships you have formed with all the staff of the agency, excluding your field instructor, as that relationship will be discussed separately. Reflect on all the relationships you have developed, positive and negative, and consider the role that each of these relationships has played in your development as a social worker. Think about what you would like to share with these coworkers before you leave. Just as we have emphasized planning in all aspects of social work practice, planning for your last week and day is important. In fact, I tell the students I work with that you don't want your last day to be like any other day—you want this day to be significant.

As part of considering your ending with your agency, you also want to demonstrate appropriate professionalism in that you have cleaned out your office, completed all necessary work tasks, informed your coworkers and field instructor of the status on all current projects and tasks, and, of course, said all of your good-byes.

REFLECTION QUESTION 12.3

As you think about ending your working relationship with your agency (including coworkers) and your tasks, how do you want your last week and last day to go? To help you answer this question, consider the following visualization: Imagine yourself coming home from your last day of field, and answer the following questions: What do you hope happened? What specifically do you hope you did so you can say you had a good last day and feel good about how that day went?

ROOM TO REFLECT

Ending Your Relationship With Your Field Instructor

Ending your relationship with your field instructor is often significant for students, particularly given the multifaceted nature of the student–field instructor relationship. Thus, engage in a focused reflection in order to best prepare for the ending of this relationship. In all likelihood, you will have strong feelings about this relationship and realize it has been significant in your development as a social worker. It is also important to realize that this sentiment is most likely shared by your field instructor. I can only speak for myself, but when I was a field instructor, I really enjoyed the unique relationship I could build with the student I was supervising, and I acknowledged that this relationship was important to me. I also always shared with the students I supervised how much I learned from them and appreciated the opportunity to serve as their field instructor. This is often because students and field instructors are encouraged to engage in the larger discussions about the profession, what being a social worker means, and their development as a social worker. On the other hand, you may not feel a strong attachment to your field instructor, and that is okay. However, it is still important to acknowledge the ending of this experience and this unique relationship. As you can see, there is no right or wrong way to go about ending this relationship, except to be present and acknowledge that the relationship is indeed ending.

REFLECTION QUESTION 12.4

As you think about acknowledging your relationship with your field instructor, what would you like to say or do? What would you like your field instructor to say or do?

ROOM TO REFLECT

Ending Your Field Education Experience

The last thing to reflect on as you consider endings in field education is the fact that you are ending your field education experience. This entails several things worth considering. First of all, for those of you in a Bachelor in Social Work (BSW) senior field placement, this means the end of being a student, the end of your field curriculum, and the end of your undergraduate BSW education. That is a lot of endings. For those of you in a foundation MSW field placement, this is the end of this part of your field program.

These endings are often experienced with mixed emotions. I have had students tell me they feel relieved, sad, excited, and petrified all at the same time. According to the life course perspective (Elder, 1998), transitions are important to consider in that how they are experienced shapes one's future. Ending field and possibly your current social work program is absolutely a significant transition that often brings with it new stressors and questions. But before we explore those new stressors and next steps, it is important to sit with this accomplishment and relish in all that you have learned and the contributions that you have made to all the client systems you have worked with.

In fact, this is an important task of both critical thinking and professional development of self. It is necessary that you develop the ability to articulate verbally and in writing what you have learned, what you have accomplished, and what you realize you need to work on next. It is also important that you can describe the work you have done so that it relates to the overarching competencies needed by a generalist social worker. Developing this skill and being prepared to share your thoughts about the preceding information will be extremely helpful to you as you think about what is next.

Curriculum Analysis

An important part of articulating what you learned in field is reflecting on the knowledge, values, and skills you have internalized from your curriculum as well as how you integrated that curriculum in your practice in field. Just as you engaged in curriculum review as a part of your orientation when you began field, you will want to engage in curriculum analysis as a part of ending.

The purpose of analyzing your curriculum is to solidify your understanding of it and identify any gaps that may have existed. If you identified any gaps, it is my hope that, first, you were able to close those gaps while in field and, second, you will provide that information to your program, either through your course evaluation or exit survey. It is very important that field education not exist in a vacuum: that students' experiences and curriculum evaluation, either in terms of the areas that seamlessly integrate with the practice experiences of field or those where there were gaps, be incorporated into the social work program. Last, periodic review of your knowledge, values, and skills as a professional will support the expectation that social workers engage in lifelong learning. Thus, this exploration can provide an opportunity for you to develop the skills necessary to meet this expectation. Integrative Activity 12.1 will provide you the opportunity to conduct this analysis and consider the areas of strength and the gaps. In light of your field experience, what recommendations would you make with regard to your program's curriculum, if any?

INTEGRATIVE ACTIVITY 12.1
CURRICULUM ANALYSIS

Purpose: The purpose of this activity is to provide an opportunity for you to analyze your curriculum in the context of the core competencies and practice behaviors to solidify your understanding of your curriculum and preparation for practice. This will also help you identify any gaps in your training and thus inform your program's curriculum.

Directions: The first column lists the 10 core competency areas identified by the Council on Social Work Education (CSWE) educational policies and accreditation standards (EPAS; CSWE, 2008). In the second column, identify the course(s) that provided the most relevant content; in the third column, provide feedback regarding your level of preparation and how the content informed your practice in field.

In the fourth column, identify any gaps in the curriculum, that is, areas in which you were not well prepared. Last, provide an overall analysis of your curriculum, answering the foundational questions: How has your curriculum prepared you? What were the seamless points of integration, and what gaps, if any, existed between your preparation and the expectation of your field agency from a generalist perspective?

Competency 1: Demonstrate Ethical and Professional Behavior

Social workers recognize the importance of lifelong learning and are committed to continually updating their skills to ensure that they are relevant and effective.

EPAS (CSWE, 2015) Core Competency (To review a description and the component behaviors, see Integrative Activity 1.1.)	Program's Courses (refer to curriculum review)	Feedback Regarding Preparation and Applicability to Field Tasks	Gaps in Curriculum
Competency 1: Demonstrate Ethical and Professional Behavior			
Competency 2: Engage Diversity and Difference in Practice			
Competency 3: Advance Human Rights and Social, Economic, and Environmental Justice			
Competency 4: Engage in Practice-Informed Research and Research-Informed Practice			
Competency 5: Engage in Policy Practice			
Competency 6: Engage with Individuals, Families, Groups, Organizations, and Communities			
Competency 7: Assess Individuals, Families, Groups, Organizations, and Communities			
Competency 8: Intervene with Individuals, Families, Groups, Organizations, and Communities			

(Continued)

(Continued)

Competency 9: Evaluate Practice with Individuals, Families, Groups, Organizations, and Communities			

Overall Curriculum Analysis: In this section, provide your overall analysis of your program's curriculum and how prepared you were for practice. Also, include areas of strength, gaps, and any suggestions you have for improving the curriculum. Identify the areas of the curriculum that were seamless in terms of integrating into the practice experiences of field and those that were more challenging. Last, reflect on lifelong learning as it relates to what you will do next in your education or practice.

Note: Specialized curriculum is not necessarily a gap; it is just that—specialized. Only include content that relates to the core competencies or that you feel should be included.

PULLING IT ALL TOGETHER

We have discussed the importance of articulating your understanding of your field education experience in terms of the knowledge, values, and skills you have integrated into field. We also discussed the role that curriculum analysis plays in solidifying your understanding of your curriculum and identifying gaps in your experience and your plans for lifelong learning. Now, it is time to pull this all together and develop your ability to articulate what you have learned, what you have accomplished, how you applied your generalist training to your field site, and what you see as the next step in your development as a competent social worker. Integrative Activity 12.2 will assist you in this task. The outcome will be invaluable as you consider the next step in your education or as a practitioner, which we will discuss in more detail later. Regardless of what you decide to do next, Integrative Activity 12.2 will provide an excellent foundation for you to articulate your accomplishments in field, your understanding of generalist practice, how you applied your generalist training to your particular agency, and how best to apply your knowledge, values, and skills to whatever you do next, whether that is at a job, in graduate school, as a volunteer, or in your advanced field placement.

INTEGRATIVE ACTIVITY 12.2
PULLING IT ALL TOGETHER

Purpose: The purpose of this activity is to assist you in the process of articulating your learning by translating your understanding of the knowledge, values, and skills integrated and developed in field into the larger, overarching competencies of a generalist social worker.

Competency 1: Demonstrate Ethical and Professional Behavior

Social workers understand the role of other professions when engaged in interprofessional teams. Social workers recognize the importance of lifelong learning and are committed to continually updating their skills to ensure that they are relevant and effective.

- use reflection and self-regulation to manage personal values and maintain professionalism in practice situations
- demonstrate professional demeanor in behavior; appearance; and oral, written, and electronic communication

Directions: For each question, jot down your thoughts and be prepared to explain your answers verbally. For the latter, think about how you would describe what you did in field to someone who has no understanding of social work and your particular area of practice.

1. Describe your agency, its program and services, and whom it primarily serves.

2. Identify the primary multilevel tasks and roles you engaged in at your field site.

3. Identify the specific knowledge you drew on and developed in field.

4. Identify the specific personal and professional values that you used and that were tested and realized in field.

5. Identify the specific practice skills you integrated and developed in field.

6. The CSWE's (2015) EPAS state, "Baccalaureate programs prepare students for generalist practice. Master's programs prepare students for generalist practice and specialized practice" (p. 11). The EPAS define *generalist practice* as follows:

Educational Policy 2.0—Generalist Practice

Generalist practice is grounded in the liberal arts and the person-in-environment framework. To promote human and social well-being, generalist practitioners use a range of prevention and intervention methods in their practice with diverse individuals, families, groups, organizations, and communities based on scientific inquiry and best practices. The generalist practitioner identifies with the social work profession and applies ethical principles and critical thinking in practice at the micro, mezzo, and macro levels. Generalist practitioners engage diversity in their practice and advocate for human rights and social and economic justice. They recognize, support, and build on the strengths and resiliency of all human beings. They engage in research-informed practice and are proactive in responding to the impact of context on professional practice. (p. 11)

Whether you are completing your BSW senior field or your MSW foundation field, reflect on the preceding definition of generalist practice as well as the core competencies identified in Integrative Activity 12.1, and identify how you would describe yourself as a generalist practitioner and what specifically you did in field to apply your generalist training to your practice.

a. Identify the ways in which you can translate the generalist training you applied in your field to the next role you take on, whether that be employment or your advanced education.

b. Identify what you see as the next step in your development as a social worker.

WHAT'S NEXT?

The last question in Integrative Activity 12.2 asked you to identify the next step in your development as a social worker. This can mean finding a job and beginning to practice or continuing in your education. Or you may decide that you want to do something altogether different. Let's review the options that are available in order to discern what the next best step is for you.

Finding a Job

If you are completing your BSW degree and you plan to work in a state that licenses the BSW, then you may decide that you want to work before you go on to graduate school. In the 20 years that I have been a field director, every year, approximately a third of the students pursue work that may entail pursuing licensure. To determine if your state licenses the BSW degree, go to the Association of Social Work Boards website and find your state to see the licensing regulations. This same site can give you all the information you need to take the exam. If you know the state you will be practicing in, you can also contact that state's licensing board directly to gather information regarding licensure. The advantage of working before attending graduate school is that you will gain experience you can draw on later in your advanced coursework. Also, you may have a better foundation from which to decide about what concentration area you want to focus on as an advanced practitioner.

Going to Graduate School

If you are completing your BSW degree, you might want to consider going straight on to graduate school. Again, there is no right or wrong thing to do, it is just important to consider all your options. As discussed in Chapter 1, most MSW programs offer some advanced standing to students who have a BSW degree. This can be a deciding factor in terms of the time commitment. When looking into programs, determine if you indeed qualify for advanced standing and what type of program you are looking for. As you recall, the BSW degree emphasizes generalist practice, whereas the MSW degree emphasizes specialized practice in a concentration area. It will be important for you to know the type of specialized practice you want to focus on in your graduate program. When looking at programs, educate yourself with regard to the program, the concentrations the program offers, the course work, and the faculty. Also, if you have the opportunity, it can make a huge difference to visit the programs you are interested in and meet with administrators, faculty, and students. I have seen an increase in the number of students deciding to go straight on to graduate school; this may be due to the thinking that they will have better job opportunities with the MSW degree. Others state they enjoy learning and feel that continuing their education while they are still in the student mode is the best way to go.

What About Something Completely Different?

I also see several students each year pursue something completely different after their BSW degree and before employment or graduate school. This often takes the form of the Peace Corps, AmeriCorps VISTA, Jesuit Volunteer Corps, Teach for America, or even travel. Again, there is no right or wrong decision; it is more important to consider the step that is the best fit for you and your goals.

Advanced Field Education

If you are completing your MSW foundation field (where you emphasize applying your generalist practice skills in preparation for advanced field), in all likelihood, you will be pursuing your specialized field placement. As you think about the concentration you have selected for specialized practice, you will want to consider your field opportunities. Again, it is important to discuss the placement process and go on interviews to determine the agency that can provide the best fit for your professional goals.

REFLECTION QUESTION 12.5

As you think about the preceding options, what do you see as your next step and why? What, if anything, do you need to realize your next step?

ROOM TO REFLECT

FREQUENTLY EXPERIENCED SITUATIONS

I can't believe field is ending. I don't really know how to feel.

I can't believe field is ending. I don't really know how to feel. On the one hand, I am so happy and relieved to be done. On the other hand, I am so sad to leave he agency, my clients, my coworkers, and my field instructor. It's also kind of frustrating, because I finally get it and fell about to do my job well, and now it's over.

The above sentiment is very common, and the wash of mixed emotions is perfectly normal. On the one hand, field has been a long haul; it is normal to feel a sense of relief that it is over. If you are in a concurrent program, in all likelihood, you have been juggling many things—coursework, field, and paid employment—not to mention other things you have been involved with on your campus or in the community. Also, for undergraduate students, the full completion of field often coincides with graduation, which can bring a whole new set of stressors. Thus, it is normal to feel sad and apprehensive.

Some students even express a sense of frustration due to the fact that many say they finally "get it." This means they know their agency and roles and feel competent to practice as a social worker, and now it's over.

What I tell students about this sense of frustration is that learning is often exponential; you will experience leaps and bounds with regard to both your competence and awareness of what you can and can't do. You are not the same person you were that first day of field, and when you enter into whatever you do next, you will find yourself doing things that you previously either had to be told how to do or had to consciously think about how to do them. So, don't worry about ending as you will now be able to enter into whatever you do next and hit the ground running and that is an exciting experience. I have had many students tell me that they didn't realize all that they could do until they began doing that thing. That is what is so exciting about endings. You often don't fully appreciate something until it is over and you look back at it. Be joyful, sad, frustrated, and excited. You have accomplished something significant and you should be very proud.

Suggested Field Tasks

- Explain the knowledge, skills, and values you developed as a result of your field experiences.

- Demonstrate the ability to conceptualize practice.

- Use reflection to explore your role, tasks, and experiences of field.

- Articulate learning from the tasks.

- Plan for and implement agency termination and client termination.

- Evaluate your progress in meeting the goals and objectives of field and core competencies and practice behaviors.

- Discuss next steps after field with your supervisor.

References

Baum, N. (2006). End-of-year treatment termination: Responses of social work student trainees. *British Journal of Social Work*, *36*, 639–656.

Council on Social Work Education (CSWE). (2015). *Educational policy and accreditation standards*. Alexandria, VA: Author.

Elders, G., Jr. (1998). The life course as developmental theory. *Child Development*, *69*(1), 1–12.

Gelman, C. (2009). MSW students' experience with termination: Implications and suggestions for classroom and field instruction. *Journal of Teaching in Social Work*, *29*, 169–187.

Sheafor, B., & Horejsi, C. (2015). *Techniques and guidelines for social work practice* (10th ed.). Boston, MA: Pearson Education.

INDEX